CLUNY AND THE MUSLIMS OF LA GARDE-FREINET

CLUNY AND THE MUSLIMS OF LA GARDE-FREINET

HAGIOGRAPHY AND THE PROBLEM OF ISLAM IN MEDIEVAL EUROPE

SCOTT G. BRUCE

CORNELL UNIVERSITY PRESS
Ithaca and London

First published 2015 by Cornell University Press

First paperback printing 2020

Library of Congress Cataloging-in-Publication Data

Bruce, Scott G. (Scott Gordon), 1967– author.
    Cluny and the Muslims of La Garde-Freinet :
hagiography and the problem of Islam in medieval
Europe / Scott G. Bruce.
        pages cm
    Includes bibliographical references and index.
    ISBN 978-0-8014-5299-4 (cloth)
    ISBN 978-1-5017-4843-1 (pbk.)
    1. Christianity and other religions—Islam—Early
works to 1800.   2. Islam—Relations—Christianity—
Early works to 1800.   3. Islam—Controversial
literature—Early works to 1800.   4. Muslims—
France—La Garde-Freinet—History—To 1500.
5. Christian hagiography—History—To 1500.
6. Cluny (Benedictine abbey)—History.   7. Peter,
the Venerable, approximately 1092–1156.   8. Majolus,
Saint, Abbot of Cluny, approximately 906–994.
I. Title.

BP172.B776 2015
261.2'709440902—dc23

                                                    2015014595

For Vivienne

The youngest in a family of dragons is still a dragon
from the point of view of those who find dragons alarming.
—Margaret Atwood,
Negotiating with the Dead: A Writer on Writing

De Monte
Mons Iovis ab Iove, quem prisci coluere profani,
Dictus, non, ut vulgus ait, de calle iocoso,
Quemque viatores per multa pericula repunt.

Concerning the Mountain
The mountain of Jupiter takes its name from the god
whom the ancient pagans worshipped and not, as some say,
from the jovial path on which travellers creep past a myriad
 of perils.
 —Egbert of Liège, *Fecunda ratis*

❧ CONTENTS

✒ ACKNOWLEDGMENTS

I first encountered the story of the kidnapping of Abbot Maiolus of Cluny more than a decade ago, when as a graduate student I read through the corpus of Cluniac hagiography in search of raw material for my dissertation. It captured my imagination then, as it once captivated the monks of Cluny, and has never let go. But the idea for the book grew slowly and I did not begin writing in earnest until 2010, when a sabbatical leave coupled with a semester-long College Scholar Award from the University of Colorado gave me many months of unencumbered time to put these thoughts to paper. Even so, I would not have finished the book in a timely manner were it not for a semester of parental leave afforded by the birth of our second daughter, Vivienne. This allowed me to complete the first draft of the manuscript at the Institute for Advanced Study in Princeton, New Jersey, in the spring and summer of 2012. There is simply no better place in the world to be a medievalist at work. I am deeply grateful to the intellectual virtuosity of my wife, Anne E. Lester, whose fellowship at IAS gave us the opportunity to return to our old home, and to the generosity of the faculty and fellows whose company we shared that semester: Emmanuel Bermon, Paschale Bermon, Glen Bowersock, Jeremy Cohen, Paul Hayward, Samantha Herrick, Christopher P. Jones, Heinrich von Staden, Chris Stray, Jorie Woods, and especially Giles Constable and Patrick Geary.

Many listeners, readers, and institutions had a hand in shaping this book. Those who attended conference sessions and public lectures at which I shared this material were always generous with questions and comments, many of which helped me to improve the arguments presented here. I am grateful to hosts and audiences at Harvard University, Mount Holyoke College, Plymouth State University, Université Lilles (France), Universiteit Gent (Belgium), the University of Auckland (New Zealand), the University of Illinois at Urbana–Champaign, Université Laval (Quebec, Canada), the University of Leeds (United Kingdom), the University of Pennsylvania, the University of Tennessee–Knoxville, and Western Michigan University. A Solmsen Fellowship from the Institute for Research in the Humanities at the University of Wisconsin–Madison fostered my first thoughts about this project in 2001–2. My thanks as well to the editors and external readers who improved the articles related to this book that have already appeared in print: "An Abbot between Two Cultures: Maiolus of Cluny Considers the Muslims of La Garde-Freinet," *Early Medieval Europe* 15 (2007): 426–40; and "Local Sanctity and Civic Typology in Early Medieval Pavia: The Example of the Cult of Abbot Maiolus of Cluny," in *Cities, Texts and Social Networks, 400–1500: Experiences and Perceptions of Medieval Urban Spaces*, edited by Caroline Goodson, Anne E. Lester, and Carol Symes (Aldershot, England, 2010), 177–91.

The book took its final form with the help of several acute readers who offered incisive comments. Thanks to Giles Constable, Brianna Gustafson, William Chester Jordan, Anne E. Lester, Constant Mews, Jonathan Shepard, and the anonymous readers for Cornell University Press. Drew Jones lent his expertise with the poem that appears in the appendix, and for this I am most grateful. Many thanks also to Tom Burman for sharing with me his microfilm copy of Paris, Bibliothèque nationale, MS Latin 3669. And I am especially grateful to Peter Potter and the staff at Cornell University Press for shepherding this project from manuscript to published book with tantamount professionalism.

Many friendships abide in these pages. While I wrote this book, Paul Cobb, Ryan Flahive, Drew Jones, Jessica Leigh, Myles Osborne, Denise Powell, and Suman Seth shared with me their wisdom, laughter, and insights at our table or theirs, in warm embrace or far away. They are scholars, teachers, parents of extraordinary children, and exceptional human beings; I am profoundly fortunate to call them my friends. The love of my family sustains me in this and all other pursuits. I am grateful for the support of Bev Bruce, Steve Bruce, Lynn and Paul Dickinson, Eric and Audrey Lester, Bob and Matthew Lester, and Lucille Lester. My wife and two children remind me always that life is bigger than the books we write and the work we do. Anne inspires me with her energy, her integrity, and the scope of her ambition. Mira, our eldest, always lives up to her name; she is a marvel, full of mirth and mischief. Vivienne is the youngest of our brood of dragons, endowed with a fierce beauty. I dedicate this book to her.

✒ ABBREVIATIONS

AASS   *Acta sanctorum quotquot toto orbe coluntur*, ed. Jean Bolland et al. (Antwerp, 1643–).

BC   *Bibliotheca Cluniacensis*, ed. Martin Marrier and André Duchesne (Paris, 1614; reprint, Mâcon, France, 1915).

BHL   *Bibliotheca hagiographica latina antiquae et mediae aetatis*, 2 vols. (Brussels, 1898–1901), with supplemental volumes published in 1911 and 1986; cited by BHL number.

CCCM   *Corpus Christianorum: Continuatio Mediaevalis* (Turnhout, Belgium, 1966–).

CCM   *Corpus consuetudinum monasticarum* (Siegburg, Germany, 1963–).

CCSL   *Corpus Christianorum: Series Latina* (Turnhout, Belgium, 1953–).

CMR   *Christian-Muslim Relations: A Bibliographical History*, ed. David Thomas and Alex Mallett, 5 vols. (Leiden, 2009–13); cited by volume and page number.

CSEL   *Corpus Scriptorum Ecclesiasticorum Latinorum* (Vienna, 1866–).

MGH SRG   *Monumenta Germaniae Historica: Scriptores rerum Germanicarum in usum scholarum separatim editi* (Hanover, 1871–)

MGH SS   *Monumenta Germaniae Historica inde ab anno christi quingentesimo usque ad annum millesimum et quingentesimum: Scriptores in folio*, 32 vols. (Hanover, 1826–1934).

MGH SSRL   *Monumenta Germaniae Historica: Scriptores rerum Langobardicarum et Italicarum, Saec. VI-IX* (Hanover, 1878).

PL   *Patrologia Cursus Completus: Series Latina*, ed. Jacques-Paul Migne, 221 vols. (Paris, 1844–88).

SC   *Sources chrétiennes* (Paris, 1941–).

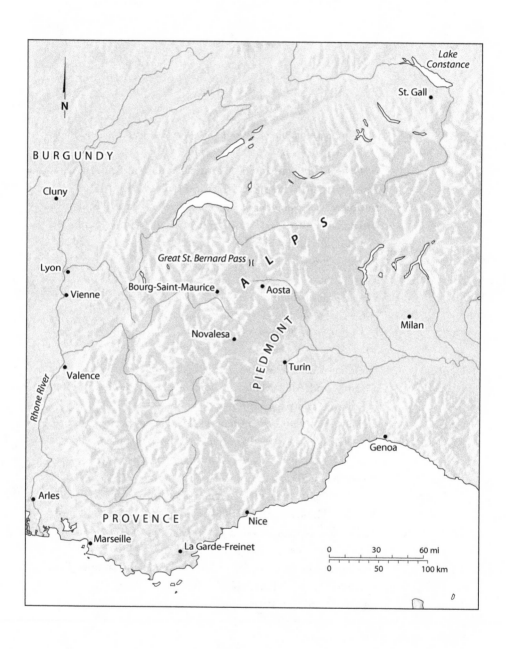

Lake Constance

St. Gall

BURGUNDY

Cluny

A L P S

Great St. Bernard Pass

Lyon

Bourg-Saint-Maurice

Aosta

Vienne

Milan

Novalesa

P I E D M O N T

Valence

Turin

Rhone River

Genoa

Arles

P R O V E N C E

Nice

Marseille

La Garde-Freinet

N

0   30   60 mi

0   50   100 km

Introduction
Hagiography and Religious Polemic
in the Cluniac Tradition

In the summer of 972, Muslim adventurers waylaid Abbot Maiolus of Cluny (ca. 909–94) and his entourage as they crossed the Great Saint Bernard Pass through the Alps on their way home from Rome to Burgundy. These brigands had held sway over the southern coast of Provence for most of the tenth century, unhindered by local Christian lords who lacked the organization and resources necessary to curb their activities from their base at Fraxinetum (present-day La Garde-Freinet, near Saint-Tropez).[1] Their forte was kidnapping, and they were able to exact a heavy toll in ransom from the families and patrons of wealthy captives; those who could not raise a ransom were sold into slavery. In Maiolus's case, a note sent from captivity explained his plight to the brethren of Cluny, who quickly raised the funds to free their spiritual father. The abbot returned home safely,

---

1. Modern research into the Muslim presence in early medieval Provence generally and Fraxinetum in particular began with Joseph Toussaint Reinaud, *Invasions des sarrazins en France et de France en Savoie, en Piémont et dans la Suisse, pendant les 8e, 9e et 10e siècles de notre ère* (Paris: A la libraire orientale de Vᵉ Dondey-Dupré, 1836), 157–225; translated by Haroon Khan Sherwani as *Muslim Colonies in France, Northern Italy and Switzerland* (Lahore, Pakistan: Ashraf, 1955), 129–69. More recent studies include Jean-Pierre Poly, *La Provence et la société féodale (879–1166): Contribution à l'étude des structures dites féodales dans le Midi* (Paris: Bordas, 1976), 3–29; Philippe Sénac, *Musulmans et sarrasins dans le sud de la Gaule du VIIIe au XIe siècle* (Paris: Sycomore, 1980); Philippe Sénac, *Provence et piraterie sarrasine* (Paris: Maisonneuve et Larose, 1982); and Mohammad Ballan, "Fraxinetum: An Islamic Frontier State in Tenth-Century Provence," *Comitatus* 41 (2010): 23–76.

but the audacity of his abductors outraged Christian leaders and galvanized the will of local lords. Shortly after the incident a Christian army laid waste to Fraxinetum, effectively erasing the Muslim presence from Provence.

The monks of Cluny did not soon forget this incident. In fact, Cluniac authors would tell the story of Maiolus's abduction over and over again in the decades to come. They produced at least four written accounts of this episode between the years 1000 and 1050—a sure sign that the story was making the rounds in monastic circles. While modern scholars have not exactly overlooked the story of Maiolus's kidnapping, no one has yet explored it from the perspective of cross-cultural commerce between Christians and Muslims in the Middle Ages. With this in mind, my goal in this book is to examine the literary representation of the Muslims of La Garde-Freinet in Cluniac hagiography from the eleventh century. As we will see, the telling and retelling of this unique historical episode provided Cluniac authors with choices about how to depict the abbot's captors. The choices that these writers ultimately made are illuminating for what they tell us about the ways in which Cluniac monks constructed images of Islam in the eleventh century. In essence these stories give us the rare opportunity to gauge changing perceptions of Muslims over time, during the century before the First Crusade (1096–99) when information about Islam in northern Europe was sporadic and ill informed at best.

Medieval hagiography has been the focus of intense study over the past few decades, but historians are only beginning to consider the influence of stories about the saints outside of the narrow devotional context in which they were written and read. An important but overlooked aspect of the tales told about the abduction of Maiolus is the impact they would have on the formation of religious polemic against Islam at the Abbey of Cluny in the twelfth century. There is one account in particular that puts forward the example of Maiolus challenging the prophetic claims of Muhammed by means of arguments based on reason. As we will see, this story would have a powerful influence on the future abbot of Cluny, Peter the Venerable (1092–1156), who was the first Christian prelate to commission a translation of the Qur'an from Arabic into Latin in order to refute its teachings.

Abbot Maiolus lived another twenty-two years after his kidnapping in the summer of 972 in the Alpine passes. He left behind no sermons, treatises, or other compositions that would give us insight into the cares and concerns of his abbacy, but the flowering of devotional literature in the decades after his death in 994 speaks volumes to the extent of his posthumous popularity. By the middle of the eleventh century, monks at Cluny and its many dependencies were commemorating the anniversary of his death (11 May) with great solemnity and celebrating the virtues of his life and his miraculous intercession on behalf of faithful Christians in narrative works of pious biography known to modern scholars as hagiography.

The devotional expectations of the genre of hagiography played an important role in shaping the narrative contours of each new retelling of the story of Maiolus's abduction. It was the primary goal of medieval hagiographers to present their subjects as models of virtuous behavior and active intercessors between heaven and earth. Their work provided examples of moral conduct and affirmed faith among pious readers. As a genre, hagiography drew its authority from the repetition of literary conventions drawn from a long-standing tradition of sacred Christian biography dating back to the New Testament and the lives of the earliest saints.[2] As a result, many medieval saints' lives followed established narrative patterns and borrowed themes, motifs, and even entire episodes verbatim from earlier works. But at the same time, it is clear that some hagiographers departed from received tradition and tailored their work to address contemporary concerns in the authoritative voices of their holy subjects. The novelist Margaret Atwood sums up this phenomenon very well:

> Although in every culture many stories are told, only some are told and retold, and . . . these recurring stories bear examining. If such stories were parts of a symphony you'd call them leitmotifs, if they were personality traits you'd call them obsessions, and if it were your parents telling them at the dinner-table during your adolescence you'd call them boring. But, in literature, they hold a curious fascination both for those who tell them and for those who hear them; they are handed down and reworked, and story-tellers come back to them time and time again, approaching them from various angles and discovering new and different meanings each time the story, or a part of it, is given a fresh incarnation.[3]

Historians of medieval saints' lives examine both the conventions of this literary genre and the incidental details in hagiographical texts for myriad

---

2. For a brief but insightful introduction to hagiography and related genres in early Christian literature, see Susan Ashbrook Harvey, "Martyr Passions and Hagiography," in *The Oxford Handbook of Early Christian Studies*, ed. Susan Ashbrook Harvey and David G. Hunter (Oxford: Oxford University Press, 2008), 603–27.

3. Margaret Atwood, *Strange Things: The Malevolent North in Canadian Literature* (Oxford: Clarendon Press, 1995), 11.

purposes related to the reconstruction of the medieval past.[4] This book follows in the footsteps of these scholars by treating every retelling of the kidnapping episode as an opportunity to reconstruct how the aims of different authors and the function of their respective works shaped their account of this story and added new and different meanings about the Muslims of La Garde-Freinet for the Christian audiences of these texts. The tale of the abduction of Maiolus is particularly noteworthy in this regard in that it provided ample historical details for generations of hagiographers to draw upon, thanks no doubt to firsthand accounts of the kidnapping related by the abbot himself and members of his entourage and the living memory of the repetition of these stories at Cluny and elsewhere.

While historians have rightly concentrated on the devotional uses of medieval hagiography, there is evidence to suggest that early medieval readers were not limited in the ways in which they read and understood the content of saints' lives. It is the contention of this book that stories about Maiolus and the Muslims of La Garde-Freinet exerted a significant and hitherto overlooked influence on later monastic readers as they considered the problem of Islam for western Europeans. The most important of these readers was Abbot Peter the Venerable, who was unrivaled among his contemporaries in the energy that he spent on combatting with words the errant beliefs of heretics, Jews, and Muslims.[5] Peter is best remembered for commissioning translations of the Qur'an and other Muslim historical and devotional works from Arabic into Latin for the purpose of refuting them.[6] The corpus of

---

4. Amid a vast literature, two discussions will have to suffice: Paul Fouracre, "Merovingian History and Merovingian Hagiography," *Past and Present* 127 (1990): 3–38, reprinted in Paul Fouracre, *Frankish History: Studies in the Construction of Power* (Farnham, England: Variorum, 2013), no. 2; and Patrick J. Geary, "Saints, Scholars, and Society: The Elusive Goal," in *Living with the Dead in the Middle Ages* (Ithaca, NY: Cornell University Press, 1994), 9–29. On the rewriting of saints' lives in the early Middle Ages, see *L'hagiographie mérovingienne à travers ses réécritures*, ed. Monique Goullet, Martin Heinzelmann, and Christiane Veyrard-Cosme (Ostfildern, Germany: Thorbecke, 2010), with references to earlier scholarship.

5. The most extensive modern study of Peter's life and work is Jean-Pierre Torrell and Denise Bouthillier, *Pierre le Vénérable et sa vision du monde: Sa vie, son oeuvre, l'homme et le démon* (Leuven, Belgium: Spicilegium Sacrum Lovaniense, 1986). For the fullest treatment of his polemical works, see Dominique Iogna-Prat, *Ordonner et exclure: Cluny et la société chrétienne face à l'hérésie, au judaïsme et à l'islam (1000–1050)* (Paris: Aubier, 1998), translated by Graham Robert Edwards as *Order and Exclusion: Cluny and Christendom Face Heresy, Judaism, and Islam (1000–1150)*, (Ithaca, NY: Cornell University Press, 2002).

6. The pioneering research of Marie-Thérèse d'Alverny and James Kritzeck remains formative and influential, despite the corrections made to their work by later scholars. See, for example, D'Alverny, "Deux traductions latines du Coran au Moyen Âge," *Archives d'histoire doctrinale et littéraire du Moyen Âge* 22–23 (1947–48): 69–131, reprinted in D'Alverny, *La connaissance de l'Islam dans l'Occident médiéval* (Aldershot, England: Variorum, 1994), no. 2; and Kritzeck, *Peter the Venerable and Islam*

Latin texts produced by his initiative did not have a collective title in the Middle Ages and it is known today by a number of different appellations, all of which are modern confections with varying degrees of accuracy. This book uses the most widely recognized name for Peter's translation project: the Toledan Collection (*Corpus toledanum* or *Collectio toledanum*), a name given to it because of the alleged though unsubstantiated association of some of its translators with the city of Toledo in Spain.[7]

Almost without exception, scholars have framed their discussions of the Toledan Collection within the narrow confines of the history of religious polemical writings.[8] This is understandable for many reasons. Peter commissioned the Toledan Collection with the intent of providing Latin-speaking Europeans with the raw material to craft a refutation of the prophetic claims of Muhammed. While Thomas E. Burman has argued persuasively that the translators employed by Peter did not willfully distort the Muslim texts they were paid to render into Latin, annotations to the Qur'an translation made shortly after its completion in the 1140s were written with obvious derogatory intent, for they were incessant in their insistence that the Qur'an was an "insane" and "impious" document.[9] Moreover, Peter himself wrote two polemical texts against Muslim beliefs: a short summary of the contents of the Toledan Collection titled *A Summary of the Entire Heresy of the Saracens* (*Summa totius haeresis Sarracenorum*) composed around 1143 and a longer treatise directed to a Muslim audience titled *Against the Sect of the Saracens* (*Contra sectam Saracenorum*) written shortly before his death in 1156.[10] Questions

---

(Princeton, NJ: Princeton University Press, 1964). On the Qur'an translation of Robert of Ketton commissioned by Peter the Venerable and its reception history, see especially Thomas E. Burman, *Reading the Qur'an in Latin Christendom, 1140–1560* (Philadelphia: University of Pennsylvania Press, 2007).

7. On the city of Toledo as a center of translation from Arabic to Latin in this period, see Marie-Thérèse d'Alverny, "Translations and Translators," in *Renaissance and Renewal in the Twelfth Century*, ed. Robert L. Benson and Giles Constable with Carol D. Lanham (Cambridge, MA: Harvard University Press, 1982), 421–62, esp. 444–57; and Robert I. Burns, "The Coherence of the Arabic-Latin Translation Program in Toledo in the Twelfth Century," *Science in Context* 14 (2001): 249–88. Other names for Peter's translation project include the *Corpus Cluniacense*, because the earliest manuscripts of the translations were produced at Cluny, and the *Corpus Islamolatinum*, which emphasizes the goal of the collection to make information about Islam accessible in the Latin language.

8. Norman Daniel's classic *Islam and the West: The Making of an Image*, first published in 1960 and again in a revised edition in 1993, has exerted a formative influence on all subsequent studies. For his treatment of the contribution of Peter the Venerable, consult the index of his book under the heading "Cluniac collection."

9. See Burman, *Reading the Qur'an*, 60–87.

10. These works have been edited with a German translation by Reinhold Glei in *Petrus Venerabilis, Schriften zum Islam* (Altenberge, Germany: CIS Verlag, 1985).

regarding the influences on the formation of Peter's stance against Islam have invariably involved a genealogical methodology that has attempted to uncover the roots of his inspiration in the polemical traditions of patristic literature or in early medieval Mozarabic writings against Muslim beliefs or in the works of near contemporary authors like Peter Alfonsi, who likewise produced treatises in the defense of the Christian faith (though not specifically against Islam).[11]

This book is the first study to consider the role of hagiographical literature in the formulation of Peter the Venerable's approach to Islam. In the twelfth century, the lives of the saints and the homilies of the church fathers saturated the imagination of the monks of Cluny, including their venerable abbot. Whether imbibed publically during the celebration of the liturgy or digested privately through reading, works of hagiography and other devotional genres played a vital role in the formation of monastic thought in the abbeys of western Europe. It is for this reason that Peter could presume that his reading audience was intimately familiar with the homilies and hagiographical texts composed by Pope Gregory the Great, for "[t]hey are recited and heard and read and understood daily and almost without interruption by innumerable and even unlearned and simple brothers."[12] Evidence for the circulation of stories about Maiolus in the twelfth century is equally evocative. Such was his renown that when Peter compiled a collection of miracle stories in the 1140s, he could boldly state that more legends were told about the virtues of Maiolus throughout all of Europe (*in tota Europa*) than about any other saint in Christendom with the exception of the Virgin Mary.[13]

This book unfolds in two parts, like a diptych. The first half comprises two chapters on the abduction of Maiolus in 972 and the legacy of this story in Cluniac hagiography written in the early eleventh century. In chapter 1, "News of a Kidnapping," I reconstruct the context of the plight of the abbot of Cluny using contemporary evidence from the tenth century. I interweave three distinct but related topics: the perils and promises of transalpine travel

---

11. See John V. Tolan's formative contribution, "Peter the Venerable on the Diabolical Heresy of the Saracens," in *The Devil, Heresy and Witchcraft in the Middle Ages: Essays in Honor of Jeffrey B. Russell*, ed. Alberto Ferreiro (Leiden: Brill, 1998), 345–67, reprinted in John V. Tolan, *Sons of Ishmael: Muslims through European Eyes in the Middle Ages* (Gainesville: University Press of Florida, 2008), 46–63.

12. Peter the Venerable, *Contra Petrobrusianos hereticos*, 256, ed. James Fearns, CCCM 10 (Turnhout, Belgium: Brepols, 1968), 151. This excerpt has been translated by Giles Constable in *Three Treatises from Bec on the Nature of Monastic Life*, ed. Giles Constable (Toronto: University of Toronto Press, 2008), 11n28.

13. Peter the Venerable, *De miraculis*, 2.32, ed. Denise Bouthillier, CCCM 83:162.

in the decades around the year 1000 for merchants and pilgrims who made the journey between northern Europe and Rome; the impact of the Muslims of Fraxinetum on Provençal society in general and on traffic through the Alpine passes in particular; and the career of Maiolus himself, who traveled back and forth through the Alps repeatedly during his tenure as abbot of Cluny (954–94). My argument is that the Muslims of Fraxinetum were above all an entrepreneurial community that took advantage of the lawlessness of tenth-century Provence to pursue profitable enterprises like kidnapping and slave trading. Although they were not recognized as a polity or colony of any Islamic government and produced no documents describing their political goals or internal organization, the inhabitants of La Garde-Freinet were highly visible in contemporary Latin Christian sources like monastic charters and regional chronicles. An analysis of these documents allows us to chart the range of their activity and to weigh the cost and consequences of their presence in southern Europe. While the enslavement of Europeans was a tragic reality of life in the tenth century, the inadvertent capture of one of the foremost abbots of the time was not inconsequential, for Christian leaders responded to this perceived affront by mounting a unified military campaign that eventually extirpated the Muslims of Fraxinetum.

In chapter 2, "Monks Tell Tales," I examine the episode of the kidnapping as it appears in a cluster of texts written by Cluniac monks in the early eleventh century. These comprise the three earliest accounts of the life of Abbot Maiolus (dating from ca. 1000–1030) and the *Five Books of Histories* (*Historiarum libri quinque*) written in the 1040s by the monastic historian Rodulfus Glaber. The primary goals of this chapter are to demonstrate how the telling of the story changed over time, to explain why these changes occurred, and to infer what these changes reveal about the spread of knowledge of Muslim peoples and their religion in northern Europe in the early eleventh century. What emerges from this analysis is the fact that none of these hagiographers was wedded to an impartial retelling of the events of 972. Instead, each of them related the abduction episode to fulfill the expectations of his respective audience and to forward the aims of his individual devotional enterprise.

A brief interlude provides the hinge between the two halves of the book. In it I examine the evidence for a failed missionary expedition to Muslims in Spain allegedly undertaken in the 1070s by a Cluniac hermit named Anastasius at the behest of Pope Gregory VII and Abbot Hugh the Great of Cluny (1024–1109). The evidence for this undertaking is provocative, but frustratingly opaque: a little-known hagiographical account of the life of Anastasius provides the only details of his missionary strategies, which involved proving the superiority of his faith to Muslims through an ordeal by fire. Correspondence preserved in an Arabic translation between "a monk of France" and the ruler of Saragossa hints at a more ambitious agenda in the minds of those who dispatched the hermit to Spain. Although the story involves the agency of an abbot of Cluny, the unsuccessful mission of Anastasius does not seem to have been inspired by the actions of Maiolus in captivity, nor does it seem to have been commemorated by Cluniac monks in the twelfth century.

The second half of the book focuses on Peter the Venerable, and specifically the influence of Cluniac hagiography on the formation of his Muslim policy. In chapter 3, "Peter the Venerable, Butcher of God," I offer a new interpretation of the polemical career of this twelfth-century abbot. Some scholars have attributed a cohesion to Peter's writings against heretics, Jews, and Muslims and have presented him as a sympathetic figure whose "tolerant" views toward Islam heralded modern sensibilities.[14] In contrast, I argue that the abbot's work against the Muslims differed markedly from his other treatises against unbelievers for two reasons. First, Peter was doing something entirely new in addressing a polemical treatise directly to a Muslim audience. Unlike his writings against heretics and Jews, which drew from the reservoir of centuries-old literary traditions, his pastoral approach toward Islam had no precedent in the Latin language. Second, his application of reason to his argument against the Muslims was not the first impulse of a tolerant man, as some scholars have presumed. Rather, as I contend in this chapter, it was his last recourse in the aftermath of the Second Crusade, which witnessed the decisive defeat of the marshaled hosts of Christendom against the armies of Islam. As we will see, Peter only turned to words in his confrontation against Muslims when the weapons of the crusaders had proven to be ineffective against them.

In chapter 4, "Hagiography and the Muslim Policy of Peter the Venerable," I examine the impact of the eleventh-century stories about Maiolus's

---

14. This tendency is especially prevalent in the work of Iogna-Prat, who often refers to Peter's polemical works collectively as a "global project" and a "triptych" with "ideological coherence." See Iogna-Prat, *Order and Exclusion*, 23, 117, and 121n3. For the depiction of the abbot as a tolerant figure, see, in particular, Kritzeck, *Peter the Venerable and Islam*. The earliest work of revisionist history on this topic, ignored by Kritzeck, is Virginia Berry, "Peter the Venerable and the Crusades," in *Petrus Venerabilis, 1156–1956: Studies and Texts Commemorating the Eighth Centenary of His Death*, ed. Giles Constable and James Kritzeck (Rome: Herder, 1956), 141–62, which argues forcefully that Peter was an active supporter of the Second Crusade. Despite evidence to the contrary, the notion that Peter acted with a disposition of religious tolerance that heralded the most enlightened sensibilities of our own age remains tenacious. See Pope Benedict XVI's address in Rome on 14 October 2009, titled "On Peter the Venerable, Abbot of Cluny"; http://www.zenit.org/article-27203?l=english.

kidnapping on the formation of Peter the Venerable's enterprise to convert Muslims to Christianity by means of rational argument. The earliest account of Maiolus's life written at Cluny presented a late tenth-century debate on religious truth between the abbot of Cluny and his Muslim captors that exercised a powerful influence on Peter's thinking about how best to confront and refute Islamic beliefs in the aftermath of the Second Crusade. Before making the case for the impact of this hagiographical text on the formulation of Peter's approach to Islam, I survey the use of reason in polemical writings against Jews and heretics in the late eleventh and early twelfth centuries to weigh the influence of contemporary intellectual currents in the shaping of the abbot's thoughts. I also consider the degree to which the ninth- or tenth-century work of Arab-Christian apologetic against Islam known as the *Apology of al-Kindi*, which Peter had translated into Latin as part of the Toledan Collection, may have informed the abbot's final foray against the religious claims of the Muslims. I conclude by making the case for the currency of stories about Maiolus among twelfth-century Cluniacs, with particular attention to the rewriting of the *Life of Maiolus* during Peter's abbacy. I argue that the abbot of Cluny drew inspiration from his tenth-century predecessor in his adoption of rational argument as the most effective way to win Muslims to the Christian faith after the failure of the Second Crusade.

A carapace of fear and anger appears to envelope medieval authors of religious polemic so completely that we can forget to immerse ourselves in the devotional texts that did so much to inform their thinking. Separated from us by the gulf of centuries, it is easy for historians to underestimate the complexity of medieval lives. Yet recognizing this complexity is vital if we are to comprehend in the fullest way possible how medieval thinkers like Peter the Venerable drew upon the full range of their cultural experience, including their knowledge of exemplary episodes in hagiographical texts, when they confronted the issues that were most pressing in their minds. No life is uncomplicated, and in the twelfth century the life of the abbot of Cluny was arguably more complicated than most. Understanding the anxieties and apprehensions that motivated Peter to write his polemical works and reconciling how different these works were from one another in their aim and audience allows us to evaluate with new clarity the influence of the hagiography of his tenth-century predecessor on the formation of his ideas about how best to confront the problem of Islam in medieval Europe.

◆ CHAPTER 1

News of a Kidnapping

In the middle of the night on 21–22 July 972, Muslim adventurers abducted Abbot Maiolus of Cluny and his entourage as they camped near the top of the Great Saint Bernard Pass in the western Alps while en route from the city of Rome to their monastery in Burgundy. Kidnapping by Islamic brigands was one of many dangers facing those who braved the precipitous Alpine passes in the tenth century. These Muslims arrived in Provence in the late ninth century and established a stronghold at Fraxinetum (present-day La Garde-Freinet, near Saint-Tropez). From there, they made frequent forays into the Provençal countryside, where they plundered local towns and religious communities and took many captives, whom they ransomed for cash or sold as slaves in Islamic principalities around the Mediterranean rim. In so doing they took advantage of political instability that was endemic in the region following the death of Charles III the Fat (d. 888), the last Carolingian emperor of western Europe. At the height of their activity, the Muslims of Provence cast a long and foreboding shadow from the Côte d'Azur across the Alps to the shores of Lake Constance.

The Islamic settlement at La Garde-Freinet thrived for many decades as an autonomous entrepôt for the export of European captives to the slave markets of the Muslim world. Although its inhabitants produced no documents of their own, they appeared frequently in contemporary Latin sources, as European chroniclers related with dismay stories of their fearful deeds even

as they railed against the Christian lords who made alliances with them to the detriment of all. The Muslims of Fraxinetum were an ominous presence in tenth-century Provence, but they were in fact latecomers in a wave of Islamic military and entrepreneurial activity dating back to the early ninth century that disrupted Christian settlements along the northwestern Mediterranean shore. While they shared many of the same commercial priorities as their ninth-century predecessors, the inhabitants of La Garde-Freinet distinguished themselves in two important ways. First, they recognized that the merchant and pilgrim traffic crossing the highest passes of the Alps in the summer months could provide them with a steady supply of human chattel with little risk of retribution from Christian authorities, who in the tenth century were more concerned with advancing their own interests at the expense of their neighbors than policing the heights of local mountain ranges. As a result, the Muslims of Fraxinetum penetrated much farther north into Europe than any Islamic group since the Muslim expedition that fought Charles Martel at the Battle of Tours in 732. Second, while the threat of Muslim slavers in the Alps haunted the minds of tenth-century travelers, the abduction of Maiolus of Cluny in the summer of 972 brought them an unparalleled notoriety throughout western Christendom. So great was the offense of the capture of this holy man that it galvanized the will of local Christian lords, who put aside their quarrels to launch a united campaign that led to the destruction of La Garde-Freinet and the elimination of the Muslim presence in the Alps.

Despite a burgeoning interest in evidence for cross-cultural commerce between Christians and Muslims in the Middle Ages, no study of this topic has given full attention to the abduction of Maiolus of Cluny. This chapter begins by reconstructing the context of his kidnapping. Many Christian travelers crossed the Alpine passes in the tenth century, merchants and pilgrims being the most frequent among them. These travelers were particularly vulnerable to robbery and kidnapping because merchants often carried considerable wealth with them in the form of goods for sale and most pilgrims were unable to afford the security of an armed escort. After establishing the motives for transalpine travel in the decades around 1000, I then examine the historical circumstances that brought Muslims to the shores of Provence and the political contingencies that allowed them to thrive commercially in the region for decades. I argue that the Muslim community of La Garde-Freinet was distinct from other Islamic settlements in Christian territory in this period not only in terms of its longevity but also with respect to the range of its influence in Provence, northern Italy, and throughout the Alpine passes. And finally, in the last portion of the chapter I treat the earliest textual evidence for the abbot's abduction in July 972: a ransom letter sent by Maiolus to the monks of Cluny to inform them of his plight and to request payment for the release of him and his fellow captives. This letter is the only contemporary record of the kidnapping incident, a precious yet hitherto neglected witness to an encounter between a prominent Christian intellectual and his Muslim captors near the close of the first millennium.[1] Although it is very brief, the document allows us to make some tantalizing inferences about the abbot of Cluny's understanding of the religion of his Muslim captors.

❧ The Perils and Promises of Transalpine Travel

The Great Saint Bernard Pass was one of the most heavily used arteries through the Alpine ranges in the early Middle Ages.[2] Merchants were among the most common travelers over the pass in the tenth century. These individuals were much more than purveyors of goods; they also played important roles as information couriers, cultural ambassadors, and agents of the saints. Some of them traveled regularly between the palaces of northern Europe and the entrepôts of the eastern Mediterranean. Their business contacts, proficiency in languages, and experience with long-distance travel made them respected figures in the royal courts of the north. It is not surprising that in the year 949 Emperor Otto I chose as his ambassador to Constantinople a wealthy merchant from Mainz named Liutefred, whose commercial experience in the East provided him with the necessary credentials for this

---

1. While several scholars have drawn attention to the abduction of Maiolus, none of them has scrutinized the text of his ransom letter. See Richard Southern, *Western Views of Islam in the Middle Ages* (Cambridge, MA: Harvard University Press, 1962), 28n25; and Benjamin Kedar, *Crusade and Mission: European Approaches toward the Muslims* (Princeton, NJ: Princeton University Press, 1984), 42–43. The episode does not figure at all in John V. Tolan, *Saracens: Islam in the Medieval European Imagination* (New York: Columbia University Press, 2002), or in the relevant volume of CMR, where it appears instead as an aside in an entry on another tenth-century abbot; see Elizabeth Dachowski, "Abbo of Fleury," in CMR 2:530.

2. The itinerary of a late tenth-century Anglo-Saxon archbishop who visited Rome to obtain his pallium sheds light on the way stations available to travelers over the pass in this period. See Veronica Ortenberg, "Archbishop Sigeric's Journey to Rome in 990," *Anglo-Saxon England* 19 (1990): 197–246. The name Great Saint Bernard had nothing to do with the renowned twelfth-century monk and theologian Saint Bernard of Clairvaux, as is often presumed. Rather, it preserves the memory of the efforts of Bernard of Menthon, archdeacon of Aosta (d. 1081), to restore way stations for travelers over this and other passes in the western Alps. Little is known for certain about this eleventh-century prelate; see Joseph Auguste Duc, "À quelle date est mort Saint Bernard de Menthon?" *Miscellanea di storia Italiana* 31 (1894): 341–68.

sensitive diplomatic position.[3] Similarly, in 953, merchants from Verdun accompanied Abbot John of Gorze on his ill-fated embassy to the court of 'Abd al-Rahman III in Cordoba.[4] Other early medieval merchants acted as brokers between the saints of Rome and the abbeys of northern Europe. Agents of these entrepreneurs haunted the Roman catacombs, where they obtained for eager monastic communities the most precious commodity of all: the relics of the martyrs. Einhard's early ninth-century account of the translation of the relics of Saints Marcellinus and Peter from Rome to Germany for the dedication of his new church at Mulinheim (now Seligenstadt) provides the clearest testimony of a lucrative traffic in holy remains that thrived well into the tenth century.[5]

For medieval merchants, the promise of transalpine travel was profit; mundane commercial items crossed the mountain passes in great abundance. Around the year 960, Bishop Giso of Aosta issued a list of toll charges to merchant caravans that entered his town en route to the Great Saint Bernard Pass.[6] This list shows that itinerant traders carted a diverse inventory of stock on pack animals and horseback to the fair towns and palaces of the north. Military equipment formed the bulk of trade moving over the Alps in this

3. Liudprand, *Antapodosis*, 6.4, ed. Paolo Chiesa, in *Liudprandi Cremonensis Opera Omnia*, CCCM 156:146; and Michael McCormick, *Origins of the European Economy: Communications and Commerce, AD 300–900* (Cambridge: Cambridge University Press, 2001), 971 (no. R814). See also Krijnie Ciggaar, *Western Travellers to Constantinople: The West and Byzantium, 962–1204: Cultural and Political Relations* (Leiden: Brill, 1996).

4. John of Saint Arnulf, *Vita Iohannis Gorziensis*, 5.115–36, in *La Vie de Jean, Abbé de Gorze*, ed. and trans. Michel Parisse (Paris: Picard, 1999), 142–61. For more on John's embassy to Spain and Cordoban diplomacy with Christian polities in general, see Abdurrahman Ali el-Hajji, *Andalusian Diplomatic Relations with Western Europe during the Umayyad Period (A.H. 138–366/A.D. 755–976): An Historical Survey* (Beirut: Dar al-Irshad, 1970), esp. 207–27; Nicholas Drocourt, "Christian-Muslim Diplomatic Relations: An Overview of the Main Sources and Themes of Encounter (600–1000)," in CMR 2:29–72; and Michael Frassetto, "John of St. Arnoul," in CMR 2:475–79. On the elision of the role of ambassador and merchant in this period, see Anthony Cutler, "Gifts and Gift Exchange as Aspects of the Byzantine, Arab, and Related Economies," *Dumbarton Oaks Papers* 55 (2001): 266: "Indeed, on occasion it would not be excessive to say that a foreigner's designation as 'ambassador' or 'merchant' is a function of the purpose of his visit rather than a clear-cut distinction in the minds and attitudes of those upon whom he called."

5. Einhard, *Translatio et miracula sanctorum Marcellini et Petri*, ed. Georg Waitz, in MGH SS, 15.1:239–64. On the early medieval relic trade and the literature it inspired, see Martin Heinzelmann, *Translationsberichte und andere Quellen des Reliquienkultes*, Typologie des sources du moyen âge occidental 33 (Turnhout, Belgium: Brepols, 1979); Patrick J. Geary, *Furta Sacra: Thefts of Relics in the Central Middle Ages*, 2nd ed. (Princeton, NJ: Princeton University Press, 1990); and Julia M. H. Smith, "Old Saints, New Cults: Roman Relics in Carolingian Francia," in *Early Medieval Rome and the Christian West: Essays in Honour of Donald A. Bullough*, ed. Julia M. H. Smith (Leiden: Brill, 2000), 317–39.

6. Joseph-Antoine Besson, *Mémoires pour l'histoire ecclésiastique des diocèses de Genève, Tarantaise, Aoste, et Maurienne, et du dècanat de Savoye* (Nancy, France: Sebastien Henault, 1759), 479 (no. 111), where the document is dated "environ 960."

period: the bishop of Aosta claimed tolls in money or in kind on a large number of swords, spears, shields, and armor, as well as horses, spurs, and reins, made in Italy for the armies of the Ottonians. Common goods likewise flowed into Mediterranean markets from northern Europe. An early eleventh-century account of the duties of imperial officials at the Ottonian court in Pavia (the so-called *Honorantiae Civitatis Papiae*) painted a vivid portrait of a southbound artery of trade stretching from England to Venice, along which moved a slow and steady stream of service animals, slaves, cloth, precious metals, and weapons.[7]

Early medieval merchants also carried exotic wares from Africa and the East northward over the Great Saint Bernard Pass. Despite Muslim dominance in the Mediterranean Sea in this period, there is evidence of sustained trade between Italian cities and Constantinople. At the turn of the millennium, Venetian merchants were renowned as importers of Byzantine silks and spices.[8] Their port city was ideally situated for the distribution of these goods over the Alpine passes. It was not unusual, for instance, for German and Frankish prelates to purchase silk vestments of Eastern origin from Italian merchants and then grant them as gifts to important northern monasteries.[9] In the year 908, Bishop Adalbero of Augsburg presented the abbot of Saint Gall with splendid purple robes from Tyre.[10] Great quantities of eastern spices also crossed the Alps. Tenth-century records show that the Abbey of Corbie, located near Amiens in northern France, purchased large amounts of pepper, cinnamon, ginger, myrrh, and other spices for culinary and medicinal use.[11] Around 965 a diplomat from Muslim Spain named Ibra-

---

7. *Honorantiae Civitatis Papiae*, edited by Adolf Hofmeister as "Instituta regalia et ministeria camerae regum Longobardorum et honorantiae civitatis Papiae," in MGH SS, 30.2:1444–60.

8. In a well-known vignette from the early tenth century, Venetian merchants were portrayed as aggressive and enthusiastic in offering their wares—cloaks and spices (*uel pallia uel pigmentorum species*)—to Gerald of Aurillac as he passed near Pavia on his way north from Rome; see Odo of Cluny, *Vita sancti Geraldi Auriliacensis*, 1.27, in *Odon de Cluny, Vita sancti Geraldi Auriliacensis: Édition critique, traduction française, introduction et commentaires*, ed. and trans. Anne-Marie Bultot-Verleysen (Brussels: Société des Bollandistes, 2009), 172–74 (and 295n40 for previous literature). For more on Pavia as a hub of commercial activity in this period, see chapter 2 of the present volume.

9. Wilhelm Heyd, *Histoire du commerce du Levant au moyen âge*, 2 vols. (Leipzig, Germany: O. Harrassowitz, 1923), is unsurpassed in its scope on the general topic of trade between eastern Mediterranean entrepôts and western Europe in the Middle Ages. On the silk trade in particular, see McCormick, *Origins of the European Economy*, 719–26.

10. Aloys Schulte, *Geschichte des mittelalterlichen Handels und Verkehrs zwischen Westdeutschland und Italien mit Ausschluss von Venedig* (Leipzig, Germany: Verlag von Duncker & Humblot, 1900), 1:72; and Heyd, *Histoire du commerce du Levant*, 1:86.

11. *Polyptyque de l'abbé Irminon ou dénombrement des manses, des serfs et des revenus de l'abbaye de Saint-Germain-des-Prés sous le règne de Charlemagne*, ed. Benjamin Guérard (Paris: A l'Imprimerie Royale,

him marveled to find pepper, ginger, cloves, and other exotic spices at the court of Emperor Otto I in Mainz: "An extraordinary thing is that, though this city is in the farthest West, they have spices there which are only to be obtained in the farthest East."[12] These goods were so precious to northern Europeans that Thietmar of Merseberg, an eleventh-century German chronicler, reported the shipwreck of four Venetian spice galleys among the most memorable events of the year 1017.[13] Exotic animals were also profitable commodities in transalpine trade. In the tenth century, apes from Africa passed through the town of Aosta on their way over the Great Saint Bernard Pass. Bishop Giso noted with apparent disgust that, even though it was an absurd little animal (*quamvis sit ridiculosum animal*), the toll charge for an ape was three times that of a horse, undoubtedly because apes brought a much higher price for their importers in the elite markets of northern Europe.[14]

Merchant traffic shared the Great Saint Bernard Pass with pilgrim caravans en route to and from the city of Rome.[15] In contrast to the worldly ambitions of commercial enterprise, pilgrimage was first and foremost a devotional act undertaken for the love of Christ (*pro amore Christi*), most often willingly, though sometimes as a penitential debt.[16] In the tenth century, the Alpine passes provided the only route to those northern Europeans motivated by Christian piety to visit the tombs of the Roman saints because the Muslim presence in Provence all but eliminated river traffic in the Rhône valley and prevented pilgrims from sailing along the Mediterranean coast

1844), 2:336 (no. 2): "Istae sunt pigmentae quas ad Camaracum debemus comparare de singulis tantum, si pretium habemus: piper libras cxx, ciminum similiter, gingimber libras lxx, gariofile libras x, cinammum libras xv, galingan libras x. . . ."

12. The translation is from Bernard Lewis, *The Muslim Discovery of Europe* (New York: W. W. Norton, 1982), 187. For more on Ibrahim and the surviving sources of his lost travel log, see *Ein arabischer Berichterstatter aus dem 10. Jahrhundert über Fulda, Schleswig, Soest, Paderborn und andere Städte des Abendlandes: Artikel aus Qazwînîs Âthâr al-bilâd*, trans. Georg Jacob, 3rd ed. (Berlin: Mayer & Müller, 1896); and Abdurrahman Ali el-Hajji, "Ibrahim ibn Ya'qub at-Tartushi and His Diplomatic Activity," *Islamic Quarterly* 14 (1970): 22–40.

13. Thietmar of Merseberg, *Chronicon* 76, ed. Robert Holtzmann, in MGH SRG, n.s. 9:492: "Quatuor naves Venetorum magne diversisque pigmentis referte naufragium sunt in predicto anno perpessae."

14. Besson, *Mémoires pour l'histoire ecclésiastique*, 479.

15. On the allure of Rome in the early Middle Ages see, generally, the studies collected in *Early Medieval Rome and the Christian West*; *Roma nell'alto medioevo*, 2 vols., Settimane di Studio del Centro Italiano di Studi sull'Alto Medioevo 48 (Spoleto, Italy: Presso la Sede del Centro, 2001); and *Roma fra oriente e occidente*, 2 vols., Settimane di Studio del Centro Italiano di Studi sull'Alto Medioevo 49 (Spoleto, Italy: Presso la Sede del Centro, 2002).

16. The literature on medieval pilgrimage is vast. The articles in *Encyclopedia of Medieval Pilgrimage*, ed. Larissa J. Taylor et al. (Leiden: Brill, 2010), provide a useful bibliography of recent research.

from Marseilles to Ostia. A few exceptional individuals, like the seventh-century Anglo-Saxon abbot Benedict Biscop, made multiple journeys to Rome in their lifetimes, but most early medieval pilgrims were not seasoned travelers and were therefore much more vulnerable to the hardships of the road.[17] Some found themselves stranded in foreign lands without any money. Prelates feared especially for women who resorted to prostitution to survive in these circumstances. In 747 Boniface advised Archbishop Cuthbert of Canterbury to prohibit religious women (*velatis feminis*) from making the pilgrimage to Rome because "a great many of them perish and few retain their virtue."[18] The number of Anglo-Saxon pilgrims who had become harlots in the towns of Lombardy, East Francia, and Gaul had already become "a scandal and disgrace to your whole Church."[19]

For medieval pilgrims the promise of transalpine travel to Rome was proximity to the physical remains of the saints, particularly the bones of Saints Peter and Paul. Anglo-Saxon pilgrims were by far the best documented foreign constituency in early medieval Rome; they traveled to Italy primarily by donkey or on foot, but a network of friends, allies, and compatriots supported them on their long journey and sustained them when they arrived at their goal. Abbeys usually extended their hospitality to foreign monks on pilgrimage, while lay pilgrims stayed in hostels and inns along the road and sought refuge in shrines in the more remote parts of the countryside.[20] In the eighth century, Carolingian rulers granted safe passage, freedom from tolls, and the use of hospices throughout the Frankish realm to pilgrims bound for Rome.[21] Once they had reached the ancient city and paid their respects to Saints Peter and Paul, Anglo-Saxon pilgrims proceeded to the *schola Saxonum*, a district near the Portico of Saint Peter settled by people from England.[22]

---

17. On Benedict's six trips to Rome in the seventh century, see Bede, *Historia abbatum*, 1–13, in *Abbots of Wearmouth and Jarrow*, ed. and trans. Christopher Grocock and I. N. Wood (Oxford: Clarendon Press, 2013), 22–53.

18. Boniface, *Epistola*, 78, ed. Michael Tangl, in MGH Epistolae Selectae, 1:169.

19. Ibid.: "Perpauce enim sunt civitates in Longobardia vel in Francia aut in Gallia, in qua non sit adultera vel meretrix generis Anglorum. Quod scandalum est et turpitudo totius aecclesiae vestrae."

20. For an example, see Michael Matheus, "Borgo San Martino: An Early Medieval Pilgrimage Station on the Via Francigena Near Sutri," *Papers of the British School at Rome* 68 (2000): 185–99.

21. See, for example, Pippin, *Capitulare*, 4:754–55, ed. Alfred Boretius, in MGH Capitularia regum Francorum, 1:32; and Charlemagne, *Capitulare missorum generale*, 27 (802), ed. Alfred Boretius, in MGH Capitularia regum Francorum, 1:96.

22. Wilfrid J. Moore, *The Saxon Pilgrims to Rome and the Schola Saxonum* (Fribourg, Switzerland: Society of St. Paul, 1937), remains unsurpassed on this topic.

The neighborhood had its own church (Santa Maria) with its own cemetery, where all Anglo-Saxons, rich or poor, who died within the limits of the district had the right to be buried. Many pilgrims made it their goal to live out their final days in this transplanted community, so that they could rest in death near the tombs of the apostles.

The perils of transalpine travel were considerable for merchants and pilgrims alike.[23] Early medieval prayers for people about to embark on long voyages beseeched God specifically to protect them from the dangers of wild animals, hostile weather, and brigands.[24] Wild animals were the least of the threats facing premodern Alpine travelers, but they nonetheless aroused considerable fear and anxiety. Wolves received special mention in prayers for safe passage, perhaps because they carried the added freight of demonic association in early medieval thought.[25] The devil sometimes took the form of a wolf or used this animal as the agent of his will.[26] For example, in the year 988, a wolf suddenly appeared in the cathedral church at Orléans. Much to the amazement of those present, it seized the bell rope in its jaws and unnerved the congregation by ringing the church bells before it was driven away. According to the eleventh-century chronicler who narrated this event, the unusual activity of this beast portended the great fire that destroyed the entire city with all of its churches the very next year.[27] Wolves may have posed some risk to lone travelers because they could easily startle or injure horses and donkeys and thereby threaten their riders, but despite the anxiety that they provoked, there is no evidence to suggest that wild animals were a significant threat to large pilgrim and merchant caravans crossing the Alps.

---

23. For a learned discussion of the myriad weather-related dangers facing Alpine travelers informed both by ancient sources and personal experience, see the treatise by the pioneering mountaineer Josias Simler, *De alpibus commentarius* (1574), esp. chap. 14, "De itinerum alpinorum difficultatibus et periculis, et quomodo haec superari possint," in *Josias Simler et les origines de l'alpinisme jusqu'en 1600*, ed. W. A. B. Coolidge (Grenoble, France: Allier Frères, 1904), 210–37.

24. Adolph Franz, *Die kirchlichen Benediktionen im Mittelalter* (Graz, Austria: Akademische Druckund Verlagsanstalt, 1960), 2:261–71. For more on long-distance travel around the year 1000 and the hazards associated with it, see Heinrich Fichtenau, "Reisen und Reisende," in *Beiträge zur Mediävistik: Ausgewählte Aufsätze* (Stuttgart: Hiersemann, 1986), 3:1–79.

25. On the image of the wolf in the medieval imagination, with an emphasis on British and Scandinavian evidence, see Aleksander Pluskowski, *Wolves and the Wilderness in the Middle Ages* (Woodbridge, England: Boydell, 2006).

26. See, for example, Odilo, *Vita sancti Maioli*, AASS Maii, 2:683–88, reprinted in PL 142, cols. 959–62. For further discussion of this text, see chapter 2 of the present volume.

27. Rodulfus Glaber, *Historiarum libri quinque*, 2.8, ed. and trans. John France, in *Rodulphus Glaber: The Five Books of Histories and the Life of St. William* (Oxford: Clarendon Press, 1989), 66.

Hostile weather, on the other hand, was perilous to even the most expe-rienced travelers. Traffic over the Great Saint Bernard Pass was heaviest in the summer months—particularly in July and August, when warm weather promised an uneventful crossing. Travel during any other season involved substantial risks. Only the most seasoned or desperate individuals dared to cross the Alps during the winter, because heavy snows could bury the paths and strand travelers in remote mountain villages for months until the weather cleared. Medieval authors spoke with fear about precipitous trails made treacherous by ice and the threat of lethal avalanches. When Emperor Henry IV and his entourage crossed the Mont Cenis Pass during the harsh winter of 1076–77, they had little trouble reaching the apex of their route with the help of local guides (marones), but had to endure a frightful descent down the frozen mountainside.[28] The toll on their horses was particularly brutal: "Some of the horses were lowered on various contrivances, others were dragged down with their feet tied. Some were killed in the process, many were maimed, only a few surviving the danger whole and sound."[29] Like-wise, in 1128 a pilgrim caravan attempting to cross the Great Saint Bernard Pass shortly after Christmas found their path blocked by snow. Retreating to a nearby church, they also hired local guides to negotiate a route through the drifts while they prayed for safe passage.

> When these devotions were taking place with the utmost fervency in the church, a most sorrowful lament sounded throughout the village, for as the scouts were advancing out of the village in one another's steps, an enormous mass of snow like a mountain slipped from the rocks and carried them away, as it seems to the depths of Hell. Those who had become aware of the mysterious disaster had made a hasty and furious dash down to the murderous spot, and having dug out their guides, were carrying them back, some of them quite lifeless and others half-dead upon poles, and dragging others with broken limbs in their arms. . . . When the poor pilgrims came out of the church, they were

28. Lampert of Hersfeld, *Annales*, anno 1077, ed. Oswald Holder-Egger, in MGH SRG, 38:286. On these local Alpine guides, who are often referred to as *marones* in the sources, see Coolidge, *Josias Simler*, 51**–56** (Pièce annexe, no. 17), esp. 51**: "L'étymologie et l'histoire du mot «marron» sont fort obscures."

29. Lampert of Hersfeld, *Annales*, anno 1077, ed. Oswald Holder-Egger, in MGH SRG, 38:287: "Equorum alios per machinas quasdam summittebant, alios colligatis pedibus trahebant, ex quibus multi, dum traherentur, mortui, plures debilitati, pauci admodum integri incolumnesque periculum evadere potuerunt." Translated by John E. Tyler in *The Alpine Passes: The Middle Ages (962–1250)* (Oxford: Basil Blackwell, 1930), 30.

terrified by this horrible accident, hesitated a little while, and then fled back down the mountain as fast as they could.[30]

After spending a week in a town farther down the mountainside waiting for good weather, the pilgrims returned to "the death-dealing village, fear of death lending them wings, now crawling, now stumbling" as they made their way over the pass.[31] Fortunately for them, the weather remained clear during their crossing, allowing them "to escape from the horrid sanctuary of Jove" and reach their own homes in safety.[32]

Tales of brigandage, kidnapping, and murder also troubled the minds of early medieval travelers. Merchants and pilgrims were particularly vulnerable to robbery because they usually carried substantial amounts of gold and supplies with them. In premodern Europe, banditry was a common problem even in the shadow of city walls.[33] In the late fourth century, Quintus Aurelius Symmachus knew for certain that he would be vulnerable to robbery if he abandoned the safety of Rome; the fact that he was the prefect of the city offered him no protection from bandits.[34] While the inexorable tide

---

30. Gislebertus de Saint-Trond, *Gesta Abbatum Trudonensium*, 12, ed. Paul Tombeur, in CCCM 257A:72:

> Cumque hęc in ęcclesia cum summa deuotione agerentur, percrepuit per plateam luctuosissimus luctus. Nam marones per ordinem de uilla egressos subito lapsus rupibus instar montis densissimus niuis globus decem inuoluit, et usque ad inferni locum uisus est extulisse. Qui huius infausti mysterii aliquando conscii fuerant, precipiti cursu ad hunc homicidam lacum uelocissime ruerant, et effossos marones, aliios exanimes in contis referebant, alios semiuiuos, alios contritis ossibus in manibus trahebant. . . . Tam horribili occursu peregrini exeuntes de ęcclesia exterriti, paululum hesitauerunt, et idem timentes sibi futurum, quantocius Restopolim refugerunt.

Translated by Tyler in *Alpine Passes*, 28–29.

31. Gislebertus de Saint-Trond, *Gesta Abbatum Trudonensium*, 12, ed. Tombeur, 72–73: "Ibi acta epyphania Domini et expectato sereno aere, conductis maronibus, mortiferam uillulam repetunt, et timore mortis pedibus uelocitatem prebente, die illa usque ad medium montis, modo reptando, modo ruendo, vix tandem perueniunt." Translated by Tyler in *Alpine Passes*, 29.

32. Gislebertus de Saint-Trond, *Gesta Abbatum Trudonensium*, 12, ed. Tombeur, 73: "Sequenti die recępto aliquantulum spiritu, prophana Iouis sacra effugiunt, et ad patrium solum tendentes, sine graui difficultate perueniunt." Translated by Tyler in *Alpine Passes*, 29. Over a century ago, Frederick Pollock suggested that tenth-century Anglo-Saxon charters cursing those who broke the conditions of their agreements with "frigid winds of ice" (*perpessus sit gelidis glaciarum flatibus*) were the work of scribes who had experienced firsthand the hardships of crossing the Alps in the winter. For Pollock's comment, see Hubert Hall, *Studies in English Official Historical Documents* (Cambridge: Cambridge University Press, 1908), 198–99. For more on the so-called glacial curse in these charters, see Petra Hofmann, "Infernal Imagery in Anglo-Saxon Charters," (PhD diss., University of Saint Andrews, 2008), 87–95.

33. The classic study remains Brent Shaw, "Bandits in the Roman Empire," *Past and Present* 105 (1984): 3–52. No comparable synthesis of this quality exists for early medieval Europe.

34. Symmachus, *Epistola*, 2.22 (*Flaviano fratri*), ed. Jean-Pierre Callu, in *Symmaque: Lettres* (Paris: Les Belles Lettres, 1972), 1:167.

of pilgrims visiting the holy sites of early medieval Rome explains the reports
of bandit activity in the vicinity of the city, robbery was most prevalent on
roads that ran through remote hinterlands, like the Alpine passes, where out-
laws could harass wayfarers with little fear of reprisal from civic authorities.
Martin of Tours (d. 397) was one such victim. In the early 360s, a decade
before he became bishop, brigands (*latrones*) waylaid the holy man after he lost
his way crossing the Alps.[35] He narrowly avoided murder at their hands and
escaped only after compelling his pagan captor to convert to Christianity.[36]
The threat of violence along Alpine routes was endemic throughout the early
medieval period.[37] A capitulary of Louis II issued in Pavia in 850 ordering
counts and their retainers to seek out and capture "bands of brigands who
plunder and often wound or murder those en route [from the Frankish king-
dom] to Rome for the purpose of prayer" is one voice in a litany of futile
responses to what was by the Carolingian period an age-old problem.[38]

   While the fear of brigandage troubled the minds of transalpine travelers
throughout the early Middle Ages, at no time was it more acute than during
the tenth century, when a new danger emerged in the Alps. From the 890s
onward, Muslim adventurers held sway over the southern coast of Provence
from their citadel at Fraxinetum. In the summer months they made forays
into the Great Saint Bernard Pass to tap the rich vein of merchant and pilgrim traffic that stretched across the Alps. Even though this Muslim community was relatively new to the shores of Europe, they were in fact the last
breaker of a century-long tide of Islamic expansion into the northwestern
Mediterranean in the early medieval period. While their presence so far north
in the Alpine passes distinguished them from other Muslims who had conquered and settled farther south on the Italian Peninsula, these groups nonetheless shared many similarities, especially in the way that they exploited
the weaknesses of local Christian populations in pursuit of their primary
economic concern: the capture of Europeans for the slave markets of the
Islamic world.

---

35. Sulpicius Severus, *Vita Martini*, 5.4, ed. Jacques Fontaine, in *Sulpice Sévère: Vie de saint Martin*, SC
133, 1:262.

36. Despite some clear similarities, this story does not seem to have influenced accounts of the
captivity of Maiolus of Cluny.

37. The laconic report in 931 of the murder of Bishop Robert of Tours and his entourage in the
Alps by brigands is but one example; see Flodoard, *Annales*, anno 931, in *Les Annales de Flodoard*, ed.
Philippe Lauer (Paris: Alphonse Picard et Fils, 1905), 48.

38. Louis II, *De rebus vero saecularibus* 1, ed. Georg Pertz, in MGH Capitularia regum Francorum,
2:86: "Perventum est ad nos, quod eos, qui Romam orationis causa pergunt vel qui negotiandi gratia
per regnum nostrum discurrunt, collecti latrones diripiant eosque aliquotiens vulnerent vel occidant
et eorum bona diripiant."

☞ The Muslims of La Garde-Freinet

Muslim penetration into Christian territories along the northwestern Mediterranean rim (excluding Spain) began in earnest in the early ninth century and was felt most acutely in Italy. The Islamic campaign to conquer Sicily that began in 829 with the fall of Mazara and Mineo and the capture of the Apulian port of Bari in 847 by the Aghlabids of North Africa realigned the political axis of southern Italy, which had been dominated for decades by the Carolingians, the Lombard kings, and the viceroys of distant Constantinople.[39] Christians were indirectly complicit in these conquests because competing local rulers in the Lombard kingdoms took to hiring Islamic warriors in their civil wars, which increased instability in the region. In 835, for example, the city of Naples paid Muslim adventurers to defend their interests against their antagonistic Lombard neighbors.[40] Similarly, in 842, quarrelling Beneventans invited Muslims from North Africa to serve as mercenaries (*auxiliatores*) in their conflict only to watch helplessly as their cities fell prey to the depredations of these so-called guests.[41] After the Muslim sack of Rome in 846, the Carolingians recognized the danger of the Islamic presence in the Lombard territories and sent Lothar's son Louis II to reconcile the competing interests among the Lombards to obviate their need for foreign mercenary support.[42]

While it is not unusual to find Muslims serving as hired henchmen for Christian lords in southern Italy, they were in fact most active in the ninth-century Mediterranean as seafaring pirates who preyed on littoral settlements between the coast of Provence and the Straits of Messina. Muslim entrepreneurs had been active in these waters since the time of Charlemagne; as early as 806, they abducted sixty monks from the island of Pantelleria between

---

39. For reliable surveys of these developments, see Hugh Kennedy, "The Muslims in Europe," in *The New Cambridge Medieval History, vol. 2: c. 700–c. 900*, ed. Rosamond McKitterick (Cambridge: Cambridge University Press, 1995), 249–71; and Alex Metcalfe, *The Muslims of Medieval Italy* (Edinburgh: Edinburgh University Press, 2009), 4–43.

40. John the Deacon, *Gesta Episcoporum Neapolitanorum*, 57, ed. Georg Waitz, in MGH SSRL, 431.

41. *Annales Bertiniani*, anno 842, ed. Georg Waitz, in MGH SRG, 5:28. It took three years for the Beneventans to restore order; see *Annales Bertiniani*, anno 843 and anno 845, ed. Waitz, 30 and 33.

42. The result was a treaty enacted in 849; see *Radelgisi et Siginulfi Divisio Ducatus Beneventani*, ed. Georg Pertz, in MGH Leges, 4:221–25. These efforts were largely ineffectual, as the many letters of Pope John VIII (ca. 872–82) to Charles the Bald, Charles the Fat, and Emperor Basil I reporting the devastation wrought by the Saracens in southern Italy and requesting a military response to their activities make clear. For a summary of John VIII's concerns about the Saracens with reference to previous literature, see Dorothee Arnold, "Pope John VIII," in CMR 1:804–9.

Sicily and Tunisia and transported them to the slave markets of Spain.[43] In 838, another group targeted the religious houses of the city of Marseilles, carrying off every religious woman and all men, lay and clerical, as well as a substantial amount of church treasure.[44] In 842, Muslim pirates sailed up the Rhône to ravage the land around Arles.[45] The aim of these raids was primarily the harvesting of slaves. As Michael McCormick has shown, the demand for European slaves in Muslim principalities around the Mediterranean rim fueled a thriving maritime commerce in human beings well into the Carolingian period.[46] Islamic law prohibited Muslims from enslaving other Muslims, so enterprising merchants turned their eyes northward to Europe and paid handsomely for Christian men, women, and children. The most vivid testimony of this economy comes from the account of Bernard, a Frankish monk who made a pilgrimage to the Holy Land in 867.[47] He traveled to the Amirate of Bari to obtain letters of safe conduct from Emir Sawdan (r. 857–71) before proceeding to the port of Taranto to find a ship that would take him to Alexandria.[48] There he observed many Muslim slave galleys, the hulls of which were crammed with thousands of captured Christians bound for the markets of Africa and Lebanon.[49] Bernard underscores the "tragic banality" of the European slave trade in this period by boarding one of these ships without protest as a paying passenger protected by the emir's documents.[50]

In one case, ninth-century Muslim raiders active along the European coastline kidnapped a church prelate to collect a ransom for his release. Among the most noteworthy events of 869, the *Annals of Saint Bertin* re-

---

43. Einhard, *Vita Karoli*, 17, ed. Oswald Holder-Egger, in MGH SRG, 25:21. Charlemagne purchased the freedom of many of these monks, allowing them to return to their homes. See *Annales Regni Francorum*, anno 807, ed. Georg Pertz, in MGH SRG, 6:124; and McCormick, *Origins of the European Economy*, 893 (no. R272).

44. *Annales Bertiniani*, anno 838, ed. Waitz, 24; and McCormick, *Origins of the European Economy*, 917 (no. R441). Greek pirates attacked the city a decade later; see *Annales Bertiniani*, anno 848, ed. Waitz, 36.

45. *Annales Bertiniani*, anno 842, ed. Waitz, 28.

46. For what follows, see McCormick, *Origins of the European Economy*.

47. Bernard, *Itinerarium*, ed. Josef Ackermann, in *Das "Itinerarum Bernardi Monachi": Edition—Übersetzung—Kommentar*, MGH Studien und Texte, 50:115–27. For more on Bernard's travels, including a map of his route to the Holy Land, see McCormick, *Origins of the European Economy*, 134–37, 940 (nos. R579–80).

48. Bernard, *Itinerarium*, 3, ed. Ackermann, 116.

49. Bernard, *Itinerarium*, 4, ed. Ackermann, 117.

50. The phrase "tragic banality" is from Michael McCormick, "New Light on the Dark Ages: How the Slave Trade Fuelled the Carolingian Economy," *Past and Present* 177 (2002): 54.

lated at length the abduction of Roland, the archbishop of Arles and abbot of Saint Caesarius.[51] Muslim pirates slaughtered three hundred of the prelate's followers on an island owned by the abbey at the mouth of the Rhône and took Roland prisoner on board their ship. His captors negotiated the payment of 150 pounds of silver, 150 cloaks, 150 swords, and 150 slaves for his release. Roland died in captivity, but this did not prevent the Muslims from concluding the transaction. Upon receiving the ransom they dressed the corpse of the abbot in his priestly regalia, propped him up on a chair, and returned him to the island. His liberators greeted their archbishop with joy, only to discover with shock and dismay that he was dead. Even though accounts of kidnapping episodes like this one are exceedingly rare in the ninth century, the amount of human capital offered as ransom, even if exaggerated, is indicative of the exponential profit that the abduction of prominent individuals could yield.

Slave harvesting was the primary occupation of Muslim pirates in the ninth-century Mediterranean, but their most notorious raid in this period shows that material gain motivated their activities as well. In August 846, an enormous force of Muslims from Palermo attacked the towns of Ostia and Portus at the mouth of the Tiber in preparation for an assault on the city of Rome. Their goal was the treasury of the Church of Saint Peter, which the Carolingians and the papacy had spent decades embellishing with lavish gifts of eastern silks, ornate liturgical objects, and richly adorned reliquaries. Almost every chronicler of the period commented on the audacity of this raid, the desecration of the holy sites caused by the invaders, and the reprisals taken against them by Christian forces.[52]

Toward the end of the ninth century a group of Islamic adventurers intensified Muslim activity along the Provençal coast by establishing a permanent base of operations in a fortified citadel called Fraxinetum.[53] Unlike the inhabitants of Aghlabid Sicily (829–1091) or the Emirate of Bari (847–71), there is no evidence to suggest that the Muslims of La Garde-Freinet were

---

51. *Annales Bertiniani*, anno 869, ed. Waitz, 106–7.

52. For an eyewitness account, see *Life of Pope Sergius II*, 45–47, in *Le Liber Pontificalis*, ed. Louis Marie Olivier Duchesne (Paris: Ernest Thorin, 1892), 2:99–101. Other ninth-century accounts include *Annales Bertiniani*, anno 846, ed. Waitz, 34; *Annales Xantenses*, anno 846, ed. Berhard von Simson, in MGH SRG, 12:15–16; *Annales Fuldenses*, anno 846, ed. Friedrich Kurze, in MGH SRG, 7:36; and John the Deacon, *Gesta Episcoporum Neapolitanorum*, 60, ed. Waitz, 432–33. See also McCormick, *Origins of the European Economy*, 923 (nos. R476–78).

53. On the location and topography of Fraxinetum, see Philippe Sénac, "Contribution a l'étude des incursions musulmanes dans l'occident chrétien: La localisation du Gabel Al-Qilal," *Revue de l'Occident Musulman et de la Méditerranée* 31 (1981): 7–12; and Philippe Sénac, *Provence et piraterie sarrasine* (Paris: Maisonneuve et Larose, 1982), 17–32.

recognized as a polity or outpost of any Islamic central government in the Iberian Peninsula or in the East. Some scholars have argued that the Umayyads of Cordoba directed the activities of these brigands and provided them with material support, but with one exception the evidence for this supposition is largely circumstantial.[54] Abbot John of Gorze's embassy to the court of Caliph 'Abd al-Rahman III in Cordoba in 953 has often been interpreted as a diplomatic response by Emperor Otto I to Muslim raids in Provence, which implies that the emperor inferred Umayyad support for the inhabitants of La Garde-Freinet.[55] The surviving account of the embassy speaks only generally, however, about the problem of Muslim brigandage, which was endemic along the western Mediterranean coast and throughout the Alpine passes in this period, and does not mention Fraxinetum by name.[56] Likewise, archaeologists have been overly eager to link early medieval shipwrecks off the coast of Provence with the inhabitants of Le Garde-Freinet. A total of four such wrecks dating from the tenth century have been found with Spanish cargo (amphorae, bronze ingots, and lamps from Cordoba) in their holds.[57] The destination of these boats is unknown, but some scholars have nonetheless asserted on very little evidence that they were pirate vessels from Fraxinetum or supply ships from Spain en route to support the Muslim enclave in Provence.

The most compelling testimony for the relationship between La Garde-Freinet and Umayyad Cordoba comes from the *Antapodosis*, an unfinished

---

54. See Mohammad Ballan, "Fraxinetum: An Islamic Frontier State in Tenth-Century Provence," *Comitatus* 41 (2010): 66–75, following the work of Sénac and others.

55. For the case that Fraxinetum was the specific issue that propelled the embassy, see El-Hajji, *Andalusian Diplomatic Relations*, 207–27. One scholar has recently suggested that the purpose of these embassies was "to forge an alliance against a common foe, the pirates of La Garde-Freinet" (Michael Frassetto, "John of St. Arnoul," in CMR 2:476), but this seems highly unlikely given that the inhabitants of Fraxinetum posed no discernable threat to the Umayyads of Cordoba.

56. John of St. Arnulf, *Vita Iohannis Gorziensis*, 130, ed. Parisse, 156: "[A]micitiam pacemque de infestatione latrunculorum Sarracenorum quoquo pacto conficiat." More than a decade later, in a letter dated 968, Otto did express his desire to destroy the Muslim enclave at La Garde-Freinet, but made no explicit connection between this community and the Umayyads; see Widukind, *Res Gestae Saxonicae*, 3.70, ed. Georg Waitz and K. A. Kehr, in MGH SRG, 60:147: "[P]er Fraxinetum ad destruendos Sarracenos, Deo comite, iter arripiemus."

57. On these wrecks, see Daniel Brentchaloff and Philippe Sénac, "Note sur l'épave sarrasine de la rade d'Agay (Saint-Raphaël, Var)," *Archeologie islamique* 2 (1991): 71–79; A. J. Parker, *Ancient Shipwrecks of the Mediterranean and the Roman Provinces* (Oxford: Tepus Reparatum, 1992), 42 (no. 8), 70 (no. 97), and 314 (no. 821); Jean-Pierre Joncheray and Philippe Sénac, "Une nouvelle épave sarrasine du haut moyen âge," *Archeologie islamique* 5 (1995): 25–34; Marie-Pierre Jézégou, Anne Joncheray, and Jean-Pierre Joncheray, "Les épaves sarrasines d'Agay et de Cannes," *Archéologia* 377 (1997): 32–39; Jean-Pierre Joncheray, "The Four Saracen Shipwrecks of Provence," in *Barbarian Seas: Late Rome to Islam*, ed. Sean Kingsley (London: Periplus, 2004), 102–7; and McCormick, *Origins of the European Economy*, 598–99, table 20.4.

history of Germany, Italy, and Constantinople composed around 960 by
Bishop Liudprand of Cremona (c. 920–73) and dedicated to Recemund, the
Christian bishop who served as 'Abd al-Rahman III's ambassador to the court
of Otto I.[58] According to Liudprand, the Muslims of Fraxinetum hailed
originally from Spain and arrived in Provence against their will on a ship
blown off course by coastal winds.[59] Once this small band of twenty individuals had established themselves by murdering the residents of a Christian stronghold, they sent messengers back to Spain with word that the
inhabitants of Provence offered no resistance against them and as a result
bolstered their number to well over a hundred. Addressing Recemund,
Liudprand called the residents of La Garde-Freinet "tributaries of your
king, that is, 'Abd al-Rahman."[60] There are reasons to question, however,
the bishop's depiction of the relationship between Fraxinetum and Cordoba. Liudprand dedicated his *Antapodosis* to a bishop who lived among
Muslims and—from the perspective of a European Christian—served an
impious sovereign. As Karl Leyser has argued, Liudprand's primary aim in
this was to remind Recemund where his loyalties lay and to instruct him
about the perils facing European Christendom from Muslims and other
unbelievers.[61] By presenting the inhabitants of La Garde-Freinet at the onset
of his history both as the "tributaries" of 'Abd al-Rahman and as the
authors of the destruction of Provence, Liudprand relayed a powerful
message to Recemund about the moral consequences of compliance with
the Muslim ruler he had chosen to serve. This agenda introduces a shadow
of doubt about the veracity of the bishop's claim.

The Muslim community at La Garde-Freinet produced no documents of
its own, so little is known about the size and composition of the settlement
except what can be gleaned from Christian sources like Liudprand.[62] While
the bishop of Cremona made the explicit distinction between this group from

---

58. Liudprand's work has been edited by Chiesa, and translated with an excellent introduction by
Paolo Squatriti in *The Complete Works of Liudprand of Cremona* (Washington, DC: Catholic University of America Press, 2007).

59. For what follows, see Liudprand, *Antapodosis*, 1.1–4, ed. Chiesa, 5–7.

60. Liudprand, *Antapodosis*, 1.2, ed. Chiesa, 6: "[S]unt tributarii regis, Abderahamen."

61. Karl Leyser, "Ends and Means in Liudprand of Cremona," in *Byzantium and the West, c. 850–c.
1200: Proceedings of the XVIII Spring Symposium of Byzantine Studies, Oxford, 30 March–1 April 1984*,
ed. J. D. Howard-Johnston (Amsterdam: Hakkert, 1988), 119–43, esp. 126–29; reprinted in Karl
Leyser, *Communications and Power in Medieval Europe: The Carolingian and Ottonian Centuries*, ed.
Timothy Reuter (London: Hambledon Press, 1994), 125–42.

62. La Garde-Freinet received mention in several Arabic geographies from the tenth to the thirteenth centuries, but these texts do not provide any details about the composition of the tenth-
century Muslim community. See Paul-Albert Février, *La Provence des origines à l'an mil: Histoire*

Spain and the African Muslims active in central and southern Italy in this period, whom he considered to be much more savage, the inhabitants of Fraxinetum could have comprised opportunistic individuals from Islamic lands around the Mediterranean rim.[63] The aborted effort of Hugh of Arles, the king of Italy, to destroy their base in 942 with a coordinated assault by land forces and a blockade of Byzantine ships wielding Greek fire implies that the community was substantial, perhaps numbering several hundred fighting men at the time.[64] The longevity of La Garde-Freinet—some eight decades from its putative founding in the 890s to its destruction in the early 970s—suggests that the settlement may have indeed had periodic support from outside Provence and that its numbers were bolstered further by the presence of women and children, like those at a contemporary Muslim enclave near Mount Garigliano in Italy.[65] Little else is known for certain about its size and organization.

The Muslim settlement at Fraxinetum is best understood as an autonomous, entrepreneurial community whose inhabitants flourished for decades as mercenaries and slavers during a time of acute political instability in Provence.[66] In 888 the death of Charles the Fat heralded a crisis that lasted for several decades as local magnates who had grown powerful in the service of his family seized authority at the expense of his underage though other-

---

et archéologie (Rennes: Ouest-France Université, 1989), 487–91; and Ballan, "Fraxinetum," 61–65.

63. Liudprand, Antapodosis, 2.44, ed. Chiesa, 53. I disagree with Ballan's use of the homogenizing name Andalusi to characterize the Muslims of La Garde-Freinet; see Ballan, "Fraxinetum," 23n1.

64. Liudprand, Antapodosis, 5.9, ed. Chiesa, 128; and McCormick, Origins of the European Economy, 970 (no. R812). On the failure of this offensive, see Archibald R. Lewis, Naval Power and Trade in the Mediterranean, A.D. 500–1100 (Princeton, NJ: Princeton University Press, 1951), 150; and Ekkehard Eickhoff, Seekrieg und Seepolitik zwischen Islam und Abendland: Das Mittelmeer unter byzantinischer und arabischer Hegemonie (650–1040) (Berlin: De Gruyter, 1966), 317–18.

65. Liudprand, Antapodosis, 2.44, ed. Chiesa, 53.

66. While brigandage, mercenary employment, and slave trading were the primary activities of the Muslims of La Garde-Freinet, Arabic sources make reference to the agricultural activities at the site as well. Some scholars have also ascribed metallurgical expertise to the community, though on the basis of the very flimsy evidence of the reference to Saracens in the names of local mines ("le trou de Sarrasins," "gallerie sarrasine," etc.) and the discovery of medieval forges nearby, the provenance of which is sketchy at best. By and large these activities were probably attempts at self-sufficiency and did not represent the economic rationale for the existence of the community. See Ballan, "Fraxinetum," 61–65, which follows Philippe Sénac, Musulmans et sarrasins dans le sud de la Gaule du VIIIe siècle au XIe siècle (Paris: Sycomore, 1980), in overstating the importance of the nonmilitary activities of the community. Ballan's article also suggests, on the basis of one Arabic source, that the Muslims of La Garde-Freinet were mujahideen who were actively engaged in jihad with the Christians of Provence. I find this hypothesis untenable without the support of further documentation.

wise legitimate son.[67] "After his death," wrote Regino of Prüm, "the kingdoms which had obeyed his authority behaved as though a legitimate heir was lacking and dissolved into separate parts. Without waiting for their natural lord, each decided to create a little king from its own innards. This was the cause of great wars . . ."[68] Just as Aghlabid Muslims had sold their swords to the warring factions of southern Italy in the ninth century, the inhabitants of Fraxinetum bolstered the modest armies of the quarreling kinglets of Provence. Liudprand remarked on the cleverness of these Muslims, who "having defeated one faction with the help of another . . . began to hunt down by all means those they at first seemed to defend."[69] Their perfidious duplicity was catastrophic for the entire region: "They ravaged, they exterminated, they made it so that no one was left."[70]

No one was left: Liudprand's ominous description of the impact of the Muslims of La Garde-Freinet on Provençal society speaks plainly to the fact that the primary goal of their escalated brigandage was slave harvesting. After the devastation of Provence the bishop reported that they ravaged the countryside of northern Italy as well, leaving many cities empty of people (*depopulatis plurimis urbibus*), just as the Aghlabids had done a century earlier in Campania.[71] The depopulation of the rural hinterland placed a strain on the income of local monasteries, which relied on the inhabitants of their domains for the production of grain and other foods. The testament of Rostang, archbishop of Arles, from 897 lamented how the onslaught of the Muslims had emptied the lands of his abbey and many others.[72] Under such

---

67. Simon MacLean, *Kingship and Politics in the Late Ninth Century: Charles the Fat and the End of the Carolingian Empire* (Cambridge: Cambridge University Press, 2003).

68. Regino of Prüm, *Chronicon*, anno 888, ed. Friedrich Kurze, in MGH SRG, 50:129: "Post cuius mortem regna, que eius ditioni paruerant, veluti legitimo destituta herede, in partes a sua compage resolvuntur et iam non naturalem dominum presolantur, sed unumquodque de suis visceribus regem sibi creari disponit. Quae causa magnos bellorum motus excitavit." Translated by Simon MacLean in *History and Politics in Late Carolingian and Ottonian Europe: The Chronicle of Regino of Prüm and Adalbert of Magdeburg* (Manchester: Manchester University Press, 2009), 199 (slightly altered).

69. Liudprand, *Antapodosis*, 1.4, ed. Chiesa, 7: "Saraceni . . . alteram alterius auxilio partis debellantes . . . quos primo defendere videbantur modis omnibus insecuntur."

70. Ibid.: "Saeviunt itaque, exterminant, nil reliqui faciunt."

71. Liudprand, *Antapodosis* 2.43, ed. Chiesa, 53. This occurred in the 930s. On the activity of the Aghlabids in Campania, see Barbara M. Kreutz, *Before the Normans: Southern Italy in the Ninth and Tenth Centuries* (Philadelphia: University of Pennsylvania Press, 1991), 53: "Aside from two major monasteries, the south Italian countryside could hardly have yielded much in the way of riches; one might therefore wonder at the continuous Muslim sweeps through rural areas, and we can only conclude that the loot was primarily human."

72. "Testament de Rostang, archevêque d'Arles," in *Gallia christiana novissima: Histoire des archevêchés, évêchés et abbayes de France d'après les documents authentiques recueillis dans les registres du Vatican et les*

pressure, some religious communities simply abandoned the region altogether, as was the case with the monks of Psalmodi, whose new abbey Charles the Simple confirmed in a diploma from 909.[73] Similarly, the monks of the Abbey of Novalesa in Piedmont fled before the Muslim advance, leaving behind not only their home but the thousands of books in their library.[74] An eleventh-century account of the life of a Provençal lay saint named Bobo, a warrior-aristocrat who allegedly waged a meritorious war against the Muslims of Fraxinetum, suggests that their encroachment did meet with periodic local resistance, but the consensus of the surviving evidence makes it clear that these efforts were largely ineffectual.[75]

Throughout the early tenth century, the Muslims of La Garde-Freinet were active in the countryside and coastal waters of Provence, but they also made forays into the Alpine passes to harry and waylay pilgrim and merchant traffic.[76] Fearful responses to their presence in Christian sources from this period allow us to chart their range of activity in the region. In 927, Archbishop Aimery of Narbonne complained that he was unable to travel to Rome because Saracens blocked the route through the Alps.[77] It was shortly thereafter, in the 930s, that Liudprand reported the devastation wrought by the Muslims of La Garde-Freinet in the foothills of northern Italy and

archives locales, ed. J.-H. Albanés and Ulysse Chevalier (Valence, France: Valentinoise, 1901), vol. 3, cols. 94–96, no. 233 (dated 6 June 897): "[O]ppressione tamen Paganorum seviente ipsius loci unde Deo sacrate sustentabantur deserte facte sunt, sicut et multe alie."

73. "Diplôme de Charles le Simple pour l'abbaye de Psalmodi," ed. Claude de Vic and Joseph Vaissete, in *Histoire générale de Languedoc avec des notes et les pièces justificatives* (Toulouse: J.P. Paya, 1840), 2:707: "[Q]uod per oppressionem paganorum monasterium Psalmodiense mutatum est in locum qui dicitur Corneliacensis, ubi ecclesiae contructae sunt . . . nuper a Sarracenis destructae."

74. *Chronicon novaliciense*, 4.26 [*sic*, correctly 4.25], ed. Georg Pertz, in MGH SS, 7:108. On the structure and content of this chronicle, which was written in the eleventh century after the return of the community to Novalesa, see Patrick J. Geary, *Phantoms of Remembrance: Memory and Oblivion at the End of the First Millennium* (Princeton, NJ: Princeton University Press, 1996), 115–33.

75. For more on Bobo, who is consistently cast as a herald of crusader sensibilities, see Claude Carozzi, "La vie de saint Bobon: un modèle clunisien de sainteté laïque," in *Guerriers et moines: Conversion et sainteté aristocratiques dans l'occident médiéval (IXe–XIIe siècle)*, ed. Michel Lauwers (Antibes, France: APDCA, 2002), 467–91; and Damien Carraz, *L'ordre du temple dans la basse vallée du Rhône (1124–1312): Ordres militaires, croisades et sociétés méridionales* (Lyon: Presses Universitaires de Lyon, 2005), 48–50.

76. The persistent activity of the Muslims in the Mediterranean is suggested by the *Annals of Flodoard*, ed. Lauer, 47, which reported in 931, "Graeci Sarracenos per mare insequentes usque in Fraxinidum saltum, ubi erat refugium ipsorum et unde egredientes Italiam sedulis praedabantur incursibus, Alpibus etiam occupatis." See also Eickhoff, *Seekrieg und Seepolitik*, 311; and McCormick, *Origins of the European Economy*, 970 (R806).

77. *Gallia Christiana in provincias ecclesiasticas distributa*, ed. Monks of the Congregation of Saint-Maur (Paris: Coignard, 1734), vol. 6, col. 27, no. 24: "[S]ed tamen nondum sibi liberum iter Romanum esse propter Sarracenos, qui Alpium fauces insidebant."

the fall of the city of Acqui.[78] By 940 they had penetrated deeply into the Alpine ranges, attacking the town of Chur and occupying the Abbey of Saint-Maurice-en-Valais.[79] Their reach extended as far north as Lake Constance. An eleventh-century chronicler from the Abbey of Saint Gall remembered them as a persistent menace, lurking in the nearby peaks and often venturing close enough to harass the monks with projectiles as they walked in procession outside of the safety of the cloister.[80] In their very repetition, however, the *Annals of Flodoard* come closest to evoking the creeping dread caused by these relentless incursions. According to this source, the Muslims of Fraxinetum menaced and murdered transalpine travelers repeatedly in 921, 923, 929, 931, 933, 936, 939, 940 and 951.[81]

The occupation of the Alpine passes by Muslim brigands galled contemporaries who recognized that ill-advised alliances of Christian lords were at least in part responsible for their presence there. In his *Antapodosis*, Liudprand snarled his disapproval of Hugh of Arles, who had the opportunity to destroy Fraxinetum once and for all when he assaulted the enclave in 942 with the help of a Byzantine fleet.[82] Hugh and his forces burned the ships of the Muslims and forced them to flee to the safety of Moor's Mountain (*montem Maurum*), a rural hideout nearby surrounded by an expanse of thorny woods.[83] Although he had routed his foes and could have defeated them utterly with a short siege of their refuge, Hugh's thoughts turned to the threat of his rival Berengar, who had been gathering troops north of the Alps in Francia and Swabia for an assault on northern Italy.[84] Following bad advice, Hugh forged an alliance with his Muslim foes, inviting them to inhabit the mountain passes that connected Swabia to Italy and charging them specifically with preventing the advance of Berengar's army. Liudprand roared his

---

78. Liudprand, *Antapodosis* 2.43, ed. Chiesa, 53.

79. On the situation at Chur, see the diploma issued in April 940 by Emperor Otto I providing reparations to Bishop Waldo of Chur due to losses incurred by the Saracen presence: "Conquerens nobis suum episcopium continua depraedatione saracenorum ualde esse desolatum, nos uero rationabili eius petitioni assensum accommodantes. Concessimus ei duas ecclesias . . . ," in *Codex Diplomaticus: Sammlung der Urkunden zur Geschichte Cur-Rätiens und der Republik Graubünden*, ed. Theodor von Mohr (Cur, Switzerland: L. Hitz, 1848), 1:66 (no. 44). On the capture of the lands around Saint-Maurice-en-Valais, see Flodoard, *Annales*, anno 940, ed. Lauer, 79.

80. Ekkehard, *Casus Santi Galli*, 126, ed. Hans F. Haefle, in *St. Galler Klostergeschichten* (Darmstadt, Germany: Wissenschaftliche Buchgesellschaft, 1980), 244.

81. Flodoard, *Annales*, ed. Lauer, 5, 19, 44–45, 47, 57, 65, 74, 79, and 132.

82. Liudprand, *Antapodosis*, 5.9, ed. Chiesa, 128.

83. Liudprand, *Antapodosis*, 5.16, ed. Chiesa, 132.

84. On the career and ambitions of Berengar, see Barbara H. Rosenwein, "The Family Politics of Berengar, King of Italy (888–924)," *Speculum* 71 (1996): 247–89.

dismay at the consequences of this pact: "And actually what a vast amount of blood of Christians heading to the thresholds of the blessed apostles Peter and Paul was spilled by this treaty God alone knows, who keeps their names written in the books of the living. How unjustly you attempted to defend your kingdom, King Hugh!"[85]

Despite the shrill testimony of tenth-century Christian authors, the Muslims of La Garde-Freinet did not always act with lethal intent. To be sure, in the earliest accounts of their activities their methods were crude and brutal. In the early 920s they reportedly murdered Anglo-Saxon pilgrims by triggering avalanches in narrow passes and then looted the pilgrims' corpses.[86] When the Muslims realized, however, that they could exact a heavy and renewable toll for granting safe passage through the Alps and by taking captives for ransom or sale, they changed their method from murder to extortion and kidnapping. In 951, the *Annals of Flodoard* reported that "[t]he Saracens blockaded a passage of the Alps and took tribute from travelers on their way to Rome, who then were allowed to pass."[87] And two decades later, in the summer of 972, raiders from Fraxinetum captured one of the most influential Christian prelates of the tenth century, Abbot Maiolus of Cluny. From captivity this holy man composed a ransom note requesting payment for the release of him and his fellow captives. This short document deserves close attention because it is the only firsthand source for the experience of a Christian captured by the Muslims of La Garde-Freinet. Moreover, it provides unparalleled insight into the abbot's perception of the religion of his captors.

⌁ "The Hordes of Belial Have Surrounded Me"

Maiolus of Cluny (954–94) remains very much in the shadow of his abbatial successors, Odilo (994–1049) and Hugh the Great (1049–1109), in part because the tenures of these long-lived and influential abbots coincided with a period of unprecedented growth at the great Burgundian abbey.[88] Over

---

85. Liudprand, *Antapodosis*, 5.17, ed. Chiesa, 132: "Eo vero constituti, quam multorum christianorum ad beatorum apostolorum Petri et Pauli limina transeuntium sanguinem fuderint, ille solus scit numerum, qui eorum nomina scripta tenet in libro viventium. Quam inique tibi, rex Hugo, regnum defendere conaris!"

86. Flodoard, *Annales*, anno 921, ed. Lauer, 5, 19.

87. Flodoard, *Annales*, anno 951, ed. Lauer, 132.

88. Most general studies of Cluny's history emphasize the eleventh century as a period of unprecedented expansion. See Noreen Hunt, *Cluny under Saint Hugh, 1049–1109* (Notre Dame, IN:

the course of the eleventh century, monastic vocations at Cluny tripled from approximately a hundred individuals to more than three hundred, an increase that strained the resources of the community and challenged the integrity of personal discipline among the brethren.[89] Moreover, the physical fabric of the abbey complex expanded apace with this dramatic rise in vocations. In the autumn of 1095, a month before preaching the First Crusade at Clermont, Pope Urban II consecrated the high altar of Cluny's new basilica (known to historians as Cluny III), which upon its completion became the largest church in western Christendom.[90] When Hugh the Great died in 1109, few alive could remember a time when he was not the abbot of Cluny and no monastic community in Europe could rival the Cluniacs in terms of their religious and political influence and the awe-inspiring opulence of their primary place of worship.

The eleventh-century achievements for which the Cluniacs are best remembered were constructed on a foundation laid in the tenth century.[91] Much of Cluny's success as a religious community belongs to the active promotion by Abbot Maiolus and his successors of the efficacy of Cluniac prayer for the dead. According to Dominique Iogna-Prat, donations of revenue-producing land to Cluny in exchange for monastic prayers on behalf of Christian souls increased exponentially in the second half of the tenth century. Contracts expressing the terms of these agreements survive in modest numbers from Cluny's early years—29 from the abbacy of Berno (910–26); 126 from the abbacy of Odo (926–42); and 194 from the abbacy of Aymard (942–54)—before rising to unprecedented heights under Maiolus (1096 charters dating from 954 to 994), when the reputation of the Cluniacs as intercessors for the dead reached its peak.[92] The creation of a

University of Notre Dame Press, 1967); and Joachim Wollasch, *Cluny, Licht der Welt: Aufstieg und Niedergang der klösterlichen Gemeinschaft* (Düsseldorf, Germany: Patmos, 1996).

89. For a summary of the evidence, see Hunt, *Cluny under Saint Hugh*, 82–83. On the strategies employed by the Cluniacs and others to prevent lapses in discipline in large monastic communities, see Scott G. Bruce, "Lurking with Spiritual Intent: A Note on the Origin and Functions of the Monastic Roundsman (*Circator*)," *Revue bénédictine* 109 (1999): 75–89.

90. On Cluny III, see Neil Stratford, "The Documentary Evidence for the Building of Cluny III," in *Studies in Burgundian Romanesque Sculpture* (London: Pindar, 1998), 1:41–59.

91. On Cluny's place in tenth-century monasticism, see Barbara H. Rosenwein, *Rhinoceros Bound: Cluny in the Tenth Century* (Philadelphia: University of Pennsylvania Press, 1982); and Giles Constable, "Cluny in the Monastic World of the Tenth Century," in *Il secolo di ferro: Mito e realtà del secolo X (Spoleto, 19–25 aprile 1990)*, Settimane di studio del Centro italiano di studi sull'alto medioevo 38 (Spoleto, I~~ Centro Italiano di Studi sull'Alto Medioevo, 1991), 391–437, reprinted in Giles Constable, ~~m the Tenth to the Twelfth Centuries: Further Studies (Aldershot, England: Ashgate, 2000), no. 1.

~~nique Iogna-Prat, *Order and Exclusion: Cluny and Christendom Face Heresy, Judaism, and Islam* ~~), trans. Graham Robert Edwards (Ithaca, NY: Cornell University Press, 2002), 224.

special day (2 November) of prayerful intercession for all Christian souls by Maiolus's successor Odilo should be understood as a response to the popularity of prayer for the dead at Cluny that had gained its momentum during the abbacy of Maiolus.[93] Moreover, it was under Maiolus that the Cluniac scriptorium first emerged as an important venue of manuscript production in tenth-century Europe.[94] Following their abbot's direction, scribes also composed the earliest collection of the liturgical customs of Cluny, an important step toward the massive efforts to codify the abbey's received traditions and legal records that occurred in the late eleventh century.[95]

During his forty-year tenure as abbot, Maiolus traveled repeatedly over the Alps to Italy both as a religious adviser and as a broker of peace at the highest level of secular affairs.[96] The abbot's saintly reputation attracted the attention of Emperor Otto I and his wife Adelaide of Italy, who enlisted his expertise to reform several monastic communities in their Italian territories, including San Apollinare in Classe, near Ravenna.[97] Maiolus spent consider-

93. The Cluniac sources for this tradition include Jotsaldus, *Vita Odilonis*, 2.15, ed. Johannes Staub, in *Iotsald von Saint-Claude, Vita des Abtes Odilo von Cluny*, MGH SRG, 68:218–20; and Glaber, *Historiarum libri quinque*, 5.1.13, ed. France, 234–37. For more on prayer for the dead at Cluny in this period, see Dominique Iogna-Prat, "Les morts dans la compatibilité céleste des moines clunisiens autour l'an mil," in *Religion et culture autour de l'an mil: Royaume capétien et Lotharingie*, ed. Dominique Iogna-Prat and Jean-Charles Picard (Paris: Picard, 1990), 55–69, translated as "The Dead in the Celestial Bookkeeping of the Cluniac Monks around the Year 1000," in *Debating the Middle Ages: Issues and Readings*, ed. Lester Little and Barbara H. Rosenwein (Oxford: Wiley, 1998), 340–62; and Umberto Longo, "Riti e agiografia: L'istituzione della *commemoratio omnium fidelium defunctorum* nelle *Vitae* di Odilone di Cluny," *Bullettino dell'Istituto storico italiano per il Medio Evo e Archivio muratoriano* 103 (2002): 163–200.

94. For evidence of scribal industry at Cluny in the late tenth century, see Monique-Cécile Garand, "Copistes de Cluny au temps de saint Maieul (948–994)," *Bibliothèque de l'École des Chartes* 136 (1978): 5–36.

95. For a collection of studies that highlights the value of the Cluniac customaries as historical sources, see *From Dead of Night to End of Day: The Medieval Customs of Cluny / Du coeur de la nuit à la fin du jour: Les coutumes clunisiennes au moyen âge*, ed. Susan Boynton and Isabelle Cochelin (Leiden: Brepols, 2005).

96. Léon Bourdon, "Les voyages de Saint Mayeul en Italie: Itinéraires et chronologie," *Mélanges d'archéologie et d'histoire* 43 (1926): 63–89.

97. Syrus, *Vita sancti Maioli*, 2.20, ed. Dominique Iogna-Prat, in *Agni Immaculati: Recherches sur les sources hagiographiques relatives à saint Maieul de Cluny (954–994)* (Paris: Éditions du Cerf, 1988), 239. On the reform of San Apollinare in Classe, which occurred toward the end of 971, see Syrus, *Vita sancti Maioli*, 2.23, ed. Iogna-Prat, 243–44. There is as yet no comprehensive study of the relationship between the Ottonians and the Abbey of Cluny but, for general orientation, see Robert G. Heath, *Crux Imperatorum Philosophia: Imperial Horizons of the Cluniac Confraternitas, 964–1109* (Pittsburgh: Pickwick Press, 1976), 53–71; and Sébastien Barret, "Cluny et les Ottoniens," in *Ottone III e Romualdo di Ravenna: Impero, monasteri e santi asceti, Atti del XXIV convegno del Centro Studi Avellaniti, Fonte Avellana, 2002* (Verona: Gabrielli Editori, 2003), 179–213.

able time in the city of Pavia, the seat of Ottonian power in northern Italy, where he restored the Abbeys of Santa Maria, San Salvatore, and San Pietro in Ciel d'Oro.[98] The abbot of Cluny soon became Otto and Adelaide's confidant, "the ear and repository of the imperial secrets."[99] His relationship with the royal couple was such that those who had obtained an audience with the emperor first sought out the abbot to act as an intermediary on their behalf.[100] Shortly after Otto's death in 973, Adelaide and her son Otto II nominated Maiolus as pope, but he demurred, explaining that he could not abandon the souls in his care at Cluny and predicting that the citizens of Rome would chafe under the rule of a bishop from Gaul.[101] When relations between Adelaide and Otto II soured in 978, it was the abbot of Cluny who brokered the peace between them.[102] This close relationship with the Ottonian dynasty made Maiolus one of the most powerful and influential prelates in tenth-century Europe.

Even the most formidable imperial patronage could not protect Maiolus from the perils of transalpine travel. The abbot of Cluny had spent the summer of 972 in Italy; he may have arrived as early as April to attend the wedding of Otto II and the Byzantine princess Theophanu in Rome.[103] It was a moment of high solemnity for the Ottonians and their allies, because Pope John XIII took the occasion to crown Theophanu as well.[104] A few months later Maiolus crossed the Alps once more to return to his home in Burgundy. On the night of 21–22 July, raiders from La Garde-Freinet abducted him, his entourage, and the pilgrim host who accompanied them as they crossed

---

98. On the activity of Maiolus in Pavia, see chapter 2 of the present volume.

99. Syrus, *Vita sancti Maioli*, 2.22, ed. Iogna-Prat, 242–43: "Hunc imperator habebat auricularium, hunc a secretis fidum internuntium." The translation is from L. M. Smith, *The Early History of the Monastery of Cluny* (Oxford: Oxford University Press, 1920), 105.

100. Syrus, *Vita sancti Maioli*, 2.22, ed. Iogna-Prat, 243.

101. Syrus, *Vita sancti Maioli*, 3.10, ed. Iogna-Prat, 260–63.

102. Syrus, *Vita sancti Maioli*, 3.11, ed. Iogna-Prat, 263–66. See also *Annales Magdeburgensis* (anno 978), ed. Georg Pertz, in MGH SS, 16:154.

103. No source tells us explicitly that the abbot attended the celebration, but Bourdon concluded on the basis of "quelques renseignements" in Syrus's *vita* that he probably had. See Bourdon, "Les voyages de Saint Mayeul en Italie," 76.

104. On the wedding and coronation, see Nikolaus Gussone, "Trauung und Krönung: Zur Hochzeit der byzantinischen Prinzessin Theophanu mit Kaiser Otto II," in *Kaiserin Theophanu: Begegnung des Ostens und Westens um die Wende des ersten Jahrtausends*, ed. Anton von Euw and Peter Schreiner (Cologne: Schnütgen-Museum, 1991), 2:161–74; Karl Leyser, "Theophanu Divina Gratia Imperatrix Augusta: Western and Eastern Emperorship in the Later Tenth Century," in Leyser, *Communications and Power*, 143–64; and Hans K. Schulze, *Heiratsurkunde der Kaiserin Theophanu: Die griechische Kaiserin und das römisch-deutsche Reich 972–991* (Hanover: Hahn, 2007).

the Great Saint Bernard Pass.[105] From captivity the abbot sent a desperate letter to his brethren in Burgundy. Maiolus's original ransom note is lost, but recollections of it have been preserved in two early eleventh-century accounts of the kidnapping episode written at Cluny. The earliest of these appeared in a hagiographical portrait of the abbot composed around 1010 by a Cluniac monk named Syrus (BHL 5179).[106] In this version of the story, Syrus described how Maiolus wrote the ransom letter with his own hand and had it delivered to his brethren by means of another captured monk who was released by their abductors to secure the payment.[107] In very few words the abbot evoked a situation fraught with life-threatening peril: "Maiolus, a captive, wretched and in chains, sends greetings to his lords and brothers, the monks of Cluny. The hordes of Belial have surrounded me; the snares of death have seized me. Please send a ransom payment for me and those held captive with me."[108] The text of the ransom letter also appeared around 1040 with slight, but significant, variations in Rodulphus Glaber's *Five Books of Histories*, which was dedicated to Odilo, Maiolus's successor as abbot of Cluny: "Maiolus, wretched and captive, sends his greetings to his lords and brothers, the monks of Cluny. The hordes of Belial have surrounded me; the snares of death have seized me. In view of this by all means please send a ransom for those held captive with me."[109]

The minor differences in the wording of the letter in these two accounts are more stylistic than substantive, but they indicate quite clearly that Glaber did not copy the contents of this short document directly from Syrus's text.[110] The fact that Syrus wrote about Maiolus's travails several decades before Glaber and may have even had the opportunity to hear the story from the saintly abbot himself before his death in 994 places his account closer to contemporary witnesses to the kidnapping but does not prove

---

105. On the date of this encounter, see Paul Amargier, "La capture de saint Maieul de Cluny et l'expulsion des Sarrasins de Provence," *Revue bénédictine* 73 (1963): 316–23.

106. Syrus, *Vita sancti Maioli*, 3.1–9, ed. Iogna-Prat, 247–60.

107. Syrus, *Vita sancti Maioli*, 3.5, ed. Iogna-Prat, 253.

108. Ibid.: "Dominis et fratribus cluniensibus, Maiolus miser captus et catenatus. Torrentes Belial circumdederunt me, preoccupauerunt me laquei mortis. Redemptionis pretium, si placet, mittite pro me et his qui una mecum capti tenentur."

109. Rodulphus Glaber, *Historiarum libri quinque* 1.4.9, ed. France, 18–20: "Dominis et fratribus Cluniensibus, frater Maiolus miser et captus. Torrentes Belial circumdederunt me, praeoccupauerunt me laquei mortis. Nunc uero si placet et his qui mecum capti tenentur redemptionem mittite."

110. For example, Glaber's version did not include Syrus's reference to Maiolus as "in chains" (*catenatus*). Moreover, the final plea for a ransom in Glaber's account added a note of urgency with the words "in view of this by all means" (*nunc uero*) before the request for payment, which Glaber called simply a *redemptio* in contrast to Syrus's descriptive phrase *pretium redemptionis*.

conclusively that the text of the ransom letter presented by him is a more accurate reproduction of Maiolus's original letter than the version preserved in Glaber's *Five Books of Histories*. Either author could have been working from memory, and both were in a position to consult the original ransom letter in the abbey archives if the brethren of Cluny in fact chose to preserve it.

These textual variations are of little consequence, however, because the heart of the letter, where Maiolus characterized the nature of his captivity— "The hordes of Belial have surrounded me; the snares of death have seized me" (*Torrentes Belial circumdederunt me, praeoccupauerunt me laquei mortis*)—is identical in both accounts. The abbot of Cluny drew the central images of his ransom letter directly from his memory of an Old Testament hymn of praise preserved in the second Book of Samuel and repeated with minor variations in the book of Psalms: "I will call upon the Lord, who is worthy of praise and I will be saved from my enemies, for the miseries of death surround me. The hordes of Belial frighten me. The cords of Hell have entangled me. The snares of death have hindered me."[111] In this ancient poem, a king of Israel gives thanks to God for help in defeating his enemies. The hymn begins with a confession of faith in God's protective power: "I love you, O my Lord, my strength. The Lord is my foundation and my refuge and my deliverer"; there follows the series of short metaphorical descriptions of the king's tribulations (quoted above), from which Maiolus borrowed images of entrapment and captivity to communicate the difficulty of his situation to his Cluniac brethren.[112] The hymn concludes with an account of the Lord's intervention in battle, leading to the defeat of the ancient king's enemies and his ascendancy as a ruler of an empire at peace.

Given the richness of liturgical psalmody at tenth-century Cluny and the impact of its language on the monastic imagination, it is not at all surprising that Maiolus chose to express the gravity of his plight by echoing the adversities that faced an Old Testament king of Israel, who relied on his faith in God for deliverance and victory.[113] It is the abbot's use of the name Belial,

---

111. II Samuel 22:4–6: "Laudabilem invocabo Dominum et ab inimicis meis salvus ero quia circumdederunt me contritiones mortis torrentes Belial terruerunt me funes inferi circumdederunt me laquei mortis." Compare Psalm 17:4–6: "Laudans invocabo Dominum et ab inimicis meis salvus ero circumdederunt me dolores mortis et torrentes iniquitatis conturbaverunt me dolores inferni circumdederunt me praeoccupaverunt me laquei mortis."

112. Psalm 17:2–3: "Diligam te Domine fortitudo mea Dominus firmamentum meum et refugium meum et liberator meus."

113. The tenth-century Cluniacs emulated the liturgical customs instituted in the early ninth century by Abbot Benedict of Aniane, who ordered the singing of 138 psalms on feast days. This was a substantial increase from the thirty-seven psalms prescribed in the sixth-century *Rule of Bene-*

however, that complicates our understanding of his perception of his captors. Unlike the phrase "the snares of death have seized me," which could apply generically to any dangerous situation, Belial was a proper name that was resonant with ancient and infamous associations. The discovery of the meaning of this name in a tenth-century monastic context is imperative for our comprehension of the abbot's response to his captivity and his perception of his captors.

Maiolus's application of the name Belial to the Muslims who abducted him is unprecedented in the Christian tradition of writing about Islam in the early Middle Ages. Northern Europeans were much more likely to identify the followers of Muhammed with the Ishmaelites or Hagarenes of the Old Testament, who were also known collectively as Saracens.[114] According to early medieval exegesis of the book of Genesis, the peoples who dwelled in the desert lands of the Arabian Peninsula were the descendants of Ishmael, the ill-favored son of Abraham by his slave woman Hagar. Destined by a prophecy of God to a legacy of conflict—"his hand against every man and every man's hand against him" (Genesis 16:12)—the sons of Ishmael elided easily in the western imagination with adherents to Islam whose war machine conquered the Byzantine settlements of North Africa and the Visigothic kingdom of Spain in the seventh and early eighth centuries. In late antiquity, Jerome and his contemporaries applied the name Ishmaelite (*Ishmalitae*) to pre-Islamic pagan Arabs, but early medieval exegetes understood it to be the name taken by the Muslims to claim their descent from Abraham's wife, Sarah, and thereby conceal their ignoble ancestry.[115] Before the eleventh century, this collective of names—Ishmaelite, Hagarene, and Saracen—carried a very specific religious association. In early medieval thought, people known by these names were commonly believed to be pagans who worshipped idols of Apollo, Venus, and Muhammed himself, as well as other gods of classical antiquity. Popular epic poems, like the *Song of Roland*, preserved this false perception in the European imagination even

---

dict, which served as the standard template for monastic life throughout the Middle Ages. See Kassius Hallinger, "Überlieferung und Steigerung im Mönchtum des 8. bis 12. Jahrhunderts," in *Eulogia: Miscellanea liturgica in onore di P. Burckhard Neunheuser O.S.B* (Rome: Anselmiana, 1979), 145–46.

114. On the meaning of these terms, their application by late ancient and early medieval Christian authors, and their religious associations, see Ekkehart Rotter, *Abendland und Sarazenen: Das okzidentale Araberbild und seine Entstehung im Frühmittelalter* (Berlin: De Gruyter, 1983), 77–130; Tolan, *Saracens*, 105–34; and Katharine Scarfe Beckett, *Anglo-Saxon Perceptions of the Islamic World* (Cambridge: Cambridge University Press, 2003), 18–19, 69–139.

115. See, for example, Jerome, [*Vita Malchi*] *De monacho captivo*, 4, ed. Edgardo M. Morales and Pierre Leclerc, in *Jérôme: Trois vies des moines (Paul, Malchus, Hilarion)*, SC 508:192.

centuries after more accurate information about Islamic beliefs became available in the West.[116]

In contrast, the name Belial was an ancient Hebrew noun that had no relation to the Old Testament racial taxonomies favored by Christian exegetes in their descriptions of Muslim peoples. There is no consensus of scholarly opinion with regard to its etymology, but the word is generally understood to mean "worthlessness" or "wickedness."[117] Old Testament authors used it most commonly in apposition to describe individuals who had committed crimes against the Israelite religion or sought to disrupt the social order.[118] By the Hellenistic period, however, the word took on a more specific association; in apocalyptic Jewish literature, Belial (sometimes written as Beliar) became the name of the adversarial entity who opposed the will of God— that is, the devil. He was a creature of darkness who, with the aid of attendant spirits, dominated the will of evil men and held the present age under his control. Although Belial was depicted as a powerful force in the immediate present, his future downfall was foretold as a war in which God and his angels would defeat him and his minions by imprisoning them in chains or hurling them into an everlasting fire.

It was this apocalyptic understanding of Belial as an opponent of God and an adversary of humankind that informed the only reference to his name in New Testament literature.[119] In the second letter to the Corinthians (composed ca. 57 CE), the apostle Paul deployed the name in a pronouncement on the proper relationship between Christians and pagans; using a series of rhetorical juxtapositions, he emphasized the conceptual and spiritual gulf that divided the faithful from the unfaithful: "Do not lead the yoke with unbelievers. Indeed what partnership has justice with iniquity or what fellowship has light with darkness? What accord has Christ with Belial or what does a believer have in common with an unbeliever?"[120] In Paul's mind, Belial was no less than the devil himself, the polar opposite of Christ,

---

116. See, for example, *La Chanson de Roland*, ed. Luis Cortés (Paris, 1994), 160, lines 7–8: "li reis Marsilie la tient, ki Due nen aimet. / Mahumet sert e Apollin recleimet."

117. For what follows, see Jeffrey Burton Russell, *The Devil: Perceptions of Evil from Antiquity to Primitive Christianity* (Ithaca, NY: Cornell University Press, 1977), 174–220, esp. 188n17; and *Dictionary of Deities and Demons in the Bible*, ed. Karel van der Toorn, Bob Becking, and Pieter W. van der Horst (Leiden: Brill, 1995), s.v. "Belial," with references to earlier literature.

118. See, for example, Deuteronomy 13:12–18; I Kings 21:8–14; I Samuel 25:17; and II Samuel 16:7, 20:1.

119. Russell, *The Devil*, 221–49.

120. II Corinthians 6:14–15: "Nolite iugum ducere cum infidelibus quae enim participatio iustitiae cum in iniquitate aut quae societas luci ad tenebras quae autem conventio Christi ad Belial aut quae pars fideli cum infidele."

and a spirit synonymous with iniquity, darkness, and false belief. The name Belial is not mentioned by any other New Testament author, so Paul's use of the word was particularly important for its transmission into the cultural vocabularies of early Christian communities. Moreover, his investment of Belial with such dark meanings shaped the reception and understanding of this name in the early Middle Ages.

The contrast of Belial with Christ in Paul's second letter to the Corinthians drew the attention of several early medieval exegetes whose topical concerns influenced the polemical application of the word in their writings. Most of them treated the name as a collective metaphor for religious rivals that threatened or opposed Christian society. In the mid-seventh century, Pope Martin I (649–55) applied the term to those spreading false doctrines. Just as there was no accord between Christ and Belial, he wrote, so too was there no accord between orthodox and heretical thinkers.[121] Echoing Paul's second letter to the Corinthians, the pope warned his readers to guard their hearts by avoiding all social commerce with those who denied the true faith. A few decades later, in an allegorical commentary on the books of Samuel, Bede applied the name Belial even more broadly to include not only errant Christians but also Jews. "The sons of Belial," he maintained, "are the sons of the Jewish priesthood, the blind sons of light, and those without a yoke, that is, those who are ignorant of the teaching of Christ. They do not follow the commandments of divine law, but rather the decrees of their own traditions."[122] This association of Belial was repeated in the early ninth century in a letter of complaint from Archbishop Agobard of Lyons to Emperor Louis the Pious about the mounting influence of Jews in the Frankish kingdoms. The archbishop employed Paul's juxtaposition of Christ and Belial to argue that it was inappropriate and reprehensible for devout Christians like the emperor to share company and commerce with unbelievers. As a solution to this dangerous situation, Agobard advised a strict segregation of Jewish people living in Christian society.[123]

---

121. Pope Martin I, *Epistola*, 13 (*ad ecclesiam Thessalonicensium de Pauli damnatione eiusque haeresi fugienda*), in PL 87, col. 197b.

122. Bede, *In Samuelem prophetam allegorica expositio*, 5, in PL 91, col. 512d: "*Porro filii Heli, Filii Belial, etc. Filii sacerdotii Judaici, filii caeci luminis, sive absque jugo (utrumque enim Belial sive Beliar sonat) exstitere, quotquot Christi doctrinam nesciebant; non divinae legis jussa, sed suarum statuta traditionum sequentes.*"

123. Agobard of Lyons, *De iudaicis superstitionibus et erroribus (ad Ludouicum)* 11, ed. Lieven Van Acker, in *Agobardi Lugdunensis Opera Omnia*, CCCM 52:208. On the context of Agobard's conflict with the Jews of Lyons, see Bat-Sheva Albert, "*Adversus Iudaeos* in the Carolingian Empire," in *Contra Iudaeos: Ancient and Medieval Polemics between Christians and Jews*, ed. Ora Limor and Guy G. Stroumsa (Tübingen, Germany: J. C. B. Mohr, 1996), 119–42; and Jeremy Cohen, *Living Letters of*

This reconstruction of the exegetical history of the name Belial allows us to consider Maiolus's ransom letter with new insight. The abbot's deployment of this ancient and infamous name in his characterization of his Muslim captors suggests that he recognized them as adherents to a system of belief that was opposed to Christianity. The polemical resonances of the name strongly imply that Maiolus understood the Muslims of La Garde-Freinet in the same way his contemporaries understood heretics and Jews—that is, as credible adversaries of the Christian faith. While it is impossible to ascertain the exact nature of Maiolus's understanding of Islam as a system of belief, it is plausible to assert that some recognition of his captors' religion informed the text of the ransom letter that he sent to his brethren in Burgundy. On the perilous heights of the Great Saint Bernard Pass, Maiolus of Cluny evoked an ancient appeal to God to characterize his captors as "the hordes of Belial." While awaiting the arrival of the ransom that would free him and his associates from captivity, he may have been strengthened by the promise of deliverance at the conclusion of the psalm that had come so readily to his mind: "You exalted me above my adversaries. You delivered me from men of violence. For this I extol you, O Lord, among the nations, and sing praises to your name."[124]

Abbot Maiolus of Cluny was one of many hundreds, perhaps many thousands, of tenth-century individuals who were captured in the Alpine passes by the Muslims of Fraxinetum. Ransomed by the wealth of his abbey, he was one of the fortunate ones. Countless others met their end to violence on those high mountain paths or passed silently into lives of ignominy as slaves in distant lands around the Mediterranean rim. The collection of ransoms and the sale of human chattel were two important sources of revenue for the Muslims of La Garde-Freinet, who thrived for almost a century as opportunistic entrepreneurs in an alien society where civil war and local rivalries prevented the exercise of authority. After decades of activity, the kidnapping of Maiolus marked a turning point for this community. Although the abbot went free, he was held in such high regard by secular magnates that his abduction could not be excused or forgotten. The enormity of his capture may have appeared all the greater to his contemporaries in light of

---

the Law: Ideas of the Jew in Medieval Christianity (Berkeley: University of California Press, 1999), 124–45.

124. Psalm 17:48–50: "Deus qui dat vindictas mihi et subdidit populos sub me liberator meus de gentibus iracundis et ab insurgentibus in me exaltabis me a viro iniquo eripies me propterea confitebor tibi in nationibus Domine et psalmum dicam nomini tuo."

the solemnities of imperial Christianity that took place in Rome only months before at the wedding of Otto II and Theophanu. Within a year of the abbot's abduction, Count William of Arles and his allies marshaled an army and laid waste to Fraxinetum, effectively erasing the Muslim presence from Provence and the Alpine passes.[125] The monks of Cluny did not forget the kidnapping of their spiritual father, however; in the decades following his death in 994, they told and retold the story of his abduction in numerous works that commemorated the virtues of his holy life. As chapter 2 will show, the harrowing tale of the abbot's captivity changed remarkably in the telling.

---

125. The expulsion of the Muslims from Fraxinetum loomed large in Cluniac hagiography, but left no impression in contemporary charters and other documents of practice from Provence. See Monique Zerner, "La capture de Maïeul et la guerre de libération de Provence: Le départ des sarrasins à travers les cartulaires provençaux," in *Saint Mayeul et son temps: Actes du congrès international de Valensole, 2–14 mai 1994* (Dignes-les-Bains, France: Société Scientifique et Littéraire des Alpes de Haute-Provence, 1997), 199–210. Despite the destruction of La Garde-Freinet, Muslim pirates remained active along the coast of Provence throughout the eleventh and twelfth centuries. See Carraz, *L'ordre du temple dans la basse vallée du Rhône*, 56–59.

✐ CHAPTER 2

Monks Tell Tales

The abduction of Maiolus of Cluny by the Muslims of La Garde-Freinet figured prominently in the earliest accounts of the abbot's virtuous life. In the first half of the eleventh century, the episode appeared in no fewer than three works of hagiography and one monastic chronicle and underwent significant changes in the telling. The monks who wrote about the abbot's adventures embellished their accounts with each retelling, adding details about his time in captivity, including the hardships he endured, the miracles he performed, his interaction with his Muslim captors, and the fate of those captors after his release. Many of these details were no doubt invented to forward the devotional aims of the authors who employed them; others were culled from oral traditions at Cluny, which may have originated from firsthand accounts of the event told by Maiolus and his companions or the memories of their contemporaries who had heard these stories from them. Taken together these tellings and retellings of the abduction of Maiolus deserve close scrutiny. Not only do they demonstrate that a rich literary tradition involving the interaction between an abbot of Cluny and a band of Muslim warriors had taken shape after the death of Maiolus in 994, but they also promise to shed light on the ways in which the Cluniacs constructed images of Islam in the century before the First Crusade.

The hagiographical dossier of Maiolus thus provides historians with an untapped opportunity to examine how Cluniac monks told tales about the

Muslims of La Garde-Freinet in the early eleventh century. This chapter concentrates on the stories themselves; its purpose is to demonstrate how the earliest reports of the kidnapping episode changed with each new iteration, to explain how the historical circumstances and sacred purpose of each account motivated the adaptation of the story with each retelling, and to infer what these changes tell us about the spread of the knowledge of Muslim peoples and their religion in northern Europe at that time. Cluniac monks in fact displayed an unfettered versatility in their representation of the inhabitants of Fraxinetum. It is the contention of this chapter that there is so little consistency in their portrayal of the Muslims in the reiteration of the story of their abbot's kidnapping precisely because the primary concern was not the advancement of a polemical portrait of Islamic peoples and their religion. Rather, each of these monastic authors made use of the abduction episode to forward his own literary and devotional ambitions, which centered primarily—though not exclusively—on the depiction of Maiolus as a holy man who demonstrated a saintly perseverance when faced with the hardships of his time in captivity.

By Savage Hands Restrained

Maiolus of Cluny traveled extensively during his forty-year tenure as abbot (954–94) and spent considerable time in the northern Italian city of Pavia, a seat of Ottonian power, where he restored the Abbeys of Santa Maria, San Salvatore, and San Pietro in Ciel d'Oro and negotiated a reconciliation between the estranged German empress Adelaide and her son Otto II.[1] Shortly after the abbot's death in 994, an anonymous monk of Pavia was the first to hail him as a saint by writing a *vita* to commemorate his holy life (BHL 5180).[2] The occasion for the composition of this work was in all likeli-

---

1. Léon Bourdon, "Les voyages de Saint Mayeul en Italie: Itinéraires et chronologie," *Mélanges d'archéologie et d'histoire* 43 (1926): 63–89.

2. Anonymous, *Vita breuior sancti Maioli* (BHL 5180), in BC, cols. 1763–82. The significance of this *vita* as the earliest account of Maiolus's life, rather than a redaction of the early eleventh-century *vita* by Syrus of Cluny (BHL 5177/79) as the Bollandists presumed, has been persuasively demonstrated by Dominique Iogna-Prat in *Agni Immaculati: Recherches sur les sources hagiographiques relatives à saint Maieul de Cluny (954–994)* (Paris: Éditions du Cerf, 1988), 20–29. For the sake of simplicity, I am assuming that the work had a single author, but it may well have been the collective endeavor of several members of a monastic community. On the making of popular saints in the early Middle Ages, see André Vauchez, *La sainteté en Occident aux derniers siècles du moyen âge d'après les procès de canonisation et les documents hagiographiques*, 2nd ed. (Paris: École française de Rome, 1988), 15–24; translated by Jean Birrell as *Sainthood in the Later Middle Ages* (Cambridge: Cambridge University Press, 1997), 13–21.

hood the rededication of a Pavian church in honor of his memory; in the late 990s, with the consent of Emperor Otto III and Abbot Odilo of Cluny, the abbey (*cella*) of Saint Mary became the Abbey of Saint Maiolus.[3] BHL 5180 was an important vehicle of self-promotion for the monks of Pavia in that it portrayed their city as the setting for Maiolus's miracles and exhibited its citizens as the special recipients of the saint's favor. Its anonymous author emphasized the relationship between the people of Pavia and the holy man of Cluny in several ways. He first established the saintly virtue of Maiolus by narrating the story of the hardships the abbot endured when Muslims abducted him in the nearby Great Saint Bernard Pass in 972. He then compared the city of Pavia explicitly to the ancient port towns of Sidon and Tyre, whose inhabitants Christ himself had singled out for their penitential character. Finally, he made direct reference in the *vita* both to local venues where Maiolus had performed miracles and to a prominent Pavian official healed by the abbot's prayers. His depiction of the Muslims of La Garde-Freinet is inextricable from the primary aim of his work: the glorification of the abbot of Cluny as a saint who graced the city of Pavia with the manifest power of his holiness.

BHL 5180 provides the first known narrative account of Maiolus's abduction by and captivity among the Muslims of La Garde-Freinet. The details of this harrowing episode allegedly came from eyewitnesses in the abbot's entourage who had endured the ordeal with him, some of whom were named to lend veracity to the account.[4] The anonymous author of the work explained that the capture of Maiolus was the design of God, who used the opportunity to work miracles through the abbot. Perseverance in the face of hardship is the dominant theme of the account. Maiolus and his companions endured their fearful abduction on the heights of the Great Saint Bernard Pass, from which their kidnappers spirited them away to a mountain lair and held them in chains for many days while awaiting a ransom.

---

3. See *Praeceptum Ottonis imperatoris de sancto Maiolo de Papia* (dated 999), in BC, col. 409, and PL 142, col. 1039; and Jotsaldus, *Vita Odilonis* 1.14, ed. Johannes Staub, in *Iotsald von Saint-Claude, Vita des Abtes Odilo von Cluny*, MGH SRG, 68:172. The implication is that Odilo endorsed the renaming of the abbey but did not explicitly sanction the Pavian *vita* that was written to celebrate it. For the date of this event, which is contested, see Cesare Manaresi, "La fondazione del monastero di S. Maiolo in Pavia," in *Spiritualità Cluniacense* (Todi, Italy: Accademia Tudertina, 1960), 274–85; and Maria Antonietta Casagrande, "Fondazione e suiluppo del monasterio cluniacense di San Maiolo di Pavia nei primi secoli," in *Atti del 4° congresso internazionale di studi sull'alto medioevo, Pavia-Scaldasole-Monza-Bobbio, 10–14 settembre 1967* (Spoleto, Italy: Centro Italiano di Studi sull'Alto Medioevo, 1969), 335–51. On Odilo's industry with respect to constructing new churches both at home and abroad, see Jacques Hourlier, "Saint Odilon bâtisseur," *Revue Mabillon* 51 (1961): 303–24.

4. For what follows, see Anonymous, *Vita breuior sancti Maioli*, 7–13, in BC, cols. 1769–72.

With the sign of the cross, the abbot freed himself from the leg irons that bound both him and a fellow monk named Goszonus. His captors responded by binding Maiolus with even heavier and tighter chains and subjecting him to derision and beatings. When a brother named Raimbertus protested their cruelty, one of the Muslims drew his sword to slay him, but Maiolus interceded, blocking the blow with his hand and receiving a grievous wound. He awoke the next day, however, to find himself miraculously healed. This harsh treatment of the holy man moved God to destroy the Muslims at the hands of a Christian army, even though a ransom had already secured his release. Ever afterward the road to Rome was less dangerous for pilgrim traffic, and Maiolus soon returned safely to Cluny, much to the delight of his brethren.

Relentless cruelty is the governing attribute of the Muslims depicted in BHL 5180. Time and again, the author underscored the brutality of the treatment suffered at their hands by Maiolus and his fellow captives. This was most pronounced when the monk Raimbertus implored his captors with tearful cries to stop tormenting his abbot with beatings and heavy chains, behavior characterized by the hagiographer as violence that was intended to maximize suffering with malicious intent (*tantae calamitatis et impietatis crudelitatem*). Amid this baleful depiction of the viciousness of the abbot's captors, the author of BHL 5180 betrayed no knowledge of their religious tenets, describing them variously as "the savage race of the Saracens" (*efferae gentis Saracenorum*) and "a barbarous people with no faith" (*impietatis gens barbara*). This terminology is entirely consistent with perceptions of Islamic peoples current in northern Europe in the decades around 1000.[5] The perceived cruelty and godlessness of the kidnappers forwarded the purpose of the *vita* as a whole. For the author of BHL 5180, the Muslims of La Garde-Freinet were not adherents to a rival monotheistic belief system; they were simply savage adversaries sent by God to test the steadfastness of Maiolus's faith as he endured the harsh conditions of his captivity. The depiction of the abbot's saintly patience in the face of the derision and violence of the Muslims inflected the goal of the hagiographer to promote the heroic virtue of his subject.

After his narration of Maiolus's abduction and release, the author of BHL 5180 arrived at the heart of the matter. The miraculous power of the saint manifested in the urban landscape of Pavia confirmed a privileged relationship between the Cluniac abbot and the city's inhabitants.[6] The author did

---

5. See chapter 1 of the present volume.

6. For another study of the function of early medieval hagiography as an expression of a local, civic identity, though without reference to biblical typologies, see Klaus Krönert, "Le rôle de

this by employing a typology of biblical cities to make the case that Pavia and its inhabitants enjoyed the special protection of the abbot of Cluny. In doing so, he deliberately elided the tenth-century experiences of the citizens of Pavia with those of their first-century counterparts in Sidon and Tyre, thus fostering the perception that the holiness of Christ's earthly ministry was also present in and around their city through the activity of Maiolus. Due to his eminence and his frequent sojourns in Pavia, the abbot of Cluny had become the spiritual father of several local monastic communities at the behest of a wide range of sponsors.[7] In the summer of 967 a judge of the imperial court named Gaidulf sold a small chapel in Pavia to Adalgis, a local priest, who immediately donated the property to Cluny. The chapel, rededicated to Saints Mary and Michael, became a Cluniac dependency under the direction of Maiolus.[8] A few years later, in 972, Empress Adelaide bequeathed the Abbey of San Salvatore near Pavia to the abbot of Cluny, who agreed to uphold the precepts of the *Rule of Benedict* among the brethren there.[9] And finally, in 987, Pope John XV invited Maiolus to undertake the reform of San Pietro in Ciel d'Oro in Pavia, a task that the abbot embraced with enthusiasm.[10] Ties of spiritual affiliation bound the abbot of Cluny to many of Pavia's monastic communities. By the end of his life, Maiolus was undoubtedly the most prominent figure in the religious landscape of the imperial capital and a firm fixture in the minds of its citizens.

The author of BHL 5180 compared the city of Pavia explicitly with Sidon and Tyre, biblical port towns of Phoenician origin that lay about twenty miles apart on the coastline of what is now modern Lebanon.[11] Both Sidon and Tyre were bustling commercial centers in the ancient world; they were current in the early medieval imagination through accounts of the journeys of the apostle Paul, who tarried for a week in Tyre at the end of his third mission

---

l'hagiographie dans la mise en place d'une identité locale aux Xe–XIe siècles: L'example de Trèves," in *Constructions de l'espace au Moyen Âge: Practique et représentations* (Paris: Publications de la Sorbonne, 2007), 379–89.

7. For what follows, see Jean Leclercq, "S. Maiolo fondatore e riformatore di monasteri a Pavia," in *Atti del 4° congresso internazionale di studi sull'alto medioevo*, 155–73, esp. 155–57; and Barbara Rosenwein, *Rhinoceros Bound: Cluny in the Tenth Century* (Philadelphia: University of Pennsylvania Press, 1982), 51–55.

8. For the documents relevant to this donation and the dispute that resulted from it due to the disaffection of Gaidulf's heirs, see *Recueil des chartes de l'abbaye de Cluny*, ed. Auguste Bernard and Alexandre Bruel (Paris: Imprimerie Nationale, 1880), 2:308–19 (nos. 1228 and 1229, dated 967).

9. Alessandro Colombo, "I diplomi ottoniani e adelaidini e la fondazione del monastero di S. Salvatore di Pavia," *Biblioteca della Societa storica subalpina* 130 (1932): 1–39.

10. Anonymous, *Vita breuior sancti Maioli*, 18, in BC, col. 1775.

11. Ibid., 17, in BC, col. 1775.

to Greece and Asia Minor (Acts 21:3–7) and later docked in Sidon at the beginning of his fateful voyage to Malta, which ended in shipwreck (Acts 27:3).[12] Although they are often mentioned as a pair, Tyre enjoyed a privileged place over its neighbor and rival due to its most renowned industry, the production of an expensive purple dye cultivated from the murex, a marine snail common in eastern Mediterranean waters.[13] This dye was highly prized in the ancient period and well into the Middle Ages both for its extraordinary color and for the tenacity of its hue. The widespread use of "Tyrrean purple" in the royal courts of early medieval Europe and Byzantium sustained an enduring image of Tyre as a city that had grown prosperous through commercial enterprise.[14]

By the year 1000 the comparison of Tyre and Sidon to Pavia was a plausible one. Although the evidence is not abundant, it seems quite clear that the imperial seat of the Ottonians in northern Italy was a thriving commercial center well situated on a lucrative transalpine trade route that connected northern Europe with the riches of the Mediterranean.[15] In the ninth and tenth centuries, silk and other fine goods made their way up the Po River from Venice to the markets of Pavia. In the 890s, Venetian traders active in the city sought out the saintly nobleman Gerald of Aurillac to sell him their wares, including cloaks and spices, as he camped near Pavia en route from Rome to Burgundy.[16] By the early eleventh century, Pavia and Ferrara, the latter a market town in the Po watershed near Ravenna, enjoyed a monopoly on the sale of silks in Italy. Long-distance trade made the citizens of Pavia prosperous, a fact that found expression in the rich array of religious and domestic building projects that adorned their city.[17]

---

12. In a lamentation for Tyre, the prophet Ezekiel called the city "merchant of the peoples on many coastlines" (Ezek. 27:3).

13. For what follows, see Lloyd B. Jensen, "Royal Purple of Tyre," *Journal of Near Eastern Studies* 22 (1963): 104–18.

14. See Wilhelm Heyd, *Histoire du commerce du Levant au moyen âge*, 2 vols. (Leipzig, Germany: O. Harrassowitz, 1923); and Michael McCormick, *Origins of the European Economy: Communications and Commerce, A.D. 300–900* (Cambridge: Cambridge University Press, 2001), 719–26.

15. The fullest account remains that of Aloys Schulte, *Geschichte des mittelalterlichen Handels und Verkehrs zwischen Westdeutschland und Italien mit Ausschluss von Venedig* (Leipzig, Germany: Verlag von Duncker & Humblot, 1900), 1:1–79.

16. Odo of Cluny, *Vita sancti Geraldi Auriliacensis*, 1.27, in *Odon de Cluny, Vita sancti Geraldi Auriliacensis: Édition critique, traduction française, introduction et commentaires*, ed. Anne-Marie Bultot-Verleysen (Brussels: Société des Bollandistes, 2009), 172–74.

17. Flodoard, *Annales*, anno 924, in *Les Annales de Flodoard*, ed. Phillipe Lauer (Paris: Alphonse Picard et Fils, 1905), 22. See also Donald A. Bullough, "Urban Change in Early Medieval Italy: The Example of Pavia," *Papers of the British School at Rome* 34 (1966): 119–29 ("Appendix 3: Evidence for Churches in Pavia Before the Sack of the City in 924").

Even more significant than the commercial parallels between Sidon and Tyre and their medieval counterpart was the comparison of the moral disposition of their respective inhabitants. Both ancient port cities enjoyed the special attention of Christ during his ministry, because the people who lived there were especially receptive to his message of repentance. It was in the vicinity of Sidon and Tyre that Christ encountered a Canaanite woman whose daughter had been possessed by a demon. Despite the fact that she was a Gentile, her acceptance of Christ's message allowed her daughter to be healed (Matt. 15:21–28; also Mark 7:24–30, where the woman is identified as a Greek). Moreover, residents of both cities came to hear the Sermon on the Plain and have their ailments relieved by Christ's healing presence (Luke 6:17–19). Most tellingly, however, Christ himself singled out the virtues of the people of Sidon and Tyre when excoriating many of the towns in which he had performed miracles, where the citizens were too hardhearted to change their ways: "Woe to you, Corazin! Woe to you, Beth-saida! For if the mighty works done in you had been done in Tyre and Sidon, they would have repented long ago in sackcloth and ashes. But I tell you, it shall be more tolerable on the day of judgment for Tyre and Sidon than for you." (Matt. 11:21–22). Implicit in the evocation of these biblical cities, which would have been well known to monastic readers who were familiar with these Gospel stories from their repetition in the liturgy, was the notion that the miracles of the abbot of Cluny took place in Pavia because the inhabitants of the city, like those of Sidon and Tyre, had a disposition toward repentance that merited the revealed power of the saint.

The author of BHL 5180 supported the claim that the citizens of Pavia deserved the special attention of the saintly abbot of Cluny by relating two miracles that occurred at local landmarks well known to the audience of the *vita*. As a whole, the miracles attributed to Maiolus in this work are quite modest in character, perhaps because the reservoir of available stories of the saint's interventions was not very deep so soon after his death.[18] The stories include an unanticipated discovery of mushrooms, the rescue of a ship and its crew on the Rhône, the protection of a book from a candle that was left to burn upon it, an unexpected catch of fish, and the pardon of a criminal. The two miracles that the abbot performed in Pavia are similarly mundane: the first occurred in the Church of Saint Sirius, where the prayers

---

18. A similar problem troubled Eadmer, the early twelfth-century biographer of Anselm of Canterbury, who contented himself with recording miracles of the most mundane sort precisely because grander miracles were in short supply. In the words of Richard Southern, "As compared with the ancient saints, it was not much." See Southern, *Saint Anselm: A Portrait in a Landscape* (Cambridge: Cambridge University Press, 1990), 426.

of the abbot rekindled an extinguished lantern during a nocturnal visit, and the second took place near a chapel on the outskirts of the city, where Maiolus retired on occasion to escape the bustle of the capital.[19] Here the power of God through the agency of the abbot performed a task of much-needed urban renewal by miraculously repairing the path to the chapel, which had become swampy and difficult to traverse.[20]

While these two stories anchored the miraculous power of the Cluniac saint firmly in the civic fabric of Pavia, a third presented a miracle experienced by a prominent imperial official who would have been well known to the local audience of the *vita*: Hildebrand, a master of the mint of the province of Pavia (*magister monetariorum Papiensis provinciae*).[21] Bedridden by an illness that caused him excruciating pain, Hildebrand had given up hope of returning to health until the prayers of Maiolus brought about his complete recovery. Explicit reference to an imperial official of high standing distinguishes this story from innumerable accounts of miraculous healings in contemporary hagiographical texts. By virtue of his office, Hildebrand must have been one of the most powerful individuals in late tenth-century Pavia. He was probably the master of the imperial treasury, overseeing "nine noble and wealthy masters above all other moneyers" in the supervision of the mint and the regulation of the currency.[22] While public recognition of Hildebrand would certainly have lent this miracle story a strong capital among local readers, the fact that he was an imperial official directly in charge of the mint and therefore deeply implicated in the city's commercial success reinforced the analogue of Pavia and the trade centers of Sidon and Tyre. This identification in turn underscored the hagiographer's claim that the residents of Pavia deserved the special attention of the Cluniac abbot because, like the citizens of these biblical port towns, their repentant character made them worthy vessels for the manifestations of the saint's power to work miracles. In other words, the earliest *Life of Maiolus* created the perception that Pavia was a plausible venue for the abbot's holy works by drawing an explicit comparison between the commercial activity and virtuous character of its in-

---

19. Anonymous, *Vita breuior sancti Maioli*, 17, in BC, cols. 1774–75. On the Church of Saint Sirius, see also *Instituta regalia et ministeria camerae regum Longobardorum et honorantiae civitatis Papiae* 16, ed. Adolf Hofmeister, MGH SS, 30.1:1457.

20. Anonymous, *Vita breuior sancti Maioli*, 19, in BC, col. 1775.

21. Ibid., 20, in BC, col. 1776.

22. *Honorantiae Civitatis Papiae*, 8, ed. Hofmeister, 1454: "Ministerium autem monete Papie debet habere novem magistros nobiles et divites super omnes alios monetarios." Although it is quite dated, Robert Lopez, "An Aristocracy of Money in the Early Middle Ages," *Speculum* 28 (1953): 1–43, is still useful for those new to this topic.

habitants and those of the ancient entrepôts Sidon and Tyre, for whom Christ himself had cast out demons and healed the sick.

For the author of BHL 5180, the kidnapping of Maiolus by the Muslims of La Garde-Freinet played an important role in establishing the credentials of the holy man who exhibited a saintly forbearance when God tested him with hardship. The abbot's abductors served no further purpose in the narrative other than to support the author's claim that the abbot of Cluny was indeed worthy of veneration as a saint. As a result, this account offered only a crudely wrought caricature of the inhabitants of La Garde-Freinet that emphasized their savage cruelty for the purpose of extolling the virtues of Maiolus. Written in Pavia for a local audience, the earliest *Life of Maiolus* did not enjoy a wide circulation after its composition.[23] The text or portions thereof survived in only four manuscripts and in an early seventeenth-century edition based on two Cluniac manuscripts that are no longer extant. In addition, two medieval breviaries included short excerpts from the work for liturgical use, and a twelfth-century account of the death of Maiolus paraphrased the preface and first chapter of the text. BHL 5180 did, however, attract the attention of the monks of Cluny, who did not take kindly to the veneration of their holy father on the other side of the Alps. Within a decade of the composition of the earliest *Life of Maiolus*, Abbot Odilo of Cluny commissioned a new *vita* that challenged the Pavians' claim to be the singular recipients of the saint's favor. This Cluniac composition put control of the abbot's legacy firmly in the hands of his Burgundian brethren by subsuming some of the Pavian episodes into the growing corpus of his miracles and by excising others from the tradition completely. It also offered a new depiction of the abduction of Maiolus by the Muslims of La Garde-Freinet, inflected by a dynamic portrait of the abbot as a relentless preacher of the word of God.

The Preacher's Prowess

Abbatial hagiography was not a medium of Cluniac self-perception or self-promotion in the tenth century.[24] The *Life of Maiolus* composed at Pavia around 1000 was only the second such work to extol the virtues of an abbot of Cluny. The first was John of Salerno's *Life of Odo*, an account of the holy

---

23. For what follows, see Iogna-Prat, *Agni Immaculati*, 24–27.

24. There is no adequate study of the origins of Cluniac hagiography or the formative influences on the Cluniac abbatial tradition, though Helmut Richter, *Die Persönlichkeitsdarstellung in cluniazensischen Abtsviten* (Erlangen, Germany: H. Richter, 1972), remains a fundamental point of departure.

character of Cluny's second abbot written shortly after Odo's death in 942.[25] John was not a monk of the fledgling Burgundian abbey but an Italian who had first met Odo in Rome and then accompanied him to Pavia, where he took the monastic vow. John dedicated the *Life of Odo* to his brethren at Salerno, where by the 940s he had become the spiritual father of a religious community with ties to Cluny. For these Italian monks the abbot of Cluny provided a model of personal virtue worthy of emulation. Moreover, the *Life of Odo* demonstrated the lengths to which the monks of Gaul were prepared to go to uphold the angelic ideal (*coelestis disciplina*) fostered by Odo in fulfillment of the abbey's foundation charter, which encouraged the brethren specifically "to seek and desire with full commitment and inner order the heavenly way of life."[26] Perhaps because John's enterprise was a work of local consumption written at a time when the Cluniacs were not self-conscious about controlling the public image of the sanctity of their abbots, John of Salerno's *Life of Odo* did not invite critical scrutiny from Cluny until the twelfth century, when Abbot Peter the Venerable commissioned a monk named Nalgod to rewrite the lives of some of his tenth-century predecessors.[27]

In contrast to John's work, the Pavian *Life of Maiolus* quickly drew the attention of the Cluniacs. The reason for this is clear. As discussed in chapter 1, the abbacy of Maiolus marked a turning point for Cluny in terms of the sheer number of donations that the community received in return for prayers for the dead. Maiolus's successor as abbot was Odilo (994–1049), who spent the early years of his abbacy promoting the image of Cluny as a religious house whose monks were so virtuous in their conduct that their prayers were especially efficacious in securing the release of souls from infernal punishment.[28] It was during Odilo's abbacy, for instance, that a legend began to circulate concerning a hermit who had a vision of the souls of the damned escaping the grasp of demons due to the agency of the vigils and almsgiving

---

25. John of Salerno, *Vita Odonis*, PL 133, cols. 43–86. On the *Vita Odonis* and its author, see the exhaustive study of Odo's career by Isabelle Rosé, *Construire une société seigneuriale: Itinéraire et ecclésiologie de l'abbé Odon de Cluny (fin du IXe–milieu du Xe siècle)* (Turnhout, Belgium: Brepols, 2008).

26. On the concept of *coelestis disciplina*, see Odo of Cluny, *Sermo 3 (De sancto Benedicto abbate)*, PL 133, col. 722a. For a similar ideal expressed in Cluny's foundation charter (composed in 910), see *Charta qua Vuillelmus, comes et dux, fundat monasterium cluniacense*, in *Recueil des chartes de l'abbaye de Cluny*, ed. Bernard and Bruel, 1:125–26 (no. 112).

27. In the preface of his work, Nalgod complained explicitly about John of Salerno's redundancy (PL 133, col. 85b). On the industry of this little known Cluniac author, see chapter 4 of the present volume.

28. Jacques Hourlier, *Saint Odilon, Abbé de Cluny* (Leuven, Belgium: Bibliothèque de l'Université, Bureaux de la Revue, 1964) remains the only book-length study of Odilo's abbacy.

of the brethren of Cluny. News of this vision allegedly inspired Odilo to establish the Feast of All Souls (2 November). This new feast day, unprecedented in its ecumenical approach to the souls of all Christians, made the prayers of the Cluniacs available to everyone, living and dead, while at the same time asserting their monopoly on prayerful intercession for all Christendom.

It was in this climate of self-conscious self-promotion that the Cluniacs responded to the Pavians' claim to a privileged relationship with Maiolus. There is no way to know exactly how and when they had learned that monks in northern Italy had honored their recently deceased abbot with a *vita*, but by the year 1010 a new *Life of Maiolus* appeared, commissioned by Abbot Odilo and composed by a monk of Cluny named Syrus (BHL 5177/79).[29] Through the judicious editing of miracle stories related in BHL 5180, this Cluniac work blunted the claim of the Pavians to be the special recipients of the abbot's favor. For instance, BHL 5177/79 related two of Maiolus's miracles that took place in Pavia—the rekindling of the candle in the Church of Saint Sirius and the healing of Hildebrand—but played down the local significance of both miracles through silent omissions.[30] First, Syrus stripped the local designation from Hildebrand's title, calling him simply "a minter of coins" (*monetarius*) rather than "the master of the mint of the province of Pavia" (*magister monetariorum Papiensis provinciae*); in doing so he distanced the significance of the miracle from the community in which it occurred. Second, he omitted the analogy between Pavia and Sidon and Tyre, thereby removing the rationale for the saint's activity among the penitential Pavians that loomed so large in BHL 5180. And while these miracles of illumination and healing melded easily with the growing corpus of stories that Syrus collected in his account of the abbot's life, the miracle of urban renewal that appeared in the Pavian *vita* did not find its way into the Cluniac version, most probably because it was so localized that it would have held little relevance to readers who were not familiar with the city of Pavia. In the end, the Cluniacs succeeded in undermining the distinctiveness of the Pavians' relationship with Maiolus by deploying a new narrative that rooted the holy activity of their abbot firmly at Cluny. Based on the surviving manuscript evidence, BHL 5177/79 enjoyed a much wider readership than the *vita* composed a decade earlier at Pavia, eventually overshadowing it completely.[31]

---

29. Syrus, *Vita sancti Maioli* (BHL 5177/79), ed. Iogna-Prat, in *Agni Immaculati*, 163–285.

30. Syrus, *Vita sancti Maioli* 3.15 (the healing of Hildebrand the *monetarius*) and 3.19 (the miracle at the Church of Saint Sirius), ed. Iogna-Prat, in *Agni Immaculati*, 270–71, 274–76.

31. On the manuscript tradition of BHL 5177/79, see Iogna-Prat, *Agni Immaculati*, 71–98.

Compared to BHL 5180, Syrus's *Life of Maiolus* was a sprawling production, comprising sixty chapters organized into three books. The work represented the ambition of Abbot Odilo to depict his predecessor as a model of saintly comportment both with respect to his personal conduct and to his dealings beyond the cloister. The result was a richly textured portrait of Maiolus's career informed by the collective memory of his own brethren. The first book sketched the abbot's early life, from his upbringing in Provence to his education at Lyon and his election as archdeacon in Mâcon. It culminated with his rejection of the world and his entry into Cluny, where his cultivation of virtue attracted the attention and admiration of Abbot Aymard (942–54). The second book presented the idealized portrait of a tenth-century abbot at work, both in the abbey and in the world. It began with the election of Maiolus as abbot of Cluny and offered an extended meditation on the ways in which his virtuous comportment mirrored the ascetic principles enshrined in the sixth-century *Rule of Benedict*, which by the year 1000 had become the most authoritative guide to monastic life in western Europe. The final book recounted the abbot's abduction by the Muslims of La Garde-Freinet followed by his rejection of Emperor Otto II's nomination of him for the papacy and more accounts of miracles attributed to his holiness. The *vita* closed with a brief account of the saint's final days and his death in Souvigny while en route to Paris to reform the Abbey of Saint Denis.

The idealized portrait of Maiolus promoted by his successor Odilo placed a strong emphasis on his prowess as a preacher after the model of the apostles.[32] Whatever thoughts he spoke aloud were laden with the freight of wisdom.[33] His words were purposeful; they were goads and nails that pricked the minds of his listeners and turned them toward virtue.[34] Following the *Rule of Benedict*, Maiolus tailored the tone and content of his speech to suit the specific needs of his audience. He wooed some with winsome words, coaxed others with admonitions, and sowed terror in the minds of the slow and stubborn. At a time when the brethren of Cluny embraced a code of personal discipline that was unparalleled in the strict limitations that it placed on mundane communication between individual monks, their abbot was garrulous in his dispensation of life-giving words.[35] With a holy urgency, an

---

32. In light of this testimony it is surprising that no sermons attributed to Maiolus survive.

33. Syrus, *Vita sancti Maioli*, 2.6, ed. Iogna-Prat, 217: "Quidquid loquebatur, sapientie grauitate componebatur."

34. For what follows, see Syrus, *Vita sancti Maioli*, 2.6, ed. Iogna-Prat, 218.

35. On this aspect of monastic discipline at Cluny and elsewhere, see Scott G. Bruce, *Silence and Sign Language in Medieval Monasticism: The Cluniac Tradition (c. 900–c. 1200)* (Cambridge: Cambridge University Press, 2007).

agitation of the tongue born of the knowledge of the consequences of his silence, Maiolus preached constantly to everyone who would listen.

This portrayal of Maiolus as a relentless preacher inflected Syrus's retelling of the abbot's encounter with the Muslims of La Garde-Freinet, which shared many similarities with the Pavian version of the episode but differed from it in two important ways. First, the Cluniac version preserved the earliest known copy of the abbot's ransom note, perhaps transcribed from the original preserved in the archives of the abbey.[36] Second, it presented a verbal exchange between Maiolus and his adversaries on matters of religious faith. Unlike the crude caricature of the Muslims presented in the Pavian *Life of Maiolus*, Syrus depicted them from the outset of the episode as religious rivals who disparaged the beliefs of their Christian captives.[37] According to Syrus, the abbot of Cluny responded by preaching in defense of his faith: "Like a seasoned warrior, blessed Maiolus immediately seized the shield of faith and, making the case for the Christian religion, he pierced the enemies of Christ with the blade of God's word. He attempted to demonstrate with proven and most credible arguments that the one whom they worshipped as God did not have the power to free himself from punishment, let alone to help them in any way."[38] The abbot's captors understood enough of the content of his defense of Christianity to respond with rage and violence at his apparent sacrilege. Maiolus expected to become a martyr at their hands, but instead of killing him, the Muslims bound him in heavy chains. At this point in the narrative Syrus is consistent with the account provided by the anonymous hagiographer of Pavia. Maiolus suffered considerable hardship in captivity—in a passage unique to Syrus, the abbot credited the intervention of the Virgin Mary with the relief of his suffering—but after his release divine vengeance overtook his captors: a Christian host attacked their citadel in Provence and drove them into flight.[39] Syrus's depiction of the conquest of La Garde-Freinet resonated with ancient echoes, evoking Virgil's description of the fall of Troy in the second book of the *Aeneid*.

---

36. On the text of the ransom note, see chapter 1 of the present volume.

37. Syrus, *Vita sancti Maioli*, 3.1, ed. Iogna-Prat, 249.

38. Syrus, *Vita sancti Maioli*, 3.2, ed. Iogna-Prat, 249–50: "Protinus ergo beatus Maiolus belligerator optimus scutum fidei arripiens, cuspide uerbi dei perfodiebat inimicos christi, christiane religionis cultum approbans, et eum quem deum colebant, nec se a supplicio liberare, nec illos in aliquo posse adiuuare certis et euidentissimis adgressus est rationibus demonstrare." This imagery of spiritual combat has a long history that derives from Ephesians 6:10–17. On military imagery and monastic culture more generally, see Katherine Allen Smith, *War and the Making of Medieval Monastic Culture* (Woodbridge, England: Boydell Press, 2011).

39. For Mary's intercession on Maiolus's behalf, see Syrus, *Vita sancti Maioli*, 3.4, ed. Iogna-Prat, 251–52.

Besieged like the doomed Trojans, the Muslim adventurers felt "an icy shiver run through the marrow of their bones" as the Christian army advanced.[40] After the initial assault, Syrus reported that some of the brigands were taken as slaves, but many more were captured and put to death. Here again the Cluniac author related details of the story with no precedent in the laconic account of BHL 5180. The Muslims who survived the assault on their stronghold fled into the mountains. Harried by the Christian host, they found themselves cornered on the precipice of a high peak. Faced with death, the last Muslims of La Garde-Freinet pleaded for baptism at the hands of the enemies and were saved, for—as Syrus reminded his readers—Maiolus had taught them about Christ "with life-giving words" (*uerbis salutaribus*) during his time in captivity.[41]

This debate between the abbot of Cluny and his Muslim captors about the principles of the Christian faith was unprecedented in Latin literature composed north of the Pyrenees in the early Middle Ages. According to Syrus's account, Maiolus had learned enough about the tenets of Islam from his captors to refute the claim that Muhammed was an effective advocate before God. Although the prophet was not named directly in this account, Syrus was clearly alluding to him when he depicted the abbot dismissing the intercessory power of "the one whom they worshipped as God" (*eum quem deum colebant*).[42] Nor was this exchange one-sided. Syrus reported that the Muslims ridiculed Christian beliefs as soon as they captured Maiolus, so their knowledge of Christianity obviously predated their encounter with him. This is not at all surprising given that Christian travelers were an important part of their livelihood. Moreover, the abbot of Cluny apparently taught his captors enough about the principles of Christianity that they knew to request baptism when faced with death.[43] Indeed, Syrus emphasized the fact that the surviving Muslims had learned about the saving power of baptism through the "life-giving words" of Maiolus, who had presented them with "proven and most credible arguments" (*certis et euidentissimis rationibus*) for abandoning their belief in the teachings of Muhammed.

Under the direction of Abbot Odilo, Syrus of Cluny crafted a portrait of Maiolus in captivity that contrasted markedly with the depiction of the saint

---

40. Syrus, *Vita sancti Maioli*, 3.8, ed. Iogna-Prat, 258: "Extemplo barbaris gelidus per dura cucurrit ossa tremor." Compare Virgil, *Aeneid*, 2.119–21, ed. Gian Biagio Conte (Berlin: De Gruyter, 2009), 37: "Uugli quae uox ut uenit ad auris, / obstipuere animi gelidusque per ima cucurrit / ossa tremor, cui fata parent, quem poscat Apollo."

41. Syrus, *Vita sancti Maioli*, 3.9, ed. Iogna-Prat, 259.

42. Ibid., 3.2, ed. Iogna-Prat, 250.

43. Ibid., 3.9, ed. Iogna-Prat, 259.

presented only a decade earlier by the anonymous monk of Pavia. While the earliest *Life of Maiolus* had emphasized the perseverance of the abbot in the face of the hardships endured during his abduction as proof of his holiness, which was manifest in the miracles that he had performed in Pavia, Syrus and his Cluniac brethren offered a new image of Maiolus among the Muslims consonant with their rendering of him as a relentless preacher. In their account the abbot defended his faith through active disputation with his captors, the result being that some of them elected to convert to Christianity rather than face death when vanquished by a Christian host. The story did not end there, however. Over the course of the next two decades, monks of Cluny would produce two more accounts of the kidnapping episode, each of which differed considerably from the tales that had come before.

⚔ Fulcher and the Great Wolf

Around the year 1033, twenty years or so after the composition of Syrus's *Life of Maiolus*, Odilo of Cluny had a hand in yet another retelling of the story of his predecessor's abduction by the Muslims of La Garde-Freinet.[44] While Odilo was visiting Romainmôtier, a Cluniac house in the Pays de Vaud, the brethren there asked him to suggest an appropriate reading to celebrate the anniversary of Maiolus's death (11 May). Odilo first proposed the *Homilies* of Pope Gregory the Great, because his predecessor had so admired them, but prompted by a nocturnal visit from the saint he decided to compose a new version of the *Life of Maiolus* (BHL 5182/84).[45] Appropriate to the liturgical context for which it was written, Odilo condensed the biographical details of Maiolus's life and omitted most chronological markers from his work. He emphasized instead the abbot's saintly disposition, for which prelates and princely powers alike esteemed him, and described the manifestation of his holy power through miracles of all kinds.

Odilo's short text ended with a report of Maiolus's death in Souvigny, but he appended to it a tale related to the abbot's kidnapping, apparently as an afterthought: "I wanted here to bring my account of the life and habits of blessed Maiolus, in which I tried to speak with faithful timerity and humble presumption, to a close. But I have [in the meantime] remembered

---

44. On the date of its composition, see Hourlier, *Saint Odilon*, 101n7.

45. Odilo, *Vita sancti Maioli*, AASS Maii, 2:683–88, reprinted in PL 142, cols. 959–62 (BHL 5182/84). For more on this work, see Iogna-Prat, *Agni Immaculati*, 34–40. In the preface to this *vita*, Odilo explained in detail the context of its composition.

a certain memorable portent concerning this father, which I had heard about from the accounts of some faithful men."[46] Odilo was not particularly interested in rehearsing the details of the events of 972; Syrus's *Life of Maiolus* had already accomplished this.[47] He focused instead on a "certain memorable portent" (*memorabile quoddam praesagium*) that foreshadowed the abduction of Maiolus and illustrated by analogy the power of the holy abbot over the Devil. According to Odilo, an incursion of savage wolves preceded and predicted the coming of the Muslims to Provence, the suffering of Christians at their hands, the destruction of religious communities and towns throughout the region, the abduction and ransom of Maiolus in the Alps, and the subsequent downfall of Fraxinetum as an act of God's will.[48] An unusually large and fierce beast with a penchant for blood and the capacity to swallow human limbs whole led this lupine invasion. It was none other than Maiolus's father, a warrior named Fulcher with landed interests in Provence, who made a stand against the marauding wolf.[49] Girding his sword and donning his armor, Fulcher spent his nights in a sheepfold covered with a sheepskin, laying in wait to confront the beast. When the great wolf pounced on him, he seized it in his iron grip and dragged it back to his companions, who paraded it before the frightened populace before killing it. The death of this monster dispersed the roving packs of wolves and restored calm to the countryside.

For Odilo the downfall of the great wolf at Fulcher's hands had a typological significance worthy of liturgical rumination: "Anyone who wants to understand these things correctly should be able to infer a spiritual significance to this incident."[50] The attack of the wolves foretold the savagery of the Muslims of Fraxinetum, while Fulcher's defeat of their leader anticipated his son's victory not only over the Muslims but also over a much more dan-

---

46. Odilo, *Vita sancti Maioli*, 14, AASS Maii, 2:687–88, and PL 142, col. 959: "Cum enim huic sententiae vellem finem imponere, in qua de beati Maioli vita et moribus fideli temeritate et humili praesumptione nisus sum aliquid dicere, venit in [mente] [PL: memoria] memorabile quoddam praesagium, quod in genitore illius quorumdam fidelium relatione audiveram gestum." Translated by Paul Dutton in *Medieval Saints: A Reader*, ed. Mary-Ann Stouck (Peterborough, Ontario: Broadview Press, 1999), 262 (slightly altered).

47. See Odilo, *Vita sancti Maioli* 15, AASS Maii, 2:688, and PL 142, col. 960, for the author's brisk recapitulation of the events leading up the kidnapping of Maiolus in 972.

48. Odilo, *Vita sancti Maioli* 15, AASS Maii, 2:688, and PL 142, cols. 960–61.

49. On the family of Maiolus, his ties to Provence specifically, and the influence of Cluny in the region generally, see Eliana Magnani Soares-Christen, *Monastères et aristocratie en Provence milieu Xe–début XIIe siècle* (Münster, Germany: LIT Verlag, 1999), 24–97, esp. 54–58.

50. Odilo, *Vita sancti Maioli*, 17, AASS Maii, 2:688; and PL 142, col. 962: "Si quis haec prudenter intelligi voluerit, aliquid spiritale inde conjicere poterit."

gerous adversary, the devil himself, whom Odilo called "the invisible wolf."[51] Why did Odilo choose an incursion of wolves as a fitting analogy for the arrival of the Muslims in Provence? The Gospel of Matthew makes explicit reference to false prophets who come like wolves dressed in sheep's clothing (7:15), which has led at least one scholar to suggest that Odilo deployed the wolf analogy to present the Muslims of La Garde-Freinet as promoters of a false religion.[52] It would be misleading, however, to impute to Odilo a critique of Islam on this basis, since the wolves in his story practice no deception about their character; it is Fulcher who disguises himself as a sheep to confront them. Rather, it seems that Odilo was simply drawing a parallel between an incursion of wild animals and the invasion of Provence by outsiders who laid waste to the region in a predatory manner.

✒ Enter Muhammed

The tale of Maiolus's kidnapping also found its way into a monastic history finished in the 1040s by a former monk of Cluny named Rodulphus Glaber (d. ca. 1046).[53] By his own account a wayward soul unfit for the religious life, Glaber was only a resident at Cluny for a few years (ca. 1030–35), but it was there that he gathered much of the material for his *Five Books of Histories*, which he dedicated to Abbot Odilo, perhaps in the hope of reconciling himself with his former spiritual father after his premature dismissal from the abbey.[54] Although narrower in scope than his ambitions imply, Glaber claimed that he wrote this chronicle "to tell of what happened in the four parts of the globe" (*quoniam de quatuor mundani orbis partium euentibus relaturi sumus*) to a contemporary audience bereft of historical writing comparable with Bede and Paul the Deacon.[55] His account of Maiolus's abduction

---

51. Odilo, *Vita sancti Maioli*, 17, AASS Maii, 2:688; and PL 142, col. 962.

52. Michael Meckler, "Wolves and Saracens in Odilo's *Life of Mayeul*," in *Latin Culture in the Eleventh Century: Proceedings of the Third International Conference on Medieval Latin Studies, Cambridge, September 9–12, 1998*, ed. Michael W. Herren, C. J. McDonough, and Ross Arthur (Turnhout, Belgium: Brepols, 2002), 2:125–26.

53. Rodulfus Glaber, *Historiarum Libri Quinque*, ed. and trans. John France, in *Rodulfus Glaber: The Five Books of Histories and the Life of St. William* (Oxford: Clarendon Press, 1989), 1–253.

54. Most of what we know about Glaber's character comes from self-referential statements in the *Histories*. See, in particular, Glaber, *Historiarum Libri Quinque*, 5.3, ed. France, 218–21. On his relationship with the abbey of Cluny and the degree to which he espoused Cluniac sensibilities, see John France, "Rodulphus Glaber and the Cluniacs," *Journal of Ecclesiastical History* 39 (1988): 497–508; and John France, "Glaber as a Reformer," *Studia Monastica* 34 (1992): 41–51.

55. Glaber, *Historiarum Libri Quinque*, 1.1, ed. France, 2.

appeared in the first book of the *Histories*, in which he related many stories about the early history of Cluny and its abbots.[56] It comes as no surprise that Glaber's version of the tale owed much to the content of Syrus's *Life of Maiolus*, to which the chronicler would have had ready access during his time at Cluny.

Glaber was not, however, a slavish imitator of Syrus's work. Embellishments abound in the *Histories*. Two particular details warrant our attention because they lend Glaber's version of the abduction narrative a vividness that belies the decades separating the chronicler from the events he describes and thereby suggest that he may have learned them at Cluny from older monks who had heard the story from sources much closer in time to the kidnapping. According to Glaber, when the Muslims stripped the abbot of his belongings, they asked him directly if he had the resources to ransom himself from captivity. The abbot allegedly responded that he had no wealth of his own, but admitted that he nonetheless had great authority among men of station.[57] This exchange may be a literary flourish on Glaber's part, but it is not unrealistic given the context. As chapter 1 has shown, captured individuals with no means to ransom themselves would have been sold into slavery, for there was a high demand for European slaves throughout this period in the Muslim principalities around the Mediterranean rim. Likewise, as in Syrus's *Life of Maiolus*, Glaber's account of the kidnapping included a copy of the ransom note sent by the abbot from captivity, but the *Histories* is the only version of the story to refer explicitly to the quantity of the ransom paid: one thousand pounds of silver—which, as Glaber explained, amounted to a share of one pound for every Muslim warrior involved in the abduction.[58] The number may well be an exaggeration, but it compares to the amount demanded a century earlier for the release of Roland, archbishop of Arles and abbot of St. Caesarius, which provides our only comparison: 150 pounds of silver, 150 cloaks, 150 swords, and 150 slaves in exchange for a single prelate.[59]

---

56. Glaber, *Historiarum Libri Quinque*, 1.9, ed. France, 18–23.

57. Ibid., 18.

58. Ibid., 18.

59. On the ransom demanded for Roland, see chapter 1 of the present volume. Evidence from the eastern Mediterranean is equally thin, but the archives of Mount Athos preserve an early eleventh-century charter that records the sale of a field by a widow to the abbot for fifteen gold pieces in her effort to raise a ransom for her son held in Muslim captivity. See *Actes d'Iviron, pt. 1: Des origines au milieu du XIe siècle*, ed. Jacques Lefort, Nicolas Oikonomidès, and Denise Papachryssanthou (Paris, 1985), vol. 1, no. 16 (dated ca. 1010), cited in Alice-Mary Talbot, "Searching for Women on Mt. Athos: Insights from the Archives of the Holy Mountain," *Speculum* 87 (2012): 1006. Sources from late medieval Spain provide much more explicit evidence for the price of ransoms and the resources

What makes Glaber's *Histories* so distinctive in the literary tradition of Maiolus's abduction, however, is an aside about the beliefs of the abbot's captors. The context for this digression is two short episodes about Maiolus's experience in captivity, both of which Glaber employed to illuminate the sanctity of the holy man. The chronicler's comment is prompted by the discursive activity of the characters that populate his text, the details of which have no parallel in the earlier accounts of the kidnapping but may hark back to oral tradition at Cluny. In the first episode the Muslims offered Maiolus meat and hard bread to eat in captivity, but the abbot declined, saying, "If I should be hungry, then it is the Lord who will provide. I will not eat this, for it is not what I am used to."[60] Moved by compassion (*pietate ductus*), one of the Muslims responded by rolling up his sleeves, washing his shield, and baking upon it a fresh loaf of bread, which he offered to Maiolus with great reverence, because he recognized the abbot as a man of God.[61] Not all of the Muslims interacted so sympathetically with their captive, however. While carving a piece of wood with a knife, another warrior placed his foot on the Bible manuscript (*codicem, bibliotecam uidelicet*) that Maiolus always carried with him.[62] The abbot reacted with horror and "certain of the less ferocious" Muslims (*aliqui minus feroces ex ipsis perspicientes*) recognized that this action was an affront to God and reprimanded their companion. Moved by divine judgment, these warriors later attacked their friend and cut off the foot with which he had offended the Lord.[63]

The key moment in Glaber's narrative arrives when some of the Muslims recognized the prophets in the abbot's Bible as their own. This scene provided the chronicler with an opportunity to digress at length on the error of Muslim belief with respect to Christian prophecy:

---

available for captives and their families to raise funds for the release of individuals in Muslim captivity. See Jarbel Rodriguez, "Financing a Captive's Ransom in Late Medieval Aragon," *Medieval Encounters* 9 (2003): 164–81.

60. Glaber, *Libri Historiarum Quinque*, 1.9, ed. France, 20: "Nam cum ei hora prandii obtulissent cibos quibus uescebantur, carnes uidelicet panemque admodum asperum, et dicerent: 'Comede,' respondit: 'Ego enim si esuriero, Domini est me pascere. Ex his tamen non comedam, quia non mihi olim in usu fuerunt.'"

61. Glaber, *Libri Historiarum Quinque*, 1.9, ed. France, 20.

62. This Bible remained in the library of Cluny after the abbot's death. It appears in a twelfth-century catalog as "Volumen secunde bibliothece, que fuit beati Mayoli." See Léopold Delisle, *Inventaire des manuscrits de la Bibliothèque nationale: Fonds de Cluni* (Paris: Librairie H. Champion, 1884), 337 (no. 3). For the argument that the core of the catalog belongs to the abbacy of Hugh the Great (1049–1109) rather than that of Hugh III (1158–61), see Veronika von Büren, "Le grand catalogue de la Bibliothèque de Cluny," in *Le gouvernement d'Hugues de Semur à Cluny: Actes du Colloque scientifique international (Cluny, septembre 1988)* (Mâcon: Musée Ochier, 1990), 245–63.

63. Glaber, *Libri Historiarum Quinque*, 1.9, ed. France, 20.

Certain of the less ferocious Saracens who had seen the incident reprimanded their companion, saying that great prophets should not be
so scorned that he should tread their words under his feet. For the
Saracens read the Hebrew prophets (or rather, those of the Christians), claiming that what they foretold concerning Jesus Christ, Lord
of all, is now fulfilled in the person of Mohammad, one of their
people. To support them in their error, they have in their possession
a genealogy of their own, similar to that found in the Gospel of
Matthew, who recounts the descent of Jesus from Abraham through
Isaac, in whose seed was the promise and prediction of universal
blessing. But theirs says that 'Ishmael begat Nabajoth' and continues
with an erroneous fiction which, in deviating from the holy catholic
account, strays equally from the truth.[64]

This aside has a significance out of proportion with its brevity, for here Glaber
provides the first known reference to Muhammed by any medieval writer
north of the Pyrenees before the First Crusade (1095–1101).[65] Glaber's
direct and precise criticism of the Muslims' claim about Muhammed's prophetic authority probably has nothing to do with Maiolus's experience in
captivity but instead reflects the slow infiltration of knowledge of Islamic
beliefs into Europe by the middle of the eleventh century. Modern scholars
are unanimous in attributing Glaber's information about Muhammed to the
arrival at Cluny in 1032 of a diplomatic embassy of Spanish monks sent by
Sancho III, king of Navarre.[66] These individuals carried with them first-

---

64. Glaber, *Libri Historiarum Quinque*, 1.9, ed. France, 20–22: "Aliqui minus feroces ex ipsis perspicientes suum increpuerunt comparem, dicentes non debere magnos prophetas sic pro nichilo
duci ut illorum dicta pedi substerneret. Siquidem Sarraceni Hebreorum, quin potius Christianorum, prophetas legunt, dicentes etiam completum iam esse in quodam suorum, quem illi Mahomed
nuncupant, quicquid de uniuersorum Domino Christo sacri uates predixerunt. Sed ad errorem illorum comprobandum etiam ipsorum genealogiam penes se habent, ad similitudinem uidelicet
Euangelii Mathei qui scilicet ab Abraham narrat genealogiae catalogum usque ad Ihesum per Isaac
successionem descendens, in cuius uidelicet semine uniuersorum promissa atque predicta est bene-
dictio. Illorum inquiens 'Hismahel genuit Nabaiot,' ac deinceps usque in erroneum illorum descendens figmentum, quod scilicet tantum est a ueritate alienum quantum a sacra et catholica auctoritate
extraneum."

65. Richard Southern, *Western Views of Islam in the Middle Ages* (Cambridge, MA: Harvard University Press, 1962), 28.

66. See, for example, the comment by France in the introduction to his edition of Glaber's text
(liii–liv). Glaber mentions Spanish monks several times in his work. See, for example, Glaber, *Libri
Historiarum Quinque*, 2.18, ed. France, 82 (a report of Spanish religious in Christian armies killed
while fighting Muslims); 3.12, ed. France, 116 (where Spanish monks visiting Cluny celebrate the
Feast of the Annunciation on 18 December rather than 25 March, which caused two Cluniac
monks to have nightmares about the Spaniards cannibalizing a child); and 4.22, ed. France, 206 (in
which Glaber remarks that many Spaniards took the habit at Cluny and spread their enthusiasm for

hand knowledge of Islam from Muslim-ruled al-Andalus, which they no doubt shared in conversation with their Cluniac brethren. While Glaber's retelling of Maiolus's kidnapping provided him with the opportunity to criticize Islamic claims of Muhammed's prophetic authority, he chose not to repeat the details of the fate of the Muslims found in Syrus's account, in which the abbot of Cluny taught his captors about the principles of Christianity with life-giving words and thereby provided some of them with a means of saving themselves by asking for baptism when faced with death. Instead, in terms reminiscent of the conclusion of the episode in the anonymous *Life of Maiolus* from Pavia, Glaber described the destruction of the Muslims of La Garde-Freinet by a Christian army in no uncertain terms: "in a short space all perished, so that not one returned to his country."[67]

By the middle of the eleventh century, a rich literary tradition had coalesced around the memory of the abduction of Maiolus by the Muslims of La Garde-Freinet. The monks of Cluny demonstrated a remarkable versatility in their telling and retelling of the story of their abbot's kidnapping. None of these authors was wedded to an impartial recounting of the events of July 972; instead, each of them retold the abduction episode to fulfill the expectations of their respective audiences and to forward their individual devotional aims—which often, though not always, centered around the glorification of Maiolus as a saint. As a result, it is impossible to parse from these stories a distinctive Cluniac view of Islam in the early eleventh century. From the cruel adversaries depicted in the earliest *Life of Maiolus* to the great wolves of the Provençal countryside to the sympathetic captors who populated Rodulphus Glaber's narrative, the Muslims of La Garde-Freinet were protean antagonists in Cluniac hagiography. The diversity of their depiction resulted primarily from the fact that the Cluniacs did not have a polemical agenda in their representation of Islam in this period.

By the mid-twelfth century, however, especially in the climate of humiliation and anxiety about Islam that simmered in the aftermath of the Second Crusade, the situation had changed. Abbot Peter the Venerable of Cluny (1122–56) emerged in this period as one of the most outspoken defenders of the Christian faith in western Europe. He expressed his contempt for rival systems of belief in an outpouring of polemical treatises against Christian

---

the abbey in their homeland). On the enduring influence of Cluniac monasticism in Spain, see chapter 3 of the present volume.

67. Glaber, *Libri Historiarum Quinque*, 1.9, ed. France, 22: "Omnesque in breui perierunt, ut ne unus quidem rediret in patriam."

heresy, Judaism, and Islam. Peter stood out among his contemporaries, however, by initiating the unprecedented enterprise of translating Islamic religious
texts into Latin for the purpose of contesting them and by addressing a
formal refutation of Islam directly to a Muslim audience. As chapter 3 will
show, the novelty of this twelfth-century abbot's stance toward Islam and the
historical contingencies that shaped his Muslim policies only become apparent when viewed within the broader context of a career in religious polemics that spanned the last two decades of his abbacy. But between the early
eleventh century and the time of Peter the Venerable, a little-known work
of hagiography preserves an account of a failed mission to Muslims on the
Spanish frontier allegedly endorsed by yet another abbot of Cluny, Hugh the
Great (1049–1109). Before proceeding with our discussion of Peter the Venerable and Islam in the twelfth century, it is worth pausing to consider the
content and impact of this vignette involving a Cluniac hermit who preached
among the Muslims of Spain in the late eleventh century.

A Cluniac Mission on the Spanish Frontier

A decade or more before the birth of Peter the Venerable, Abbot Hugh the Great of Cluny (1049–1109) may have sponsored the first sanctioned mission to Muslims in the history of the medieval West. The unlikely agent of this poorly documented enterprise was a hermit. Throughout the late eleventh and early twelfth centuries, the holy reputation of the Abbey of Cluny attracted a small constellation of solitaries into its orbit. These ascetics settled in the deep forests and narrow caves that adorned the rolling hills of the surrounding countryside.[1] Some of them were Cluniac monks who had left the cloister to pursue a more rigorous program of personal withdrawal without abandoning altogether the oversight of their abbot; others were peripatetic recluses who entered the community for a short while to inspire the brethren by their holy example before their restlessness spurred them back to remote solitudes once more.[2]

---

1. Jean Leclercq, "Pierre le Vénérable et l'érémitisme clunisien," in *Petrus Venerabilis 1156–1956: Studies and Texts Commemorating the Eighth Centenary of His Death*, ed. Giles Constable and James Kritzeck (Rome: Herder, 1956), 99–120; and Germaine Chachuat, "L'érémitisme à Cluny sous l'abbatiat de Pierre le Vénérable," *Annales de l'académie de Mâcon* 58 (1982): 89–96.

2. For insight into the lives of these Cluniac hermits and the anxieties that their vocation provoked in their abbots, see the long letter by Peter the Venerable to a hermit named Gilbert, *Epistola* 20, in *The Letters of Peter the Venerable*, ed. Giles Constable (Cambridge, MA: Harvard University Press, 1967), 1:27–41.

The most celebrated of these Cluniac hermits was Anastasius (d. ca. 1085). Most of our information about this saint derives from the early twelfth-century *Life of Anastasius* (BHL 405) written by an otherwise unknown monk named Walter (*Galterius*) of Doyde.[3] Anastasius was a monk from Venice who was living in a remote retreat when Abbot Hugh invited him to Cluny.[4] There he impressed the brethren with his feats of asceticism, particularly with the denial of the needs of his body, until the solemnity of the Lenten season drew him back to his mountain refuge, where he punished his flesh with constant prayer, long fasts, sleepless vigils, and painful prostrations.

With the permission of Abbot Hugh, Anastasius departed around 1073 on a journey to Spain for the purpose of preaching to the Muslims there (*Hispaniam ad praedicandum Sarracenis ingressus est*).[5] Although Walter's laconic account is the only medieval source for this failed mission, most scholars have followed Benjamin Kedar in their inclination to believe that it actually took place.[6] The details of the journey are very thin. Walter relates that Anastasius challenged his Muslim audience to an ordeal by fire (*per rogum ardentem . . . transire*). The hermit promised to walk across a pile of flaming embers in order to prove how unwavering the faith of Christians was; if he emerged unscathed, his adversaries must agree to abandon their harsh cruelty and fly to the grace of baptism. The tactic failed. When the assembled Muslims did not assent to the conditions of the ordeal, Anastasius "shook off the dust from his feet against them" and returned to the Abbey of Cluny.[7] Little else is known beyond these sparse details. It is unclear whether the hermit had ventured into Muslim-held territory or was preaching to potential converts in a region newly conquered by the Christian armies of the *reconquista*. While there is ancillary evidence (discussed herein) to suggest

---

3. PL 149, cols. 427–32. There is an English translation of this work by Scott G. Bruce forthcoming in *The Renaissance of the Twelfth Century: A Reader*, ed. Alex J. Novikoff (Toronto: University of Toronto Press, 2015). On the career of Anastasius, see Mathieu Arnoux, "Un Vénitien au Mont-Saint-Michel: Anastase, moine, ermite et confesseur († vers 1085)," *Médiévales* 28 (1995): 55–78.

4. For what follows, see Galterius, *Vita Anastasii*, 4, in PL 149, cols. 428–29.

5. Galterius, *Vita Anastasii*, 5, in PL 149, col. 429. For a full discussion of the evidence relevant to this event, to which I am much indebted, see Benjamin Kedar, *Crusade and Mission: European Approaches toward the Muslims* (Princeton, NJ: Princeton University Press, 1984), 44–46, 56–57. There is no mention of the mission of Anastasius in the relevant volume of CMR.

6. Kedar, *Crusade and Mission*, 45: "True, the account is not corroborated by other sources, but this does not necessarily render it spurious."

7. Galterius, *Vita Anastasii*, 5, in PL 149, col. 429, evoking Luke 10:11 and Acts 13:51 on the rejection of the earliest Christian missionaries: "Excusso pulvere pedum in illos in testimonium, ad monastarium suum refressus est."

that Anastasius may have been an ambassador to the court of Saragossa, there is nothing in Walter's narrative to indicate the rank and station of the Muslim audience to whom he was preaching or the setting of the proposed ordeal. All that is certain about this mission from the *vita* is the method of persuasion employed by Anastasius, who agreed to undertake an ordeal by fire to prove the steadfastness of his faith, and his failure to win the hearts of the Muslims, which prompted his return to Cluny.

Walter's account of Anastasius's mission to Spain is poor in detail about his interaction with Muslims, but it does tell us on whose authority he undertook this unprecedented task: "by the order of our holy father Pope Gregory VII and the repeated prompting of that venerable man, his own abbot Hugh."[8] It is surprising to see the pope's name associated with this mission. To be sure, from the vantage point of Rome, Gregory VII could survey with dismay the breadth of Christendom diminished by the onslaught of Islam.[9] All around the Mediterranean—in the Taifa kingdoms of Spain, the coastal towns of Ifriqiya, and the countryside of Asia Minor—Christians lived under the dominion of Muslims. Letters written around the time of Anastasius's mission reveal the pontiff's pointed concern for the suffering of Spanish Christians under the yoke of Islam.[10] Writing to Countess Beatrice and her sister Mathilda in 1074, Gregory VII lamented the gains made by the Muslim faith due to the erosion of Christianity in Spain.[11] In a letter sent to French barons the previous year, the pope had urged them to offer their help to Count Eblo of Roucy, who sought "to wrest away from the pagans' grasp" territory in Spain that belonged rightfully to the jurisdiction of Saint Peter.[12] The perfidy of the Muslims was the latest in a litany of tragedies that had diminished the Christian faith in the kingdom of Spain, from the heresy of the Priscillians to the invasion of the Goths.[13] But unlike his namesake Pope Gregory I, whose understanding of the pastoral responsibilities of

---

8. Galterius, *Vita Anastasii*, 5, in PL 149, col. 429: "Per idem tempus praecepto sancti patris nostri papae Gregorii septimi, et frina persuasione venerabilis viri abbatis sui Hugonis."

9. On Gregory VII's attitude toward Islam, see H. E. J. Cowdrey's towering *Pope Gregory VII, 1073–1085* (Oxford: Clarendon Press, 1998), 489–94; and Tomaž Mastnak, "Gregory VII," in CMR 3:182–203.

10. On the pope's abiding concern for the *regnum Hyspaniae* and the activity of his legates there, see Cowdrey, *Pope Gregory VII*, 468–80.

11. Gregory VII, *Registrum*, 2.9 (16 October 1074), ed. Erich Caspar, in *Das Register Gregors VII*, MGH Epistolae selectae 2 (Berlin: Apud Weidmannos, 1920), 139.

12. Gregory VII, *Registrum*, 1.7 (30 April 1073), ed. Caspar, 11–12.

13. Gregory VII, *Registrum*, 1.64 (19 March 1074; addressed to King Alfonso VI of León-Castile and Sancho IV of Navarre), ed. Caspar, 93–94.

his office reached beyond the boundaries of Christendom to the pagan kingdoms of the northern world, "Gregory [VII] was concerned, not with the conversion of Muslims, but with the faithful witness of a Christian minority which would win their respect for Christianity."[14] His willingness to endorse the mission of Anastasius was exceptional unless we understand his motivation to include the shoring up of the faith of Christians living under Muslim rule in those places visited by the hermit. We know that the pope voiced his concerns about Islam to Abbot Hugh of Cluny, with whom he had cultivated a close friendship expressed in terms of a personal warmth and an emotional candor that he shared with few other correspondents.[15] Mindful of the pontiff's growing alarm about the plight of Christianity across the Pyrenees, the abbot of Cluny may have suggested Anastasius's name as a reputable and obedient representative who could forward Christian interests on the Spanish frontier.

Hugh the Great's endorsement of the hermit's mission is less surprising in light of another possible testimony for his interest in Islam. Although the evidence is thin, the mission of Anastasius may have been only one component of a much more ambitious pastoral effort launched by the abbot of Cluny among Muslims in Spain in the wake of the *reconquista*. There survives in Arabic a letter from an unnamed "monk of France" (*rahib min Ifransa*) inviting al-Muqtadir ibn Hud, the ruler of Saragossa (1049–82), to convert to Christianity. This missive inspired a lengthy and condescending rebuttal from a distinguished Andalusian scholar, Abu l-Walid Sulayman al-Baji (d. 1081), on behalf of his royal patron.[16] While the Christian letter shows some signs of redaction by a Muslim editor, its repeated references to the monks who delivered the missive to Saragossa and their interaction with their Arabic

---

14. Cowdrey, *Pope Gregory VII*, 566. The pope did not rule out the possibility that pious Christians could induce neighboring Muslims to convert by living a virtuous life, but he reserved this optimism for the inhabitants of North Africa. For a summary of the evidence, see Kedar, *Crusade and Mission*, 56–57.

15. See, for example, Gregory VII, *Registrum*, 2.49 (22 January 1075; to Abbot Hugh the Great), ed. Caspar, 189–90, where the activities of the "ancient enemy" (*antiquus hostis*) against the eastern church refer obliquely to the depredations of the Seljuk Turks. For an estimation of the friendship between these men, see Cowdrey, *Pope Gregory VII*, 672–73.

16. For a critical edition and English translation of these letters, see D. M. Dunlop, "A Christian Mission to Muslim Spain in the Eleventh Century," *Al-Andalus* 17 (1952): 259–310. For more on the scholarship inspired by these sources, see Amalia Zomeño, "Al-Baji," in CMR 3:172–75; and Sarrió Cucarella, "Corresponding across Religious Borders: Al-Bājī's Response to a Missionary Letter from France," *Medieval Encounters* 18 (2012): 31, which argues convincingly for the authenticity of the *rahib*'s letter but remains tentative about its authorship: "the most likely guess as to the identity of the high-ranking ecclesiastic who refers to himself modestly as 'the humblest of monks' is that he is a bishop or an abbot related to Cluny, perhaps Abbot Hugh himself."

interpreter suggests that it is an actual letter and not a literary confection composed by al-Baji solely for the purpose of disparaging Christianity.[17] The Christian letter introduces us to a conversation in progress.[18] The unnamed prelate has already written to al-Muqtadir ibn Hud and received a response, but there has been "no spiritual reply in accordance with our desire." For this reason, the *rahib* has decided not only to write again, but also to send "some of our brethren . . . to explain in your presence the truth of the religion of the Christians and confirm in you the knowledge of Christ, our Lord." He then makes the case that the incarnation of God in the person of Jesus Christ took place in order to restore to the world the divine order that it had lost through the disobedience of Adam and Eve. In the meantime, the devil sought to deflect the gains made by the apostles and the martyrs in their battles against idolatry; he had "deceived the children of Ishmael in regard to the Prophet, whose mission they acknowledged, and thereby drew away many souls to the punishment of Hell." The *rahib* concludes by inviting the king to convert to Christianity and thereby escape the deceptions of the devil and obtain eternal salvation. The significance of this letter cannot be overstated. In the words of Benjamin Kedar, "the crucial fact is that in this Arabic work a Catholic European is reported to have made, on his own initiative, an unequivocal offer of conversion to a Muslim ruler"; moreover, "[t]his unprecedented incident points to the emergence of a new venturesome stance toward the world of Islam, a reflection on the intellectual plane of the Catholic European military counteroffensive."[19]

Some scholars have identified the author of the Christian letter as Abbot Hugh the Great and its courier as the Cluniac hermit Anastasius.[20] Although the *rahib* and his messengers are unnamed in the surviving Arabic translation of the correspondence, historians have found support for this inference in two pieces of evidence from later in Hugh's abbacy, which suggest that he cultivated an active interest in the conversion of Muslims in Spain to Christianity. The first is a letter from 1087 addressed by the abbot to Bernard of Sédirac, a Cluniac monk who had recently been appointed as the new archbishop of Toledo after the capture of that city by King Alfonso VI

---

17. Abdelmagid Turki was the first to emphasize the influence of a Muslim redactor on the Christian letter in "La lettre du 'Moine de France' à al-Muqtadir billah, roi de Saragosse, et la réponse d'al-Bayi, le faqih andalou," *Al-Andalus* 31 (1966): 75–80. On the circumstantial evidence that points to the letter's authenticity, see Kedar, *Crusade and Mission*, 54–55.

18. For what follows, see Dunlop, "A Christian Mission to Muslim Spain," 263–66.

19. Kedar, *Crusade and Mission*, 55–56.

20. See, for example, Anthony Cutler, "Who Was the 'Monk of France' and When Did He Write?" *Al-Andalus* 28 (1963): 249–69.

on 25 May 1085.[21] In this letter Hugh encouraged Bernard to preach to the unbelievers (*infideles*) in his midst and to adopt a lifestyle that was beyond reproach in order to win their souls for Christianity by word and example.[22] The second piece of evidence is an anecdote preserved in the hagiographical dossier of Hugh the Great compiled after his death in 1109. It tells the story of the abbot's attempt to convert a Muslim in 1090 during his only trip to Spain. Hugh returned to Cluny with his new catechuman, but the Muslim had a change of heart and fled the abbey with gold stolen from Hugh's satchel. Weighed down by his loot and not knowing the way home, he was easily captured and brought back to the abbey, but the story concludes without informing us of his fate.[23]

While it is certainly possible that Hugh the Great sent the hermit Anastasius to Saragossa with a letter inviting al-Muqtadir ibn Hud to convert to Christianity, the evidence linking the abbot of Cluny to this failed missionary endeavor is largely circumstantial. There is nothing in the body of the letter to localize its composition at Cluny. Whether or not Hugh the Great was the agent behind this mission to Saragossa in the 1070s, it is telling for our purposes that stories relating to it did not circulate at Cluny and its dependencies in the twelfth century.[24] The only testimony of the affair to survive in Latin was the laconic description of the hermit's attempt to convert Muslims by subjecting himself to an ordeal by fire in Walter's early twelfth-century *Life of Anastasius*. Walter wrote this work for Peter, a subdeacon of the Church of Saint-Martin d'Oydes near Toulouse, where the saint's relics lay buried. It only survived in a single local manuscript and was unknown in the Latin hagiographical tradition until its rediscovery in the seventeenth century by Bishop Antonio Petro Bertier of Rieux, who sent a

---

21. This letter was discovered and edited by Marius Férotin in "Une lettre inédite de Saint Hugues, abbé de Cluny, à Bernard d'Agen, archevêque de Tolède (1087)," *Bibliothèque de l'École des Chartes* 61 (1900): 341–45; and Marius Férotin, "Complément de la lettre de Saint Hugues," *Bibliothèque de l'École des Chartes* 63 (1902): 682–86. The best introduction to the career of Bernard of Sédirac remains Marcelin Defourneaux, *Les Français en Espagne aux XIe et XIIe siècles* (Paris: Presses Universitaires de France, 1949), 32–43.

22. Abbot Hugh the Great "Une lettre inédite de Saint Hugues," ed. Férotin, 345: "Haec enim vita, scilicet inreprehensibilis, et bonorum operum cum cultis moribus exhibitio super omnem predicationem ad excitandos et convertendos infideles prevalebunt."

23. Gilo, *Vita sancti Hugonis abbatis* (BHL 4007), 10, ed. H. E. J. Cowdrey, in "Two Studies in Cluniac History 1049–1126," *Studi Gregoriani* 11 (1978): 60.

24. This does not preclude the fact that Anastasius himself was commemorated with many thousands of other faithful departed in the Cluniac liturgy. Someone of this name does, in fact, appear in the necrology of Cluny, which has been reconstructed by Joachim Wollasch on the basis of surviving necrologies from other houses within the orbit of the great Burgundian abbey. See *Synopse der cluniacensischen Necrologien*, ed. Joachim Wollasch (Munich: Fink, 1982), 1:69 (A 214: Anastasius).

copy of it to the great Maurist scholar Jean Mabillon.[25] In the end there is not enough evidence to conclude that the mission of Anastasius either took its inspiration from the hagiographical accounts of Maiolus in captivity or exerted any influence on the formulation of a Muslim policy at Cluny during the abbacy of Peter the Venerable.

---

25. Galterius, *Vita Anastasii*, 1, in PL 149, col. 425: "Galterius Petro Devotensis Ecclesiae subdiacono et fratri eius Bernardo, in omnibus prosperitatem, et ad effectum perducere bonam devotionem." On the discovery of the manuscript, see Mabillon's *observationes praeviae* in *Acta sanctorum ordinis sancti Benedicti in saeculorum classes distributa*, ed. Jean Mabillon (Paris: Colet, 1701), 6.2:487–88, reprinted in PL 149, col. 423–26, where he described Anastasius as "ignotum huc usque in fastis benedictinis" and Walter as "auctor nobis antea incognitus" (col. 423).

✐ CHAPTER 3

Peter the Venerable, Butcher of God

In the early months of 1142, Peter the Venerable made the long and arduous journey from Burgundy across the Pyrenees to Spain, where he proposed to inspect Cluniac dependencies and visit the shrine of Saint James at Compostella. He also had the economic interests of his abbey foremost in his mind.[1] Later that year, in July, he had an audience at Salamanca with Alphonso VII of León-Castile. At this meeting Peter promised to endorse the ruler's favored candidate for the important archbishopric of Compostella. In return, Alphonso VII granted Cluny several substantial privileges in Spain and agreed to revive the long neglected obligation made by his grandfather, Alfonso VI, to send an annual gift of gold to the great Burgundian abbey.[2] Having accomplished his goals, Peter

---

1. On the date, itinerary, and purpose of this visit, see Charles Julian Bishko, "Peter the Venerable's Journey to Spain," in *Petrus Venerabilis 1156–1956: Studies and Texts Commemorating the Eighth Centenary of His Death*, ed. Giles Constable and James Kritzeck (Rome: Herder, 1956), 163–75, reprinted with a supplementary note in Charles Julian Bishko, *Spanish and Portuguese Monasticism, 600–1300* (London: Variorum, 1984), nos. 12–13; *The Letters of Peter the Venerable*, ed. Giles Constable (Cambridge, MA: Harvard University Press, 1967), 2:257–69 (Appendix D: Chronology and Itinerary of Peter the Venerable); and Damien Van den Eynde, "Les principaux voyages de Pierre le Vénérable," *Benedictina* 15 (1968): 95–100.

2. The terms of the original eleventh-century gift were greatly reduced in the twelfth century. Compare the charters of donation from Alphonso VI in 1090 and Alphonso VII in 1142 in *Recueil des chartes de l'abbaye de Cluny*, ed. Auguste Bernard and Alexandre Bruel (Paris: Imprimerie Natio-

returned home by May 1143 after an absence of more than a year. An expedition of this magnitude was not unusual for an abbot of Cluny; Peter's predecessors, Hugh the Great and Pons of Melgueil, had both crossed the Pyrenees on diplomatic missions.[3] What made the abbot's sojourn in Spain in 1142–43 so extraordinary was the unprecedented translation enterprise that he initiated there.

While Peter the Venerable tarried at the Cluniac priory of Santa María de Nájera en route to Compostella, he initiated the idea of translating a corpus of texts on the historical traditions and religious beliefs of Muslim peoples, including the Qur'an, from Arabic into Latin. Upon the completion of these translations in the summer of 1143, the abbot of Cluny composed a short handbook titled *A Summary of the Entire Heresy of the Saracens* (*Summa totius haeresis Sarracenorum*) that summarized their contents for Christian readers and expressed a polemical purpose: to reveal Muhammed as a forerunner of the Antichrist and to expose his religious doctrines as heretical and false.[4] It was Peter's hope that this "Christian arsenal" (*armarium christianum*) of texts would inspire someone to write a refutation of Islamic teachings.[5] Despite an earnest entreaty to Bernard of Clairvaux to undertake the project, no such refutation materialized and Peter set aside his ambition for more than a decade. When he returned to the problem of Islam in the mid-1150s, his approach toward the Muslims had changed. In 1156, during the last months of his life, the abbot of Cluny composed a formal treatise against

---

nale, 1888 and 1894), 4:809–10 (no. 3638) and 5:423–26 (no. 4072). For a reevaluation of the tradition that portrays Fernando I of León-Castile (r. 1037–65) as the initiator of these donations to Cluny, see Lucy Pick, "Rethinking Cluny in Spain," *Journal of Medieval Iberian Studies* 5 (2013): 1–17.

3. On Hugh the Great's dealings with Spanish monarchs, including his journey to Burgos in 1090, see Charles Julian Bishko, "Liturgical Intercession at Cluny for the King-Emperors of Leon," *Studi Monastica* 3 (1961): 53–76, esp. 70–72, reprinted in Bishko, *Spanish and Portugese Monasticism*, no. 8; and Armin Kohnle, *Abt Hugo von Cluny, 1049–1109* (Sigmaringen, Germany: Thorbecke, 1993), 223–33. Two decades later, in 1113, Pons of Melgueil visited Spain to intercede as a papal legate in the civil strife that had erupted between Queen Urraca of León-Castile (1109–26) and King Alfonso I of Aragon (1104–34). See Charles Julian Bishko, "The Spanish Journey of Abbot Ponce of Cluny," *Richerche di Storia Religiosa* 1 (1957): 311–19, reprinted in Bishko, *Spanish and Portugese Monasticism*, no. 10.

4. A critical edition of Peter the Venerable's polemical writings against Islam with a German translation by Reinhold Glei, *Petrus Venerabilis, Schriften zum Islam* (Altenberge, Germany: CIS Verlag, 1985) has superceded that of James Kritzeck, *Peter the Venerable and Islam* (Princeton, NJ: Princeton University Press, 1964), 203–91, though the latter remains much more accessible. The author of an Italian translation of this corpus based on Kritzeck's editions displayed no knowledge of Glei's work; see Giuseppe Rizzardi, *Domande christiane sull'Islam nel medioevo: Edizioni e studi sul Corpus cluniacense a proposito dei saraceni* (San Cataldo, Italy: Lussografica, 2001).

5. Peter the Venerable, *Epistola de translatione sua*, 4, ed. Glei, 26.

the religious claims of Muhammed and his followers, *Against the Sect of the Saracens* (*Contra sectam Saracenorum*).[6] Unlike earlier works of Latin Christian polemic against Islam, however, Peter directed his exposition specifically at Muslim readers in terms that were markedly more conciliatory than his combative stance of the early 1140s: "I do not attack you, as some of us often do, with arms but with words, not with force but with reason, not out of hatred, but out of love."[7] By following the rational line of argument put forward in this treatise, the abbot hoped that Muslim readers would come to realize that the Qur'an was not a divinely inspired text and Muhammed was not a prophet in the tradition of the Old Testament prophets. While it is doubtful that his labors won any converts for Christianity, the enterprise was unprecedented in the history of religious dialogue between Christendom and the House of Islam. Taken together, the abbot's writings represent the first systematic refutation of Islamic doctrine based on a reading of Muslim texts translated into the Latin language.

Peter the Venerable's Muslim project was not his first foray into religious polemics. More so than any of his abbatial predecessors, he was deeply concerned with the erosion of faith in Latin Christendom due to the insidious influence of false beliefs. During the last two decades of his life, the abbot of Cluny applied his intellectual energy to the composition of several treatises that confronted what he viewed to be the most threatening religious ideologies of his day: heresy, Judaism, and Islam. While Peter's verbal attacks against heretics and Jews joined a swelling chorus of contempt for these adversaries of Christendom that resounded throughout twelfth-century Europe, his direct appeal to Muslims has set him apart from his contemporaries in the minds of modern historians as a tolerant and reasonable voice in the age of the first crusades.[8] Yet, as this chapter argues, the Muslim policy of the abbot of Cluny was neither as sympathetic nor as premeditated as some scholars have presumed. It is a difficult but necessary task to acknowledge that Peter was not a man we would have admired. One twelfth-century monk praised him for "butcher[ing] with the sword of the divine word" (*divini verbi gladio trucidastis*) all those who were opposed to the Christian faith.[9] In doing so this monk expressed and embodied many of the values that

---

6. Peter the Venerable, *Contra sectam Saracenorum*, ed. Glei, 30–239.

7. Peter the Venerable, *Contra sectam Saracenorum*, 1.24, ed. Glei, 62: "Aggredior inquam vos, non, ut nostri saepe faciunt, armis sed verbis, non vi sed ratione, non odio sed amore."

8. On this perception of Peter the Venerable in Cluniac historiography, see the introduction to the present volume.

9. Peter of Poitiers, *Epistola*, ed. Glei, 228. The metaphor of spiritual combat was a commonplace in monastic discourse, deriving ultimately from Ephesians 6:10–17, but Peter of Poitiers's

Christian intellectuals of that age held dear. We need not share them; in fact, we can render the originality of the abbot's Muslim project much more clearly the moment we put aside our imagined affinities with him and his contemporaries.

With the benefit of hindsight, historians have tended to overstate the unity of the corpus of Peter the Venerable's polemical writings against the perceived enemies of Christianity, imputing from them a premeditated and coherent program of intellectual engagement with rival systems of belief.[10] This presumption carries unnecessary burdens. It has had the consequence of flattening any sense of the historical development of the abbot's thinking about the threats posed by his religious adversaries and how best to confront them. Moreover, it has generally excluded from consideration the impact of one of the most consequential events of that period on Peter's approach to Islam: the catastrophe of the Second Crusade (1145–49) and the aborted efforts in its aftermath to launch military action against the Greek Christians whom many blamed for its failure. Abandoning the presumption that the abbot organized his corpus of polemical writings according to some cohesive plan, this chapter interprets the character and tone of his treatises against heresy, Judaism, and Islam with sensitivity to the specific historical contingencies that shaped each of them in turn. What emerges from this analysis is the portrait of a career in religious polemic that varied considerably from decade to decade, from treatise to treatise, and from adversary to adversary.

There are many reasons for this lack of cohesion, from the influence (or absence) of comparable traditions of polemical literature available to Peter the Venerable to the relative degree of his understanding of the religious ideologies of his enemies to the contemporary concerns that inflected the tone of his treatises. What is most important for our purposes is to recognize that in many respects Peter's approach to Islam differed markedly from his stance against heresy and Judaism. First, unlike his forays against heretics and Jews, the abbot of Cluny never intended to write a treatise against Muslim beliefs at all, but hoped instead that one of his contemporaries would do so using the translations he commissioned as a resource in their refutation. Second, when Peter did finally write a polemical tract against Islam in the final year of his life, his pastoral appeal to a Muslim audience was not the first impulse of a tolerant man. Rather, it was a matter of last recourse in the bitter aftermath of the Second Crusade, the failure of which reduced the violent

---

choice of the verb *trucidare* ("to butcher" or "to slaughter") to describe his abbot's activities adds an unprecedented vehemence to the image.

10. On this tendency in modern scholarship, see the introduction to the present volume.

ambitions of European crusaders to folly and forced the abbot of Cluny to find another way to win the hearts of his Muslim adversaries, now that the threat of arms had failed.

✤ Against the Heirs of Iniquity

Peter the Venerable was by far the most prolific abbot of Cluny in the Middle Ages.[11] The sheer volume of his literary output—especially his letters and treatises—dwarfs that of his predecessors, so much so that some scholars have marked Peter's abbacy as demonstrative of a fundamental shift in the leadership of Cluny.[12] Cluniac abbots of the tenth and eleventh centuries had cultivated an authority based largely on charismatic modes of expression like preaching, which obliged them to be peripatetic in order to make their presence felt far and wide among supporters and detractors alike.[13] Although Peter was often itinerant despite frequent bouts of illness, the character of his abbacy was different because he was the first of the Cluniac abbots to broadcast his thoughts primarily through the medium of personal letters, statutes, and polemical treatises.[14] Moreover, unlike his predecessors, he self-consciously compiled and made public a portion of his voluminous correspondence as a way to communicate his abbatial authority. The final redaction of the letter collection compiled by Peter toward the end of his life with the help of his secretary, Peter of Poitiers, numbered 195 documents addressed to a diverse group of correspondents, including kings, popes, and abbots, on a staggering range of topics from the recruitment of

---

11. There is no adequate modern biography of Peter the Venerable. Jean Leclercq's *Pierre le Vénérable* (Paris: Éditions de Fontenelle, 1946) is long out of date given the advances in monastic scholarship over the past sixty years. Although it is not a traditional work of biography, Jean-Pierre Torrell and Denise Bouthillier, *Pierre le Vénérable et sa vision du monde: Sa vie, son oeuvre, l'homme et le démon* (Leuven, Belgium: Spicilegium Sacrum Lovaniense, 1986) remains the fullest study of the abbot's life and thought.

12. For what follows, see Marc Saurette, "Rhetorics of Reform: Peter the Venerable and the Twelfth-Century Rewriting of the Cluniac Monastic Project" (PhD diss., University of Toronto, 2005), with references to earlier literature. On the abbot's correspondence in particular, see Giles Constable, "Medieval Letters and the Letter Collection of Peter the Venerable," in *Letters of Peter the Venerable*, 2:1–44.

13. The portrait of Abbot Maiolus presented by Syrus of Cluny is a prime example. See chapter 2 of the present volume.

14. Peter suffered from malaria and chronic bronchitis. Evidence from his letters led Constable to conclude that "for most of his adult life he was in delicate, if not poor, health." See Constable, *Letters of Peter the Venerable*, 2:247.

monks and the resolution of disputes to the praise of ascetics and the debate of monastic ideals. This was by no means an inclusive collection; it represented only a modest portion of the letters that Peter had written and received during his lifetime.

Peter became abbot of Cluny shortly after the tenure of Pons of Melgueil (1109–22) ended in schism and violence.[15] His early years as abbot were spent putting his house in order, which included curbing excesses in the consumption of food and drink and generally enforcing a higher standard of discipline among his charges.[16] Once he had consolidated his affairs at Cluny proper, Peter turned his attention to the many monastic communities that were dependent on the great Burgundian abbey. In 1132, the abbot called a meeting of over two hundred priors at Cluny so that they might "hear rules for a stricter observance of monastic life than they had hitherto shown."[17] Orderic Vitalis reported that Peter used the occasion to impose new fasts and to broaden the rules of silence that already governed most parts of the abbey.[18] The abbot of Cluny also issued written directives (*statuta*) on a regular basis that were sent to all of those religious houses that recognized his authority.[19] These texts carried the voice of the abbot well beyond the precincts of his cloister, allowing his influence to reach Cluniac dependencies as far away as England and Spain. Peter's imposition of these new precepts at Cluny and elsewhere was inspired primarily by his own ideals of the cloistered life, which were informed by his upbringing as an oblate at

---

15. The conflicting testimony of near contemporary evidence still clouds the motives surrounding the departure of Pons from Cluny in 1122, which prompted the election of the elderly Hugh II, who died after a few months as abbot, and then Peter the Venerable. Pons's return to Cluny in 1126 after a pilgrimage to the Holy Land and a short sojourn in northern Italy incited an uprising among monks and townspeople of Cluny who did not recognize his abdication. The violence that ensued in the cloister led to Pons's excommunication and death in a papal prison later that year. For a summary of the evidence and the history of its interpretation, see Joachim Wollasch, "Das Schisma des Abtes Pontius von Cluny," *Francia* 23 (1996): 31–52.

16. Peter the Venerable, *De miraculis libri duos*, 2.11, ed. Denise Bouthillier, CCM 83:116.

17. Orderic Vitalis, *Historia ecclesiastica*, 13.13, in *The Ecclesiastical History of Orderic Vitalis*, ed. and trans. Marjorie Chibnall, (Oxford: Clarendon Press, 1980), 6:424–25: "Petrus Cluniacensis abbas ueredarios et epistolas per omnes cellas suas tunc direxit, et omnes cellarum periores de Anglia et Italia regnisque aliis accersiit, iubens ut dominico Quadragesimae tertio Cluniaci adessent, ut precepta monasticae conuersationis austeriora quam hactenus tenuerant audirent."

18. Orderic Vitalis, *Historia ecclesiastica* 13.13, ed. Chibnall, 6:424–25. On Peter's advocacy of the discipline of silence, see Scott G. Bruce, *Silence and Sign Language in Medieval Monasticism: The Cluniac Tradition (c. 900–1200)* (Cambridge: Cambridge University Press, 2007), 149–51.

19. Peter compiled his *Statuta* in 1146–47; the earliest of them was probably issued in the late 1120s, but almost none of them can be dated precisely. See *Statuta Petri Venerabili abbatis Cluniacensis*, ed. Giles Constable, in CCM 6:19–106.

Vézelay.[20] They met with some resistance, as his own writings attest, and on several occasions he made compromises to his ideals in order to placate the less stalwart among his followers.[21] But by the early 1130s Peter had steered Cluny away from the shoals of discord and a perceived laxity that threatened the earliest years of his abbacy.

It was during this time, less than a decade after he had become abbot, that Peter made his first foray into religious polemics. In a letter from the early 1130s he admonished an anonymous Cluniac monk who had embraced the errors of Apollinarius of Laodicea, a fourth-century bishop condemned for his belief that Christ was human with respect to his body, but not with respect to his soul.[22] While Peter's reprimand was pastoral in purpose, he could not mask his anger that one of his brethren had strayed so far from correct belief. He opened the letter with an outpouring of hyperbolic vitriol, condemning the inhuman stupidity, profound foolishness, and pervasive ignorance that led the thoughts of this monk astray.[23] The harshness of the abbot's tone betrayed his anxiety about the compounded dangers of heresy. By denying the fundamental humanity of the Son of God, this wayward monk imperiled not only his own soul but also those of his brethren. The heretic himself was deemed nothing more than "a beetle born out of ancient filth" who threatened to irritate everyone around him with "his loathsome sounds."[24] Peter responded to the circulation of these mutinous ideas with a short treatise. His aim was

---

20. Constable has persuasively downplayed the notion that Peter's reforming efforts were inflected by his defense of Cluniac customs in the wake of criticism hurled from Cistercian quarters in the most vulnerable years of his young abbacy. See Giles Constable, "The Monastic Policy of Peter the Venerable," in *Pierre Abélard—Pierre Vénérable: Les courants philosophiques, littéraires et artistiques en Occident au milieu du XIIe siècle: actes et mémoires du colloque international, Abbaye de Cluny, 2 au 9 juillet 1972* (Paris: Éditions du Centre national de la recherche scientifique, 1975), 119–41, reprinted in Giles Constable, *Cluniac Studies* (London: Variorum, 1980), no. 3.

21. For Peter's anticipation of resistence to certain of his new precepts, see *Statuta*, 61, ed. Constable, in CCM 6:93. For an independent report of Peter's concessions, see Orderic Vitalis, *Historia ecclesiastica*, 13.13, ed. Chibnall, 6:426–27.

22. Peter the Venerable, *Epistola*, 37, ed. Constable, in *Letters of Peter the Venerable*, 1:117–24, esp. 117–18: "Vetustissima haec tua heresis est, et ab Apollinari quodam erroneo antiquitus adinuenta"; and 2:125. There is no internal evidence for the date of the letter's composition, but Paul Séjourné has inferred a date of 1130–32 based on its position in the collection of Peter's letters compiled by Peter of Poitiers; see *Dictionnaire de théologie catholique*, 15 vols. (Paris, 1923–50), s.v. "Pierre le Vénérable," vol. 12, col. 2069: "avant une autre lettre qui ne peut être postérieure à 1132." On the rhetorical techniques employed in the letter, see Dominique Iogna-Prat, *Order and Exclusion: Cluny and Christendom Face Heresy, Judaism, and Islam (1000–1150)*, trans. Graham Robert Edwards (Ithaca, NY: Cornell University Press, 2002), 125–26.

23. Peter the Venerable, *Epistola*, 37, ed. Constable, in *Letters of Peter the Venerable*, 1:117.

24. Ibid., 1:118: "Uelut scarabeus de ueteri putredine creatus musitas, et stridore dissono aures fratrum exasperas."

to choke the words of the heretic as he drew his breath to utter them "with persuasive reasoning and the immeasurable authority of the fathers."[25]

What is most remarkable about this letter is the tone of confidence that Peter strikes about the state of faith in Latin Christendom in this period. How monstrous it seemed to him to have to argue about Christian doctrine at a time when "the prince of the world has been cast out from the world, now when Christ holds dominion from sea to sea."[26] From his point of view the battle against the devil had almost been won, for "having abused the faith of Christ for a long time with warring pagans and quarrelsome heretics, Satan has now emptied the quiver of his wickedness; he has no arrows left with which to wound the Christian faith."[27] Peter's confidence had less to do, however, with the state of Christianity in Europe than with the integrity of belief that he took for granted within his own monastic community. It is important to remember that this exchange between Peter and the Cluniac heretic was first and foremost a domestic affair between an abbot and his charge. Although it may sound unduly harsh to modern ears, the stern paternalism of Peter's response to the rebel monk was entirely consistent with the disciplinary precepts of the *Rule of Benedict*: "In his teaching the abbot must always observe the Apostle's advice when he says, 'Reprove, appeal, rebuke' (2 Tim. 4:2)."[28] In the narrow intellectual confines of the monastery, Peter's authority as abbot was unassailable. When the blight of heresy appeared in his community, he moved swiftly and decisively to choke it off before it could spread. The fate of the errant monk is unknown. If Peter's little treatise succeeded in swaying his opinion, he would have been reconciled to the community after making satisfaction with sincere contrition and the appropriate penance; if he persisted in his error, the heretic would have found himself excommunicated and cast out from the abbey, a measure intended "to prevent the single diseased sheep from infecting the whole flock."[29]

---

25. Ibid.: "Quae mox ut spirare uisa est, patrum est ualidis rationibus et innumeris autoritatibus suffocata."

26. Ibid.: "Monstruosum quidem hoc tempore de fide disputare, quando iam princeps mundi de mundo eiectus est, quando iam dominatur Christus a mari usque ad mare" (Ps. 71.8).

27. Ibid.: "[P]ostquam Sathanas diuturno tempore paganis impugnantibus, hereticis disputantibus fidem Christi persequens, ita phaeretram nequitiae suae exhausit, ut nulla qua eam ledere possit ei iam sagitta supersit."

28. *Regula Benedicti*, 2.23, in *La règle de saint Benoît*, ed. Adalbert de Vogüé, SC 181 (Paris: Éditions du Cerf, 1972), 1:446: "In doctrina sua namque abbas apostolicam debet illam semper formam servare in qua dicit: Argue, obsecra, increpa."

29. *Regula Benedicti*, 28.8, ed. de Vogüé, SC 182, 2:552: "ne una ouis morbida omnem gregem contagiet."

Only a few years later, in the late 1130s, Peter the Venerable confronted the teachings of yet another heretical adversary, known collectively as the Petrobrusians.[30] The errant doctrines of Peter of Bruys and his "pseudo-apostle" Henry the Monk came to the abbot's attention while he was traveling through Provence en route to the Council of Pisa in the early summer of 1135.[31] Although Peter of Bruys had been murdered around 1132 in St. Gilles near Arles by a Christian mob angered by his burning of crosses, his false doctrine still clung tenaciously in the region, and whisperings of it had begun to spread eastward into Septimania and from there into Gascony.[32] Shortly before 1138, the abbot of Cluny drafted a treatise in the form of a long letter to the bishops of the dioceses of Embrun, Die, and Gap, where the remnants of this heresy were still entrenched.[33] This work summarized and refuted the five principle errors attributed to these heretics: their rejection of the baptism of infants; their denial that churches and other consecrated sites were holier than any other place; their disdain of the cross as a hateful reminder of Christ's death rather than an object of reverence; their denunciation of the Eucharist; and their abandonment of the cult of the dead, including all funerary masses and prayers.[34]

Despite the novelty of their claims and the unprecedented scope of the abbot's rebuttal, Peter the Venerable's methods of refuting the Petrobrusians

---

30. Peter the Venerable, *Contra Petrobrusianos hereticos*, ed. James Fearns, CCCM 10. See also Raoul Manselli, *Studi sulle eresie del secolo XII* (Rome: Nella sede dell'Istituto, 1953), 25–67; James Fearns, "Peter von Bruis und die religiöse Bewegung des 12. Jahrhunderts," *Archiv für Kulturgeschichte* 48 (1966): 311–35; Iogna-Prat, *Order and Exclusion*, 99–261; and R. I. Moore, *The War on Heresy* (Cambridge, MA: Belknap Press of Harvard University Press, 2012), 111–26, 144–51.

31. Peter the Venerable, *Contra Petrobrusianos hereticos*, 8, ed. Fearns, 12: "duobus tantum homuncionibus Petro de Bruis et Heinrico eius pseudoapostolo." See also Peter the Venerable, *Epistola*, 10, ed. James Fearns, CCCM 10:5 "heres nequitie eius Heinricus." The relationship between these two men is probably more obscure than Peter's writings imply; it is unclear, for instance, if they ever actually met one another.

32. Peter related the circumstances surrounding the death of his adversary in the letter prefacing his treatise: *Epistola* 10, ed. Fearns, 5. On the geographical setting of the Petrobrusian heresy and its dissemination, see Peter the Venerable, *Epistola*, 1, ed. Fearns, 3; and Peter the Venerable, *Contra Petrobrusianos hereticos* 1, ed. Fearns, 7.

33. The treatise underwent considerable revision before it appeared in 1141 in the collection of Peter's letters prepared for publication by Peter of Poitiers. A final revision may have taken place upon Peter the Venerable's return from Spain in 1143. On the date of this treatise and its subsequent revisions, see Constable, *Letters of Peter the Venerable*, 2:285–88 (Appendix G: The Date of the *Contra Petrobrusianos*).

34. Peter's summary of these principles appears in the letter prefacing his treatise (*Epistola*, ed. Fearns, 5). At the very end of the treatise he appended a short defense of monastic chant, which the heretics had abandoned because they preferred silent prayer to liturgical devotion; see *Contra Petrobrusianos hereticos*, 273–77, ed. Fearns, 163–65.

were remarkably similar to those he had honed in his earlier letter to the heretical Cluniac. While early Christian authorities testified to the antiquity of the heresy of Apollinarianism addressed in his letter to the rebel monk of Cluny, the teachings of the Petrobrusians did not descend directly from any of the villains who crowded the annals of Christian heresiology; their ravings were entirely new.[35] This may account for the length of Peter's response to them. His letter to the bishops of Provence was a polemical treatise—it later circulated as such, independent of his other letters—and was by far the longest piece of writing he had composed at this point in his career.[36] The abbot of Cluny relied first on scriptural authorities to make his case against the false beliefs of the heretics, but he also appealed to reason—that is, he made arguments from analogy that drew their authority from common sense rather than from the Bible.[37] The tone of this treatise is consistent with his earlier work as well. Propelled by his confidence that Christ was already triumphant in the world and his conviction that the Petrobrusians were immersed in error, Peter rebuked them sternly and challenged them to a confrontation of words: "Masters of error, blind men leading the blind, filth of heresy, last of the schismatics . . . I summon you to come out of your hiding places to meet us in the open. Truth has no hidden corners, as the saying goes, nor does light want to hide under a bushel nor do the things which are called catholic desire to be isolated because that which Christ's command has sent forth throughout the world is not content with parts of the world."[38]

Peter the Venerable was not the only person who attacked the religious claims of the Petrobrusians in the 1130s. After the death of Peter of Bruys,

---

35. It was common in the Middle Ages for Catholic authors to condemn the teaching of their opponents by associating them with ancient heresies (most often Arianism or Manichaeism), but Peter did not do this in his treatise. For the statement that the Petrobrusians were "new heretics," see Peter the Venerable, *Contra Petrobrusianos hereticos*, 10, ed. Fearns, 12, where the heading reads, "Prima propositio novorum hereticorum."

36. The earliest manuscript of *Contra Petrobrusianos hereticos* includes it among Peter's letters (Douai, Bibliothèque municipale 381, fols. 66r–108r, dated ca. 1144–66), but the treatise was already circulating on its own by the end of the twelfth century (Berne, Bürgerbibliothek 251, fols. 64r–147v). For more on these manuscripts, see the introduction to *Contra Petrobrusianos hereticos*, viii–xi.

37. For the fullest discussion of Peter's modes of argument in this work, see Iogna-Prat, *Order and Exclusion*, 120–47.

38. Peter the Venerable, *Contra Petrobrusianos hereticos*, 9, ed. Fearns, 12: "[M]agistri errorum, ceci duces cecorum, feces heresum, reliquie scismaticorum, uos ego, inquam, seductorum seductores conuenio et, ut de latibulis uestris ad publicum nostrum prodeatis, inuito. Non habet, ut uulgo dicitur, ueritas angulos, nec lumen sub modio uult latere, nec ea que catholica dicitur amat fieri singularis, quia, que per totum mundum Christi precepto diffusa est, mundi partibus contenta non est."

some of the most influential prelates of the period pursued the "heir of his iniquity" (*heres nequitie*), Henry the Monk, with a tenacity that underscores the seriousness of his crimes against the church. Henry was preaching openly in Bordeaux when he was captured by the archbishop of Arles in 1132.[39] Denounced by the Council of Pisa in 1135 and cast into prison, he subsequently escaped and remained active in and around Toulouse. Meanwhile, Peter Abelard attacked the doctrines of Peter of Bruys with particular attention to his denial of the fundamental teachings of the church.[40] Likewise, Hildebert of Lavardin defended the cult of the saints against Henry's outspoken denial of the power of their intercession.[41] Finally, in the early 1130s, an author known only as William the Monk wrote a short treatise against the doctrines of the Petrobrusians directed specifically to Henry.[42] After his formal condemnation at the Second Lateran Council in 1139, Henry disappeared from the historical record, the tumult raised by his teachings echoing only in the words of those prelates, like the abbot of Cluny, who had raised their voices against him.[43]

Peter the Venerable played no small part in the downfall of the teachings of Peter of Bruys and Henry the Monk because they shared more in common with his own than anyone involved would care to admit. The alarm raised by these heretics had stemmed from the fact that they claimed to represent the true teaching of the church made on the authority of the Gospels. The abbot of Cluny pointed out with scorn that they had once been Christian priests.[44] So, even though the Petrobrusians had introduced false doctrines to the faithful and had steadfastly denied the validity of the Old Testament, they still revered the Gospels. For Peter, this was enough. A

---

39. Manselli, *Studi sulle eresie*, 63–64.

40. Peter Abelard, *Theologia "Scholarium,"* 2.4, in PL 178, cols. 979–1114 (where it bears the title *Introductio ad theologiam in libros tres divisa*), at col. 1056. Constant Mews dated this work to 1133–37 and called it "the culmination of a long process of revision and development" that "synthesised Abelard's most mature ideas about God." See Constant Mews, "On Dating the Works of Peter Abelard," *Archives d'histoire doctrinale et littéraire du moyen âge* 52 (1985): 132, reprinted in Constant Mews, *Abelard and His Legacy* (Aldershot, England: Ashgate, 2001), no. 7.

41. Hildebert of Lavardin, *Epistola*, 23–24, in PL 171, cols. 237–42. Hildebert (1055 or 1056–1133), bishop of Le Mans from 1096 and archbishop of Tours from 1125, is remembered primarily for his poetry.

42. For an edition of the untitled treatise, see Raoul Manselli, "Il monaco Enrico e la sua eresia," *Bolletino dell'Istituto storico italiano per il Medio Evo e Archivo muratoriano* 65 (1953): 1–62, esp. 44–62.

43. On the ruling of the Second Lateran Council against the Petrobrusians, see Charles-Joseph Hefele, *Histoire des Conciles d'après les documents originaux*, trans. Henri Leclercq, (Paris: Letouzey et Ané, 1907), 2:731–32 (canon 23). Peter attended the council; Constable, *Letters of Peter the Venerable*, 2:252–56.

44. Peter the Venerable, *Contra Petrobrusianos hereticos*, 274, ed. Fearns, 162.

mutual respect for the teachings of Christ provided common ground in the debate that allowed the abbot of Cluny to marshal a host of patristic authorities to his side both to rebuke his heretical opponents and to shore up faith among wavering Christians tainted by their thinking. In the end an inexorable tide of Christian tradition washed away the novelties of the Petrobrusians, but this was only possible because both sides in the debate drew from the same well of scriptural authority to defend their rival claims. Peter and his heretical opponents were like faces on the opposing sides of a common coin: each drew its value from the precious metal of the Gospels, but their gazes were fixed in opposite directions.

↝ A Christian Arsenal against Islam

By the early 1140s the significance of Peter the Venerable's victory against the Petrobrusians had receded as more paramount concerns crowded his mind—namely, the erosion of the Christian faith due to the tenacity of Judaism within Europe and the success of Islam throughout the rest of the known world. In the abbot's view, these rival systems of belief presented a much greater threat to Christendom than the heretics condemned at the Second Lateran Council. For the next fifteen years, until his death in 1156, Peter was the most active prelate of his age in his campaign against the beliefs of Jews and Muslims. His polemical writings from this period were unrivaled among those of his contemporaries in two important ways. First, Peter's research into the truth claims of his adversaries involved the condemnation of religious texts from the sacred traditions of his opponents—the Talmud and the Qur'an—that few other northern European Christians had ever read, let alone scrutinized for the purpose of a systematic refutation. Second, the dawning realization of the futility of the abbot's enterprise, especially in the context of the Second Crusade, invested these polemical works with a strident tone and ultimately drained them of the confidence that characterized his treatise against the Petrobrusians. Faced with religious adversaries who did not recognize the authority of the Gospels, Peter inflected his treatises against Judaism and Islam with a shrillness born of the realization that "Satan's quiver was by no means as empty as he had first thought."[45]

---

45. Gavin Langmuir, *Toward a Definition of Antisemitism* (Berkeley: University of California Press, 1990), 197–208 (quotation at 199). Langmuir is one of the only historians to have shown due sensitivity to the development of Peter's polemical writings over time.

On his trip to Spain in 1142–43, only three years after the condemnation of the Petrobrusians at the Second Lateran Council, Peter the Venerable encountered a society of religious diversity unlike anything he had experienced in his travels through northern Europe and Italy. While the southward surge of Christian armies had liberated the interior of the Spanish peninsula from Muslim control by the late eleventh century, the kingdoms of northern Iberia preserved the iridescent patina of devotional pluralism that had long characterized the tolerant cultures of the Umayyad dynasty and the independent Taifa kingdoms that succeeded in the wake of its dissolution.[46] Like the bones of an immense prehistoric creature, the remnants of Islamic culture in northern Spain were evocative of an ancient power that would have been terrible to behold in the flesh. This firsthand experience of the magnitude of the achievement of Islam left a deep and abiding impression on the abbot of Cluny and forced nothing less than a painful reordering of the world that he had imagined from the security of his abbey in Burgundy. Peter could no longer state with the bluster of naive confidence that "Christ holds dominion from sea to sea," as he did in his letter to the heretical monk, without a measure of sober qualification. After his visit to Spain the world had grown larger in his imagination, and his place within it had diminished. With reluctance, the abbot of Cluny had to admit that Christians shared the lordship of the earth with Saracens, while the Jews—subjugated, but not silent—lurked among them both.[47]

In the wake of these unsettling realizations, Peter the Venerable grasped an unprecedented opportunity presented by the rich diversity of religious and intellectual culture of twelfth-century Spain when he commissioned a translation of the Qur'an and other Islamic devotional texts into Latin. To carry out this plan he employed three Christian scholars and prelates who were proficient in Arabic and already residing in Spain—Peter of Toledo, Robert of Ketton, and Herman of Dalmatia—as well as an otherwise unknown Muslim named Mohammed, whom he directed to check the accuracy of the translations.[48] The fruit of their labor, the so-called Toledan Collection,

---

46. For orientation, see David Wasserstein, *The Rise and Fall of the Party-Kings: Politics and Society in Islamic Spain 1002–1086* (Princeton, NJ: Princeton University Press, 1985); and Bernard F. Reilly, *The Contest of Christian and Muslim Spain, 1031–1157* (Cambridge, MA: Blackwell, 1992).

47. Peter the Venerable, *Adversus Iudeorum inveteratam duritiem* (hereafter *Adversus Iudeorum*), ed. Yvonne Friedman, CCCM 58:109.

48. On the identity of these translators, see Kritzeck, *Peter the Venerable and Islam*, 56–69. On translation activity in Spain in this period more generally, see Marie-Thérèse d'Alverny, "Translations and Translators," in *Renaissance and Renewal in the Twelfth Century*, ed. Robert L. Benson and Giles Constable with Carol D. Lanham (Cambridge, MA: Harvard University Press, 1982), 421–62.

survives in a twelfth-century manuscript (Paris, Bibliothèque de l'Arsenal 1162), which is not only the earliest witness to this enterprise, but is also almost certainly a direct copy of the original exemplars of this extraordinary compilation.[49] Peter's anthology consisted of the following texts:

1. A work of unknown provenance translated by Robert of Ketton titled both *The Fables of the Saracens* (*Fabulae Saracenorum*) and *A Lying and Ludicrous Chronicle of the Saracens* (*Chronica mendosa et ridiculosa Saracenorum*), which recounted the history of creation, a chronology of the patriarchs and prophets, and the story of the Hijrah, as well as biographical portraits of Muhammed and the first seven caliphs.[50]

2. *The Book of the Birth of Muhammad and His Upbringing* (*Liber generationis Mahumet et nutritia eius*), translated by Herman of Dalmatia, on the continuity of prophecy from Adam to Muhammed.[51]

3. *The Teaching of Muhammad* (*Doctrina Machumet*), also translated by Herman of Dalmatia, which presented the truth claims of Islam in the form of a didactic dialogue between Muhammed and a new Muslim convert.[52]

---

49. Paris, Bibliothèque de l'Arsenal, MS 1162 (hereafter Arsenal 1162), the contents of which are described in *Catalogue des manuscrits de la bibliothèque de l'Arsenal* (Paris: Plon, 1886), 2:315–17 (no. 1162). On the various names given to the collection, all of which are modern confections, see the introduction to the present volume. On the significance of this manuscript as an assemblage of copies of the archetypes of these texts—but not the archetypes themselves, as Marie-Thérèse d'Alverny first surmised—see the introduction to *Exposición y refutación del Islam: La versión latina de las epístolas de al'Hasimi y al-Kindi*, ed. and trans. Fernando González Muñoz (A Coruña, Spain: Universidade da Coruña, Servizo de Publicacións, 2005), cxv–cxvii, which modifies the findings of d'Alverny, "Deux traductions latines du Coran au moyen âge," *Archives d'histoire doctrinale et littéraire du Moyen Âge* 22–23 (1947–48): 69–131, esp. 77, 96. Both scholars agree, however, that another copy of Arsenal 1162 was subsequently made at Cluny, which became the archetype for every other surviving copy of these texts. With the exception of González Muñoz's new edition of *The Apology of al-Kindi* cited above, the only printed edition of the Toledan Collection is that of Theodore Bibliander, *Machumetis saracenorum principis eiusque successorum vitae, doctrina ac ipse alcoran*, 3 vols. (Basel: Johann Oporinus, 1543), which does not always conform with the text of Arsenal 1162. For more on the Arsenal manuscript, see Kritzeck, *Peter the Venerable and Islam*, 73–112; Glei, *Petrus Venerabilis*, xv–xix; and Iogna-Prat, *Order and Exclusion*, 332–57.

50. Arsenal 1162, fols. 5r–10v and margin of 11r; ed. Bibliander, 1:213–23. While the general contents of this work were well known in medieval Islamic traditions, neither D'Alvernay nor Kritzeck could identify an Arabic text that provided the exemplar for this specific translation. For a summary of its contents, see Kritzeck, *Peter the Venerable and Islam*, 75, calling it "a typical potpourri of Islamic traditions."

51. Arsenal 1162, fols. 11r–18r, ed. Bibliander, 1:201–12. Kritzeck identified the Arabic original as *The Book of the Lineage of the Messanger of God*; see Kritzeck, *Peter the Venerable and Islam*, 84–88.

52. Arsenal 1162, fols. 19r–25v, ed. Bibliander, 1:189–200. This text is a translation of a well-known Arabic work titled *The Questions of 'Abd Allah ibn Salam*. The fullest discussion of its contents remains Kritzeck, *Peter the Venerable and Islam*, 89–96.

4. *Lex Mahumet pseudoprophete que Arabica Alchoran id est Collectio praeceptorum uocatur*, being Robert of Ketton's translation of the Qur'an annotated for Christian readers.[53]

5. *The Apology of al-Kindi*, which Peter of Toledo translated with the titles *The Letter of a Saracen to a Christian* (*Epistola sarraceni ad christianum*) and *The Christian's Response* (*Rescriptum Christiani*), a popular ninth- or tenth-century Arab-Christian treatise against Islam couched as an epistolary exchange between a Muslim and a Christian.[54]

The abbot of Cluny departed from Spain in early 1143 while the longest of these translations was still in preparation.[55] He had a journey of many weeks to weigh how best to use this new trove of information about Islam in defense of the Christian faith.

By the time Peter the Venerable arrived back at Cluny in the spring of 1143, he had decided not to write a formal refutation of Islam. Instead he hoped to attract someone who would read the contents of the Toledan Collection and compose "a worthy response . . . to counter this contagion" (*responsionem tamen condignam . . . contra hanc pestem*).[56] In the meantime he composed a short handbook on Muslim beliefs to serve as a prologue to the translations.[57] Titled *A Summary of the Entire Heresy of the Saracens* (*Summa totius haeresis Sarracenorum*), this work was a compendium of all of the errors

---

53. Arsenal 1162, fols. 26r–138r, ed. Bibliander, 1:8–188. Thomas E. Burman treats this Latin translation of the Qur'an and its polemical annotations with admirable sensitivity to its manuscript context in *Reading the Qur'an in Latin Christendom 1140–1560* (Philadelphia: University of Pennsylvania Press, 2007), 60–87.

54. Arsenal 1162, fols. 140r–178r, ed. and trans. González Muñoz, in *Exposición y refutación del Islam*, 1–147. See also Kritzeck, *Peter the Venerable and Islam*, 101–7; Fernando González Muñoz, "La versión latina de la *Apología al-Kindi* y su tradición textual," in *Musulmanes y cristianos en Hispania durante las conquistas de los siglos XII y XIII*, ed. Miquel Barceló and José Martínez Gázquez (Barcelona: Universidad Autónoma de Barcelona, 2005), 25–40; and Laura Bottini, "The Apology of al-Kindī," in CMR 1:585–94.

55. Peter's translation team probably accompanied him on his travels through Spain and may have completed most of its work before the abbot's departure. For a summary of the evidence that this was likely the case, see Bishko, "Peter the Venerable's Journey to Spain," 168. The translation of the Qur'an was a much longer enterprise, however, that Robert did not complete until June or July 1143. On the "phases in the construction of the Toledan Collection," see James Kritzeck, "Peter the Venerable and the Toledan Collection," in *Petrus Venerabilis*, ed. Constable and Kritzeck, 182–83.

56. Peter the Venerable, *Epistola de translatione sua*, 4, ed. Glei, 26.

57. This was the full extent of Peter's intended input into the project. Kritzeck, "Peter the Venerable and the Toledan Collection," 184, expresses this point concisely: "Peter's own role, as he first

of the Muslims that the Christian reader would find in the anthology.[58] The aim of this brief but incisive text was to portray and discredit both the religious beliefs and personal character of "that most miserable and unholy Muhammad, who now denies all of the sacraments of the Christian faith . . . to almost a third of the human race."[59] According to Peter, Islam was nothing less than the sum of all previous heresies. Muslims denied the Trinity like Sabellius; they were blind to the divinity of Christ like Nestorius; and although they acknowledged the Lord's ascent to heaven, they disavowed his death like the Manichaeans.[60] Although Muhammed attributed his holy words to the archangel Gabriel, he in fact concocted the fables of the Qur'an with the assistance of learned heretics and conspiring Jews.[61] With it he poisoned the bodies and souls of his wretched followers, who abandoned their worship of many gods and made him both their king and the object of their religious devotion.[62] The Muslim conquests of Asia and Africa and Spain had now doomed "almost half of the world" (*paene dimidia pars mundi*) to damnation due to the spread of Muhammed's evil doctrines.[63] Peter's purpose in writing this summary was not to debate at length the points that he raised but to broadcast his fear about the threat of Islam in the hope of attracting a champion who would respond in the defense of Christendom.[64]

It is clear from another text that Peter the Venerable wrote at this time that he already had a worthy candidate in mind for the task of refuting the Muslims: Abbot Bernard of Clairvaux. In a missive known as the *Letter concerning his Translation Project* (*Epistola de translatione sua*), the abbot of Cluny

---

and long considered his project, was to have ceased precisely with the composition of this handbook."

58. Peter the Venerable, *Summa totius haeresis Sarracenorum* (hereafter *Summa*), ed. Glei, 2–22.

59. *Summa*, 2, ed. Glei, 4: "Sic enim docuit eos miserrimus atque impiissimus Mahumetus, qui omnia sacramenta Christianae pietatis, quibus maxime homines salvantur, abnegans iam paene tertiam humani generis partem, nescimus quo dei iudicio, inauditis fabularum deliramentis diabolo et morti aeternae contradidit."

60. *Summa*, 9, ed. Glei, 10–12. Shortly thereafter, Peter also compared Muhammed to Arius, the archheretic of the Christian tradition, because both of them denied that Jesus was the true son of God. See *Summa*, 13, ed. Glei, 14.

61. *Summa*, 7, ed. Glei, 6.

62. Ibid.

63. *Summa*, 16, ed. Glei, 18–20.

64. *Summa*, 17, ed. Glei, 20. The translation of *contremiscere* as "sound an alert" in Iogna-Prat, *Order and Exclusion*, 342, misses the sense of fearful trembling or shuddering at the root of the meaning of this word.

addressed Bernard in affectionate terms and described for him the circumstances under which he had commissioned the translation of Muslim texts from Arabic into Latin.[65] His intention in doing so, Peter explained, was to follow the example of those church fathers who had defended the faith from hateful and damnable heresies both in their writings and by means of oral debate. Islam was deemed the worst of them all, nothing less than "the filth of all heresies, in which the debris of every diabolical sect that has arisen since the coming of our Savior flows together."[66] The abbot of Cluny had created this Christian arsenal (*Christianum armarium*) so that Bernard would respond to the threat of Islam in the manner of David and Solomon. The former hoarded weapons during a time of peace, while the latter built and decorated a mighty temple to God. Neither endeavor was necessary at the time, but both paid dividends for future generations.[67] Similarly, while the Muslims did not present an immediate threat to Christian Europe, it was nonetheless important to strive against the errors of their belief, "to battle, to destroy, to trample underfoot every knowledge that raises itself against the very height of God."[68] At the outset of the letter, Peter indicated that a new Latin translation of a Muslim work—probably *The Apology of al-Kindi*—would accompany the missive to Bernard, and he promised to send the remaining bulk of the anthology to Clairvaux if he agreed to take on the task of refuting it.[69] Once his messenger had departed for Bernard's monastery, the abbot of Cluny turned his attention away from Islam to address more pressing concerns.

---

65. Peter the Venerable, *Epistola de translatione sua*, ed. Glei, 22–29. Peter had in hand a draft of this letter when he wrote his longer *Epistola* 111 to Bernard later that summer (1144). On the relationship between these two works, I have followed the reasoning of Constable in *Letters of Peter the Venerable*, 2:275–84. The *Epistola de translatione sua* took its place alongside the abbot's *Summa totius haeresis Sarracenorum* as the prologue to the Toledan Collection in most of the surviving manuscripts, including Arsenal 1162.

66. Peter the Venerable, *Epistola de translatione sua*, 3, ed. Glei, 24: "[D]e hac faece universarum haeresum, in quam omnium diabolicarum sectaru quae ab ipso salvatoris adventu ortae sunt reliquiae confluxerunt."

67. Peter the Venerable, *Epistola de translatione sua*, 4, ed. Glei, 26.

68. Ibid.: "Nec tamen ut mihi videtur opus istud etiam hoc tempore otiosum vocare debeo, quoniam, iuxta Apostolum [cf. 2 Cor. 10:5], vestrum est et omnium doctorum virorum 'omnem scientiam extollentem se adversus altitudinem dei' omni studio verbo et scripto impugnare, destruere, conculcare." This phrase appeared again in a slightly different form in the prologue to Peter's treatise *Contra sectam Saracenorum*, ed. Glei, 32.

69. Peter the Venerable, *Epistola de translatione sua*, 2, 6, ed. Glei, 22, 28.

↝ Assailing the Monstrous Beast

Peter the Venerable was not idle while he waited for a response from Bernard of Clairvaux, for it was during the very next year, 1144, that he brought to completion the first draft of his second major polemical enterprise, a treatise titled *Against the Long-Standing Stubbornness of the Jews* (*Adversus Iudeorum inveteratam duritiem*).[70] It is unclear why the abbot of Cluny chose to address the issue of Judaism at this point in his career. Following Georges Duby, historians have placed the motives for Peter's anti-Jewish writings squarely in the context of a serious and ever deepening financial crisis that afflicted Cluny in the early twelfth century.[71] It was around this time, in 1146, that Peter complained to King Roger II of Sicily that "Cluny has many debtors but few benefactors" and pleaded for a loan to keep his community solvent.[72] One of his most generous supporters was Henry of Blois (d. 1171), a younger brother of King Stephen of England who had been educated at Cluny before he became abbot of Glastonbury (1126) and bishop of Winchester (1129).[73] On several occasions Henry sent thousands of silver marks to his cherished brethren in Burgundy to help pay down the abbey's mounting debts.[74] Indeed, in a letter written in 1135, Peter expressed his relief and gratitude for Henry's financial intervention, which allowed the monks of Cluny to retrieve some liturgical vestments that were being held as collateral by Jews of Mâcon.[75] With the memory of this shameful indebtedness in

---

70. *Adversus Iudeorum*, ed. Friedman. For an English translation of this treatise, see *Peter the Venerable: Against the Inveterate Obduracy of the Jews*, trans. Irven M. Resnick (Washington, DC: Catholic University of America Press, 2013). There is a useful overview of Peter's characterization of the Jews in Jean-Pierre Torrell, "Les juifs dans l'oeuvre de Pierre le Vénérable," *Cahiers de civilisation médiévale* 30 (1987): 331–46.

71. The *locus classicus* is Georges Duby, "Le budget de l'abbaye de Cluny entre 1080 et 1155: Économie domaniale et économie monétaire," *Annales: Économies, Sociétés, Civilisations* 7 (1952): 155–71; reprinted in Georges Duby, *Hommes et structures du moyen âge: Recueil d'articles* (Paris: Mouton, 1973), 61–82. The issue of Cluny's financial woes during the abbacy of Peter the Venerable merits a thorough reinvestigation.

72. Peter the Venerable, *Epistola*, 131, ed. Constable, 1:332: "Inde est quod Cluniacus debitores multos, benefactores habet paucos." Constable dates the letter to "early 1146" (2:186).

73. See, most recently, Neil Stratford, "Un grand clunisien, Henri de Blois," in *Cluny: Onze siècles de rayonnement* (Paris: Éditions du Patrimoine Centre des Monuments Nationaux, 2010), 238–45, with references to previous literature.

74. The sources for these loans are discussed in Lena Voss, *Heinrich von Blois: Bischof von Winchester (1129–1171)* (Berlin: Ebering, 1932), 114–15, 118.

75. Peter the Venerable, *Epistola*, 56, ed. Constable, 1:177. On the use of liturgical items as securities against loans from Jews in this period, see Joseph Shatzmiller, *Cultural Exchange: Jews, Christians and Art in the Medieval Marketplace* (Princeton, NJ: Princeton University Press, 2013), 22–44.

mind, the ostentatious wealth of local Jewish communities barbed the abbot—especially since, as he alleged, they amassed their fortunes through the purchase and sale of precious ornaments stolen from Christian churches.[76] While Peter seems to have avoided borrowing from Jewish lenders again, the stark contrast between the insolvency of his community and the prosperity of the Jews may have been enough to prompt him into action against them. Whatever the catalyst, the abbot would have found affirmation of his treatise from the repetition of its central themes in the Cluniac liturgy. Year in and year out, each 21 December, the monks of Cluny listened to a sermon against the Jews by the fifth-century North African prelate Quodvultdeus as one of their office lessons.[77] It is no coincidence that Peter borrowed the opening sentence of his treatise—"I address you, you, O Jews, who even unto today deny the Son of God"—directly from this late antique sermon.[78]

In the first draft of 1144, Peter the Venerable's treatise against the Jews did not differ markedly in its content from other works of anti-Jewish polemic produced by Christian scholars in the early Middle Ages, most of which presented arguments in support of the divinity of Jesus and his role as the Messiah based on the authority of well-trodden biblical passages.[79] In his prologue, the abbot of Cluny mapped out the small patch of common ground shared by Jews and Christians—namely, the belief that the prophets of the Old Testament foretold the coming of the Messiah.[80] He then laid out the four principle errors of the Jews concerning Christ: "You do not believe that he was the son of God, you deny that he himself was God, that he ruled on earth as a king in the manner of other kings, and you maintain that the Messiah has not yet come, but will come in the future."[81] He proceeded to refute these false claims over the course of four chapters with a litany of biblical and patristic authorities.

---

76. Peter the Venerable, *Epistola*, 130, ed. Constable, 1:328. For more on Peter's depiction of the Jews in this letter, see Torrell, "Les Juifs dans l'oeuvre de Pierre le Vénérable," 339–42.

77. Quodvultdeus, *Contra Iudaeos, paganos et Arrianos*, ed. René Braun, in *Opera Quodvultdeo Carthaginiensi Episcopo Tributa*, CCSL 60:227–58. For its use in the Cluniac liturgy "die IV ante Natalem Domini," see CCM 7.4:126.

78. *Adversus Iudeorum*, prologue, ed. Friedman, 1: "Vos ego, vos, ego convenio, o Iudei, qui usque in hodiernum negatis Filium Dei." Compare Quodvultdeus, *Contra Iudaeos, paganos et Arrianos*, 11.1, ed. Braun, 241.

79. On the *adversus Iudaeos* tradition in early medieval Christian literature, see chapter 4 of the present volume.

80. *Adversus Iudeorum*, prologue, ed. Friedman, 2–3.

81. *Adversus Iudeorum*, prologue, ed. Friedman, 3: "Dissentis, quod eum Dei filium non creditis, quod Deum negatis, quod aliorum regum more temporaliter regnaturum, quod non iam venisse, sed venturum affirmatis."

When Peter returned to this treatise once more in 1146–47, he added two new sections that stand out in bold relief to the earlier chapters both in the novelty of their content and in the hostility of their tone. In the first of these sections, the abbot argued that miracles account for the success of Christianity.[82] In the time before Christ, human beings employed their innate reason (*innata ratio*) to locate the divine in objects and they expressed their devotion naively through idolatry. But by the age of the apostles, human beings had developed to such an extent in terms of their understanding of philosophy, law, and science that they could understand the signs worked by Christ and his disciples as indicative of divine power and therefore rushed to embrace the Christian faith. In Peter's mind, then, it was the efficacy of miracles that earned converts for Christianity. Here the abbot of Cluny paused to reflect on the success of Islam. How had this new religion, which shunned the miraculous, won so many converts to its cause? Based on a reading of his Latin translations of the Qur'an and *The Apology of al-Kindi*, Peter concluded that Muhammed obtained converts to Islam through the fear of armed conquest and by the irresistible lure of sexual indulgence.[83] By contrast, Christians did not compel the conversion of unbelievers by the threat of force and Christ called upon them to renounce the flesh and expect no earthly rewards for their faith. It was the belief in Christian miracles alone that inspired people to crowd the thresholds of the churches of God and gather in hopeful throngs around the tombs of the saints.

In his final foray against the Jews, written in 1147 as the last chapter of his treatise, Peter the Venerable attacked the authority that they placed in the "ludicrous and most foolish stories" that comprised the Talmud.[84] The Talmud, which means "learning" or "instruction" in Hebrew, was a collection of late ancient Rabbinic writings made up of the Mishnah, a compilation of legal interpretations of the Hebrew scriptures that circulated orally until they were put into writing around 200, and the Gemara, a collective commentary on the Mishnah made by several generations of Jewish rabbis that

---

82. For what follows, see *Adversus Iudeorum*, 4.1357–2009, ed. Friedman, 106–24. This section is closely allied with Peter's treatise *De miraculis*, which was written at the same time. On the importance of *miracula* in the abbot's thought, see Jean-Pierre Torrell and Denise Bouthillier, "*Miraculum*: Une catégorie fondamentale chez Pierre le Vénérable," *Revue thomiste* 80 (1980): 357–86, 549–66.

83. *Adversus Iudeorum*, 4.1531–56, ed. Friedman, 111.

84. *Adversus Iudeorum*, 5 (*De ridiculis et stultissimis fabulis Iudeorum*), ed. Friedman, 125–87. Peter was the first Christian intellectual to refer to the Talmud by name in a polemical context (*Adversus Iudeorum*, 5.33: "Thalmuth," ed. Friedman, 126) and only the second after Peter Alfonsi to deploy its contents in a treatise against Judaism. On Alfonsi and the possible influence of his work on the abbot of Cluny, see chapter 4 of the present volume.

was written down around 500.[85] By the early twelfth century this exegetical tradition had become even richer and more vibrant, as Rabbinic scholars like Gerschom ben Judah of Mainz (d. ca. 1028) and Rashi of Troyes (d. 1105) composed learned commentaries to explain both the Mishnah and the Gemara.[86] The Talmud has a very complex textual history that braids together several different genres; its contents include not only statements on Jewish law and its application but also homilies, exegesis, and stories with ethical or moral messages. Several of these stories couched their messages in whimsical scenarios, which depicted God with human attributes. Some portrayed God reading the Talmud with a group of Rabbinic scholars in heaven and debating their interpretation of the Bible.[87] Another related how a canny Talmudic scholar outwitted the angel of death on a tour of hell by stealing his sword.[88] Most of these tales glorified the piety of Jewish scholars who were diligent in the study of the Talmud, but they did not carry the same authority as the Torah and were not taken literally by their Jewish readers. To the abbot of Cluny, who misunderstood the Talmud as a holy text (*sacer textus*) equal in stature to the Torah and misconstrued the conventions of the genres that comprised it by reading them at face value, these stories were at best utter nonsense and at worst completely blasphemous.[89] It remains unclear how Peter obtained his knowledge of the text of the Talmud; his information was almost certainly indirect because the abbot of Cluny knew no Hebrew, and Latin translations of the Talmud would not appear until the thirteenth century. Scholars have proposed that he made use of an anthology of Talmudic legends mediated either by a Latin translation or by a Jew

---

85. *Oxford Dictionary of the Jewish Religion*, ed. R. J. Zwi Werblowsky and Geoffrey Wigoder (New York: Oxford University Press, 1997), 668–72, s.v. "Talmud," with extensive bibliography. For a good introduction to this tradition, see Adin Steinsaltz, *The Essential Talmud*, trans. Chaya Galai (London: Weidenfeld and Nicolson, 1976).

86. On the traditions of Hebrew exegesis in the Middle Ages, which are much more complex than this summary suggests, see Aryeh Graboïs, *Les sources hébraïques médiévales, 2: Les commentaires exégétiques*, Typologie des sources du moyen âge occidental 66 (Turnhout, Belgium: Brepols, 1993).

87. For Peter's criticism of the Talmud's anthropomorphic portrayal of God as an insult to divine omnipotence, see *Adversus Iudeorum*, 5.275–396, ed. Friedman, 132–35. Some medieval Jewish thinkers—most notably, Maimonides—were also critical of such depictions of God. On the state of the question in medieval Jewish studies, see Yair Lorberbaum, "Anthropomorphisms in Early Rabbinic Literature: Maimonides and Modern Scholarship," in *Traditions of Maimonideanism*, ed. Carlos Fraenkel (Leiden: Brill, 2009), 313–17.

88. Peter likewise scorned the presumptions of this story, which depicted a mortal confounding the omniscience of God. See *Adversus Iudeorum*, 5.1336–1663, ed. Friedman, 163–72.

89. For Peter's evaluation of the Talmud as a *sacer textus*, see *Adversus Iudeorum* 5.1176–79, ed. Friedman, 159.

who had converted to Christianity.[90] Peter himself is unusually cryptic on the matter, alluding only to the role of Christ in revealing the falsehood of these "Jewish secrets" (*secreta Iudaica*), but the argument of the final book of his treatise against the Jews is very clear: the Talmud is a "monstrous beast" (*portuentuosa bestia*) that lulls its readers into a bestial stupidity, stripping them of human reason and debasing their intellect until they are nothing more than cattle.[91] This, the abbot concluded, was the fate of the Jews.

It is not surprising that Peter the Venerable returned to his treatise in 1146–47 to assail the Jews once more, for this was the eve of the Second Crusade. The abbot of Cluny was a firm supporter of King Louis VII and his allies, who responded to Pope Eugenius III's call for a new crusade in 1146 after the fall of the County of Edessa in 1144 to Emir Imad ad-Din Zengi, the ruler of Aleppo and Mosul.[92] But when Peter received a letter from the king enlisting his support for this endeavor, he replied not only with a declaration of his allegiance to Louis's call to fight the Saracens in the Holy Land but also with a condemnation of dangerous adversaries much closer to home: the Jews of western Europe.[93] "What good is it," he asked the king, "to pursue the enemies of the Christian faith in far and distant lands if the Jews, vile blasphemers and far worse than the Saracens, not far from us but right in our midst, blaspheme, abuse, and trample on Christ and the Christian sacraments so freely and insolently and with impunity?"[94] Peter was not advocating a violent attack on the Jews, such as occurred in the

---

90. For a summary of Peter's probable sources, see Friedman's introduction to *Adversus Iudeorum*, xx, which posits "the existence of a post-Biblical Jewish literature which reached the Christians in this period but which has not survived in the form of a book or prepared anthology," the likes of which were "surpressed after the burning of the Talmud [in 1240]." Cf. Gilbert Dahan, *Les intellectuels chrétiens et les juifs au moyen âge* (Paris: Éditions du Cerf, 1990), 458–59, which argues more plausibly for the collaborative role of a converted Jew rather than the agency of a lost Latin translation of these traditions.

91. *Adversus Iudeorum*, 5:35–41, ed. Friedman, 126. In contrast, the abbot was much more forthcoming about how he had obtained information on the tenets of Islam. On the Talmud as a monstrous beast, see *Adversus Iudeorum*, 5.30, 5.32–33, ed. Friedman, 125–26.

92. On Peter's advocacy of the Second Crusade, see Virginia Berry, "Peter the Venerable and the Crusades," in *Petrus Venerabilis*, ed. Constable and Kritzeck, 141–62. For a judicious and thorough account of this crusade, see Jonathan Phillips, *The Second Crusade: Extending the Frontiers of Christendom* (New Haven, CT: Yale University Press, 2007).

93. Peter the Venerable, *Epistola*, 130, ed. Constable, 1:327–30. For a close study of this letter, see Yvonne Friedman, "An Anatomy of Anti-Semitism: Peter the Venerable's Letter to Louis VII, King of France (1146)," *Bar-Ilan Studies in History* 1 (1978): 87–102.

94. Peter the Venerable, *Epistola*, 130, ed. Constable, 1:328: "Sed quid proderit inimicos Christianae spei in exteris aut remotis finibus insequi ac persequi, si nequam blasphemi, longeque Sarracenis deteriores Iudaei, non longe a nobis, sed in medio nostri, tam libere, tam audacter, Christum, cunctaque Christiana sacramenta, impune blasphemauerint, conculcauerint, deturpauerint?" This

Rhineland at the outset of the First Crusade.[95] Rather, he was encouraging Louis to burden them with the financial load of the looming expedition, since they were not only the murderers of Christ but had also grown rich through their traffic in stolen goods—often relics and other devotional objects taken from churches—and their deception of Christians. Why should Christians pay for the Second Crusade when the Jews had more than enough wealth to fund the expedition? Peter concluded, "Spare their lives, but take away their money" (*Reseruertur eis uita, auferatur pecunia*).[96] It was this anger that fueled the abbot's return to his treatise against the stubbornness of the Jews and ignited his verbal assault on the traditions of the Talmud.

By 1149 the Second Crusade had ended in complete and utter failure.[97] The armies of the West retreated back to Germany and France, leaving behind them weakened allies and emboldened enemies. The tide had turned in favor of the Muslims, who in the words of William of Tyre "mocked at the shattered strength and broken glory" of the Christians.[98] The defeat of the crusading forces, combined with the death of Prince Raymond of Antioch at the Battle of Inab in 1149 and the renewed suffering of Frankish settlers throughout the Holy Land, kindled the wrath of Abbot Bernard of Clairvaux, who advocated for a new crusade in 1150.[99] But the ambivalence of the warriors who had just returned from the Holy Land in disgrace, and the hesitancy of Pope Eugenius III (who supported the mission in principle but not in practice), doomed this project to failure before it had even begun. It

---

excerpt has been translated by Jeremy Cohen in *Living Letters of the Law: Ideas of the Jew in Medieval Christianity* (Berkeley: University of California Press, 1999), 247.

95. On the legacy of the Rhineland massacres in Jewish history and modern historiography, see Robert Chazan, *European Jewry and the First Crusade* (Berkeley: University of California Press, 1987); David Nirenberg, "The Rhineland Massacres of Jews in the First Crusade: Memories Medieval and Modern," in *Medieval Concepts of the Past: Ritual, Memory, Historiography*, ed. Gerd Altoff, Johannes Fried, and Patrick Geary (Cambridge: Cambridge University Press, 2002), 279–310; and Jeremy Cohen, *Sanctifying the Name of God: Jewish Martyrs and Jewish Memories of the First Crusade* (Philadelphia: University of Pennsylvania Press, 2004).

96. Peter the Venerable, *Epistola*, 130, ed. Constable, 1:330. In the end, Peter's plea was ineffectual. According to Phillips, *The Second Crusade*, 108, "In spite of Peter's prominent position there is no sign that the king implemented such a plan, at least to any noticeable extent."

97. The classic work on the subject of the Second Crusade remains Giles Constable, "The Second Crusade as Seen by Contemporaries," *Traditio* 9 (1952): 213–79, reprinted and selectively updated in Giles Constable, *Crusaders and Crusading in the Twelfth Century*, (Burlington, VT: Ashgate, 2009), 229–300. For a synthetic overview, see Phillips, *The Second Crusade*.

98. Phillips, *The Second Crusade*, 269.

99. See Giles Constable, "The Crusading Project of 1150," in *Montjoie: Studies in Crusading History in Honour of Hans Eberhard Mayer*, ed. Benjamin Z. Kedar, Jonathan Riley-Smith, and Rudolf Hiestand (Aldershot, England: Variorum, 1997), 67–75; reprinted with revisions in Constable, *Crusades and Crusading in the Twelfth Century*, 311–20.

would take a military catastrophe on the scale of the Battle of Hattin, where in July 1187 the forces of Saladin crushed the army of the Christian kingdom of Jerusalem and a few months later captured the Holy City, to motivate Europeans to embark on a crusade once more.

✒ Recourse to Reason

In the long shadow of the disastrous crusade and the frustrated plans for a war of vengeance against the Greeks in 1150, Peter the Venerable turned his thoughts once again to his enterprise to combat the religious tenets of Islam.[100] By this time, the project had lain fallow for many years. In 1143 his invitation to Bernard of Clairvaux to undertake a refutation of Muslim beliefs had gone unanswered. It may be that Bernard had simply ignored Peter's request, but it was not unusual for letters between these men to go unanswered, as we can tell from the complaints that these silences evoked.[101] Unfortunately, the intention behind these lapses in correspondence is never certain. It was only in the aftermath of the crusade and after the death of Bernard in 1153 that the abbot of Cluny instructed his trusted secretary, Peter of Poitiers, to sketch out the contours of a treatise against the prophetic claims of Muhammed that he would write himself. Peter of Poitiers was already deeply intimate with the contents of the Toledan Collection, for he had accompanied his abbot to Spain in 1142–43 and had worked diligently there to improve the style of the Latin translation of *The Apology of al-Kindi* produced by Peter of Toledo, whose proficiency in Latin was not nearly as accomplished as his skill in Arabic.[102] More than a decade later, probably in 1154 or 1155, Peter the Venerable called upon his expertise in these matters yet again.

While his abbot was abroad in England, Peter of Poitiers set to work.[103] The result was the rough outline of a treatise comprising four books, each

---

100. Peter's frustration with the outcome of the Second Crusade and his anger with the eastern Christians (*Graeci*) upon whom he put the blame for its failure are palpable in a letter to King Roger of Sicily written in or around 1150. See Peter the Venerable, *Epistola*, 162, ed. Constable, 1:394–95, esp. 395, where the letter simmers with thoughts of violent retribution; and 2:206–7 on the probable date of the letter.

101. See, for example, Peter the Venerable, *Epistola*, 65 (written late 1137) and Bernard's reply, *Epistola*, 74 (*Rescriptum Bernardi abbatis ad Petrum Cluniacensium abbatem*, written early 1138), ed. Constable, 1:194–95, 207–8.

102. Peter the Venerable, *Epistola*, 111, ed. Constable, 1:294.

103. Peter of Poitiers, *Epistola*, 3, ed. Glei, 226–28. This letter also explains that the abbot of Cluny was in England when Peter of Poitiers finished the first draft of the outline. This early version was

consisting of several chapters, on the following topics: a refutation of the Muslim claim that the books of the Old and New Testaments had been lost and later forged, which diminished their claim to be authoritative scripture; the charge that Muhammed was not a prophet because he led a sinful life and never performed any miracles; and a discussion of the sacred tradition of Christian prophecy, in which Muhammed had no place.[104] The outline ended with an admonition to Christian readers to hold fast to their faith in the saving power of Christ through baptism as the end times approached and the ravings of the devil filled the air. In a letter that accompanied this text, Peter of Poitiers encouraged his abbot to supplement or change the outline in any way that he saw fit. The composition of Peter's refutation of Islam, *Against the Sect of the Saracens*, occupied him for the final months of his life.[105] The treatise comprised only two books rather than the four books outlined by Peter of Poitiers, and this has led to considerable debate among scholars as to whether the work was left unfinished when the abbot died on Christmas Day in 1156.[106]

The organization of *Against the Sect of the Saracens* allowed the abbot of Cluny to speak in two distinct registers. In the prologue Peter explained the rationale of his work to a Christian audience.[107] The church fathers were never silent when faced with the threat of heresy. Do the prophetic claims of Muhammed not merit a similar response? The abbot explained how

---

lost by a monk named John who was charged to carry it to Peter the Venerable in England. These circumstances forced Peter of Poitiers to rewrite the outline from scratch, but also allowed him to make improvements to it before sending it again; this time, however, he kept a file copy of the document just in case. See Peter of Poitiers, *Epistola*, 4, ed. Glei, 228–30. Peter the Venerable's presence in England dates the second draft of the *capitula* firmly to 1155. On the date of this visit to England, see Constable, *Letters of Peter the Venerable*, 2:268.

104. *Capitula Petri Pictavensis*, ed. Glei, 232–39.

105. Peter the Venerable, *Contra sectam Saracenorum*, ed. Glei, 30–224 (cited hereafter by its title alone).

106. Torrell and Bouthillier concluded from the brevity of *Contra sectam Saracenorum* in comparison to Peter's other polemic works that the work was unfinished when he died. See Torrell and Bouthillier, *Pierre le Vénérable et sa vision du monde*, 182–83, and n95. On the other hand, Kritzeck, "Peter the Venerable and the Toledan Collection," and Iogna-Prat, *Order and Exclusion*, 344–45, have both argued that the core of Peter of Poitier's outline is present in the two surviving books. The disparity between the chapter count of Peter of Poitier's outline and Peter the Venerable's treatise was disconcerting for medieval readers as well. When the Maurist scholars Edmond Martène and Ursin Durand discovered a copy of *Contra sectam Saracenorum* in a manuscript in Douai in the early eighteenth century, they noted that a medieval scribe had written in the margin of the text: "Desunt duo libri quos invenire non potui." See Martène and Durand, *Veterum scriptorum et monumentorum ecclesiasticorum et dogmaticorum amplissima collectio* (Paris: Apud Franciscum Montalant, 1733), 9:1121.

107. For what follows, see *Contra sectam Saracenorum*, prologue, 1–9, ed. Glei, 30–44.

Muslims challenged the taxonomies traditionally applied to the enemies of Christianity. Like heretics, they confused and denigrated the nature of Christ; like pagans, they scorned baptism and the other sacraments of the holy Church. It was therefore best to consider them to be both heretics and pagans and resist them accordingly.[108] The first step in this process was the translation of Muslim texts from Arabic into Latin, which Peter had accomplished in the early 1140s, because for a long time "there was no one to respond [to the claims of Muhammed] because there was no one who understood them."[109] This consideration of the linguistic chasm separating the abbot from his Muslim adversaries led him to wonder aloud whether his refutation could be translated into Arabic for their benefit, just as the errors of Islam had been rendered into Latin by his effort.[110] Even if they remained deaf to his message, his labors were not in vain, because this Christian armory (*Christianum armarium*) of texts would shield the church against any wavering Europeans who harbored "secret thoughts" (*cogitationibus occultis*) about the tenets of Islam.[111]

Having explained the purpose of the treatise to a Christian audience in the prologue, Peter the Venerable spoke in a much more conciliatory register in the remainder of the book, in which he addressed an imagined Muslim audience. He introduced himself as "Peter, Gallic in origin, a Christian by faith, an abbot by office of those who are called monks" and then justified his undertaking:

> It seems astonishing and perhaps indeed it is, that I, a man so far removed from you in place, who speaks a different language, separate from you in my calling, strange with respect to my customs and life, write to those of you living in the eastern and southern parts of the world from my home far to the west and address you with words whom I have never seen and most likely never will see. I do not attack you, as some of us often do, with arms but with words, not with force but with reason, not out of hatred, but out of love.[112]

---

108. *Contra sectam Saracenorum*, prologue, 14, ed. Glei, 50.

109. *Contra sectam Saracenorum*, prologue, 17, ed. Glei, 54: "Nam non erat qui responderet, quia non erat qui agnosceret."

110. *Contra sectam Saracenorum*, prologue, 19, ed. Glei, 56.

111. *Contra sectam Saracenorum*, prologue, 20, ed. Glei, 56–58.

112. *Contra sectam Saracenorum*, 1.23–24, ed. Glei, 62: "In nomine Patris et Filii et Spiritus Sancti, unius omnipotentis et veri dei, Petrus quidam, Gallus natione, Christianus fide, abbas officio eorum qui monachi dicuntur, Arabibus Ismaelis filiis legem illius qui Mahumetus dicitur servantibus. Mirum videtur et fortassis etiam est, quod homo a vobis loco remotissimus, lingua diversus, professione seiunctus, moribus vitaque alienus, ab ultimis Occidentis hominibus in Orientis vel meridiei

In the decade after the failure of the Second Crusade, during which Christian armies proved ineffectual against the might of Islam, Peter felt that an invitation to reasoned argument (*ratio*) was the only recourse for reaching a Muslim audience. The core of his message to them was pastoral: "I invite you to salvation, not the kind that passes away, but the kind that is permanent, not the kind that ends after this brief life, but the kind that remains forever in eternal life."[113] Unlike the Jews, whose silly fables had debased their minds and made them all but subhuman, Peter addressed Muslims as rational beings fully capable of understanding the arguments he would set forth to make the case for the truth of Christianity. His first concern, however, was that Muslim law did not permit them to listen to any words contrary to their faith without a violent response.[114] Here the abbot of Cluny made a plea for a fair hearing and evoked the example of Ethelbert, the Anglo-Saxon king of Kent, who despite his suspicions was the first of the pagan rulers of England to allow Augustine of Canterbury and his fellow missionaries from Rome to preach among his people.[115]

Peter concluded the first book of his treatise with a refutation of alleged Muslim claims that the authentic texts of the Old and New Testaments had been lost long ago during times of Jewish exile and Christian persecution. According to this tradition, the current versions of scripture used by Jews and Christians were in fact corrupt variations that lacked the authority of the prophetic utterances of Muhammed preserved in the Qur'an. The abbot contested this, acknowledging that the corruption of texts undoubtedly occurred but did not effect every single copy of the Bible. He assured his Muslim readers that the Roman Church from the time of Saint Peter onward had guarded the scriptures from corruption.[116] It was a ludicrous assertion for Muslims to make in any case, he argued, because if the Gospel is false then

---

partibus positis scribo, et quos numquam vidi, quos numquam forte visurus sum, loquendo aggredior. Aggredior inquam vos, non, ut nostri saepe faciunt, armis sed verbis, non vi sed ratione, non odio sed amore."

113. *Contra sectam Saracenorum*, 27, ed. Glei, 66: "Invito vos ad salutem, non quae transit, sed quae permanet, non quae finitur cum vita brevi, sed quae permanet in vitam aeternam."

114. *Contra sectam Saracenorum*, 29, ed. Glei, 66–68.

115. *Contra sectam Saracenorum*, 51–54, ed. Glei, 98–104. Peter knew this story from Bede, *Historia Ecclesiastica*, 1.25, in *Bede's Ecclesiastical History of the English People*, ed. Bertram Colgrave and R. A. B. Mynors (Oxford: Clarendon Press, 1969), 72–77. Manuscripts of the works of Bede were numerous in the twelfth-century library catalog from Cluny, including a copy of the *Historia*. See Léopold Delisle, *Inventaire des manuscrits de la Bibliothèque nationale: Fonds de Cluni* (Paris: Librairie H. Champion, 1884), 352 (no. 261): "Volumen in quo continetur historia gentis Anglorum ab eodem Beda composita."

116. *Contra sectam Saracenorum*, 81–82, ed. Glei, 138–40.

so too is the Qur'an, since Muhammed drew his inspiration from the life of Christ. Having defended the purity of the Old and New Testaments, Peter forecast the argument of the next book of the treatise—namely, that the Qur'an had no claim to religious truth because Muhammed was a wicked seducer rather than a prophet of God.[117]

The authenticity of Muhammed as a prophet was the issue around which Peter the Venerable organized his second—and final—book of *Against the Sect of the Saracens*. For the abbot of Cluny this was a matter of definition. Drawing on Gregory the Great's first homily on Ezekiel, Peter argued that true prophets can speak in three different temporal registers: "A prophet is one who reveals to mortals things unknown either of the past or the present or the future taught not by human reasoning but inspired by the spirit of God."[118] He supported this definition with a litany of examples from the Old Testament. Moses was informed about the distant past by divine inspiration when he spoke about creation, "that time when there was no man."[119] The great patriarch also prophesied about the present when he narrated the fall of Korah, Dathan, and Abiram as the event was taking place.[120] The foretelling of future events was the dominion of innumerable Hebrew prophets, the most important of whom was Isaiah, who from the shadows of the past predicted the virgin birth of the Lord and his baptism, miracles, and death on the cross. By contrast, the Qur'an yielded no account of prophecies attributed to Muhammed. And while the newly translated *Book of the Birth of Muhammad and His Upbringing* claimed that the so-called prophet of Islam had foretold that twelve caliphs would follow after him, Peter dismissed this text as spurious because of the Quranic injunction to reject everything that does not concur with its words.[121] Muslims could not claim with any legitimacy that Muhammed was the "seal of the prophets"—that is, the last of

---

117. *Contra sectam Saracenorum*, 88, ed. Glei, 148.

118. *Contra sectam Saracenorum*, 97, ed. Glei, 160: "Propheta est, qui res ignotas aut praeteriti temporis aut praesentis vel futuri non humana cognitione edoctus, sed spiritu dei inspiratus mortalibus manifestat." The notion that a prophet works in three different temporal registers—past, present, and future—comes from Gregory the Great's first homily on Ezekiel. See Gregory the Great, *Homilia*, 1.1, in *Grégoire le Grand, Homélies sur Ézéchiel*, ed. Charles Morel, SC 327, 1:50–52. See also Jean-Pierre Torrell, "La notion de prophétie et la méthode apologétique dans le *Contra Sarracenos* de Pierre le Vénérable," *Studia monastica* 17 (1975): 257–82.

119. *Contra sectam Saracenorum*, 98, ed. Glei, 160: "Haec verba prophetica fuerunt, non de praesenti vel futuro tempore, sed de praeterito, quae propter hoc maxime se probant esse prophetica, quia, ut quidam magnus de nostris ait: 'De illo tempore / locutus est homo, quando non erat homo'" (with reference yet again to Gregory the Great, this time *Homilia*, 1.14).

120. *Contra sectam Saracenorum*, 99, ed. Glei, 160–62.

121. *Contra sectam Saracenorum*, 120–22, ed. Glei, 186–89.

the great prophets of God who made predictions about universal truths that applied to all people. That honor, Peter insisted, belonged instead to John the Baptist, who foretold the salvation of all through the coming of Christ.[122] After the time of Jesus, all prophets, even the apostles, could only make pronouncements about particular events relevant to certain individuals. The final words of the treatise summed up the argument of its second book. In the sense of the term defined by the abbot of Cluny, "Muhammad is therefore not a prophet" (*Non est igitur propheta*).[123]

Peter the Venerable's death on Christmas Day in 1156 brought to a close his unprecedented enterprise to call Muslims to the saving grace of Christ through a reasoned refutation of Muhammed's prophetic claims grounded in the study of Islamic religious texts translated into Latin. For the last two decades of his life Peter had distributed his contempt toward unbelievers with an outpouring of polemical treatises. Writing to his abbot in 1155, Peter of Poitiers praised him as "the only one in our time who has butchered with the sword of the divine word the three worst enemies of Christianity, namely the Jews, the heretics, and the Saracens."[124] This claim has misled some scholars into thinking that this was Peter's plan all along. As we have seen, however, the abbot of Cluny had no intention of writing a treatise against Islam after the completion of the Toledan Collection in 1143. It was only in 1156—after the Second Crusade had unmasked the folly of armed combat against the forces of Islam and the death of Bernard of Clairvaux had robbed Christendom of its most eloquent champion—that Peter returned to his Muslim project in the hope that reason (*ratio*) would succeed where weapons had failed. With a refutation of Muslim beliefs grounded in his defense of the authenticity of Christian scriptures and his denial of the prophetic power of Muhammed, the abbot of Cluny urged his adversaries to recognize the errors of their pernicious religion and fly to the grace of baptism, where the promise of true salvation awaited them.

While Peter the Venerable's early treatises against heresy and Judaism had ancient antecedents in the traditions of early Christian literature, his interest in Islam set him apart from his contemporaries in the Latin West. Muslims did not fit easily into the categories of medieval polemics honed by Christian intellectuals during the early Middle Ages, primarily because they had never been a direct threat to western Europeans and very little was known

---

122. *Contra sectam Saracenorum*, 137, ed. Glei, 206.

123. *Contra sectam Saracenorum*, 154, ed. Glei, 224.

124. Peter of Poitiers, *Epistola*, ed. Glei, 228.

about their religion. While the Christian tradition had nourished robust genres of refutation against the beliefs of heretics and Jews, Peter's treatise *Against the Sect of the Saracens*, informed by the Toledan Collection, was the first of its kind, a formal censure of Muslim beliefs that brought to bear the most important intellectual tool of the early twelfth century: reason. Given the widespread application of reason in debates with unbelievers in the early twelfth century, it is sensible to assume that Christian intellectuals beyond the walls of Cluny influenced Peter's decision to employ this mode of argument in his polemical foray against Islam. But despite the currency of reason in contemporary polemical literature, especially in works against the Jews, the final chapter of this book argues that the venerable abbot found his inspiration for his Muslim policy much closer to home, in the hagiographical traditions of his saintly predecessor Maiolus of Cluny.

CHAPTER 4

Hagiography and the Muslim Policy of Peter the Venerable

Almost every scholar who has lent his or her attention to Peter the Venerable's Muslim enterprise has assumed that the abbot of Cluny seized upon the idea of translating the Qur'an and other Islamic writings while on his journey to Spain in 1142–43.[1] This is an appealing explanation for many reasons. The abbot's translation project required access to Muslim texts in Arabic, which were an exceedingly rare commodity north of the Pyrenees but common enough on the Iberian Peninsula. Moreover, it also required translators for hire who could render Arabic texts quickly and proficiently into Latin. Specialists of this kind were almost unknown in early twelfth-century Europe, but they were thick on the ground in Spain; Peter hired no fewer than three such individuals on his trip to the court of Alphonso VII.[2] While it is clear that the abbot of Cluny was able

---

1. See, for example, James Kritzeck, *Peter the Venerable and Islam* (Princeton, NJ: Princeton University Press, 1964), 14, where he characterizes the project as "probably . . . unpremeditated" and "conceived, planned, and sponsored" while on the journey to Spain. Richard Southern, *The Making of the Middle Ages* (New Haven, CT: Yale University Press, 1953), 39, is more circumspect on this question: "whether on a sudden impulse or in pursuit of a long conceived plan we cannot tell." Charles Bishko considered the question open, but was inclined to believe that the translation enterprise was a byproduct of Peter's visit. See Bishko, "Peter the Venerable's Journey to Spain," in *Petrus Venerabilis 1156–1956: Studies and Texts Commemorating the Eighth Centenary of His Death*, ed. Giles Constable and James Kritzeck (Rome: Herder, 1956), 164.

2. On the translators of the Toledan Collection, see chapter 3 of the present volume.

to gather the materials for his translation project and to find bilingual translators skilled in the relevant languages during his stay in Spain, the genesis of the Toledan Collection does not provide the context to explain why Peter elected to compose his treatise *Against the Sect of the Saracens* over a decade later and why, in contrast to his earlier polemical writings against heretics and Jews, he chose to address a Muslim audience directly in this particular work.

The gulf of time separating the translation of the Toledan Collection in 1142–43 and the composition of Peter the Venerable's treatise against Islam in 1156 seems in hindsight relatively short, but from the perspective of the abbot of Cluny the decade separating his return from Spain and the resumption of his Muslim project was a long and bitter season fraught with disappointment and frustration. It had begun with such promise in 1145 with the calling of the Second Crusade, which Peter hailed as a portentous reenactment of biblical history in the present age (*Renouantur iam nostro tempore antiqua saecula*).[3] Dispatched by the Lord to destroy the Muslims, the Capetian king Louis VII was both a new Moses, who had laid low the Amorrhites and their subject peoples, and a new Joshua, who had cast down the Canaanites with innumerable unbelievers at the command of God. But by 1149 the failure of the Second Crusade to shore up the Latin kingdoms of the East against the renewed assault of the Muslims had dashed the hopes of many western Europeans, including the abbot of Cluny. Christian prelates were unable to mask their despair that the loss of life incurred during this futile expedition had "withered the flower of the whole of Gaul and Germany."[4] Many blamed these misfortunes on the perfidy of their Greek allies, on the sins of the crusaders, or on the agency of the devil himself.[5] Whatever the cause, the legacy of disappointment in the aftermath of the crusade haunted its participants and supporters alike. "The hearts of the princes have become weak," Bernard of Clairvaux lamented to Peter in 1150. "They carry a sword

---

3. For what follows, see Peter the Venerable, *Epistola*, 130 (*ad Ludovicum Francorum regem*), in *The Letters of Peter the Venerable*, ed. Giles Constable (Cambridge, MA: Harvard University Press, 1967), 1:327–30, and 2:185, where it is dated 1146 (probably after Easter).

4. Peter the Venerable, *Epistola*, 162 (*ad regum Siciliae*), ed. Constable, 1:395: "Ut enim iuxta quod in mente mea uideo loquar, si necesse esset quantum ad monachum pertinere potest, non recusarem mori, si mortem tantorum, tam nobilium, immo pene totius Galliae et Germaniae miserabili fraude extinctum florem, iustitia dei per aliquem suorum dignaretur ulcisci." See also 2:206–7, where Constable dates the letter to 1150.

5. For contemporary responses to the crusade's failure, see Giles Constable, "The Second Crusade as Seen by Contemporaries," *Traditio* 9 (1952): 213–9; reprinted and selectively updated in Giles Constable, *Crusaders and Crusading in the Twelfth Century* (Burlington, VT: Ashgate, 2009), 281–92.

without a purpose; it is wrapped in the skins of dead animals and consigned to rust."[6]

It was the inability of the crusading armies of France and Germany to wage successful campaigns against the hosts of Islam during the Second Crusade that inspired Peter the Venerable to return to his Muslim project with renewed purpose. In his late treatise *Against the Sect of the Saracens* he attempted to win the hearts of his adversaries "not with force, but with reason" and to invite them to salvation "not the kind that ends after this brief life, but the kind that remains forever in eternal life."[7] As we saw in chapter 3, Peter did not adopt this pastoral stance toward the Muslims because he was opposed to the violent action of Christian warriors against the enemies of the Lord.[8] Rather, in the aftermath of the disastrous expedition, words were the last weapons that remained against the perceived threat of Islam now that the vanquished crusaders had abandoned their swords to rust.

Historians have long recognized the novelty of Peter the Venerable's undertaking, but they have never pursued the question of the influences that may have informed his disposition toward Islam in this, his final work. It is the contention of this chapter that stories about the abbot's tenth-century predecessor Maiolus of Cluny played an influential role in the formation of Peter's Muslim policy in those dark days following the Second Crusade. Maiolus provided both an example of a reasoned refutation of the prophetic claims of Muhammed addressed directly to a Muslim audience and also—notably—a testimony of its success. As chapter 2 has shown, every hagiographer who celebrated the virtues of Maiolus recounted his abduction by the Muslims of La Garde-Freinet. What is most compelling about these stories from Peter's perspective in the aftermath of the Second Crusade was that one of them—the account composed around 1010 by Syrus of Cluny (BHL 5177/79)—depicted Maiolus debating successfully with his captors concerning matters of faith.[9] If this story exercised an influence on Peter's method of refuting Muslim beliefs in his treatise *Against the Sect of the Saracens*,

---

6. Bernard of Clairvaux, *Epistola*, 521, ed. Jean Leclercq, in *Sancti Bernardi Opera* (Rome: Editiones Cistercienses, 1977), 8:483: "Intepuerunt corda principum; sine causa gladium portant: pellibus mortuorum animalium reconditus est, rubigini consecratus."

7. Peter the Venerable, *Contra sectam Saracenorum*, 24, ed. Reinhold Glei, in *Petrus Venerabilis, Schriften zum Islam* (Altenberge, Germany: CIS Verlag, 1985), 64: "Aggredior inquam vos, non, ut nostri saepe faciunt, armis sed verbis, non vi sed ratione, non odio sed amore." See also *Contra sectam Saracenorum*, 27, ed. Glei, 66: "Invito vos ad salutem, non quae transit, sed quae permanet, non quae finitur cum vita brevi, sed quae permanet in vitam aeternam."

8. On Peter's advocacy of the Second Crusade and participation in plans for another crusade project in 1150, see chapter 3 of the present volume.

9. See chapter 2 of the present volume.

then the abbot's approach in this work differed so markedly from his refutations of the Petrobrusian heresy and Judaism because it was informed not by a centuries-old tradition of polemical literature but by a pastoral model preserved in an account of the life of his saintly predecessor Maiolus.

Peter the Venerable lived in an age, however, when many Christian prelates applied their energy with ever greater urgency to the problem of unbelievers in their midst. Some of the most luminous thinkers of this period, from Peter Damian and Anselm of Bec to Peter Alfonsi and Peter Abelard, composed treatises that exalted the truth of Christianity at the expense of rival systems of belief. What measure of influence did their writings have on Peter's approach to Islam? This question requires considerable care to unravel. While the abbot of Cluny was clearly not alone among late eleventh- and early twelfth-century intellectuals in his application of reason in polemical discourse with non-Christians, he stood out among them as the only prelate of his time to employ what John Van Engen has called "a reasoning apparatus" in a treatise directed specifically at a Muslim audience.[10] Moreover, in his writings against Islam, Peter made no allusion to the formative influence of any of his contemporaries.[11] The novelty of his approach and his lack of reference to the authority of the intellectual currents of his own time, as they were expressed in the polemical writings of other Christian thinkers, compel us to look elsewhere for the abbot's inspiration.

Medieval Arab-Christian polemic against Islam cannot be ruled out as an influence on the formulation of Peter the Venerable's Muslim policy. Most of the Arabic texts translated for the Toledan Collection were devotional and historical works of the Muslim tradition, but one—*The Apology of al-Kindi*—was a lengthy censure of the religious claims of Islam couched as an epistolary exchange between a Muslim and a Christian. Originally written in Arabic in the ninth or tenth century, this text was representative of polemical works in circulation in the medieval Islamic world, and its author was well versed in making arguments based on evidence found in Muslim and Christian scriptures. In its twelfth-century Latin translation, *The Apology of al-Kindi* exposed Peter the Venerable to the traditions of Arab-Christian criticism of Islam. It is clear that the abbot of Cluny knew this work well, for he made several references to it in his treatises against the Jews and the Muslims. Yet despite Peter's

---

10. John Van Engen, "The Twelfth Century: Reading, Reason, and Revolt in a World of Custom," in *European Transformations: The Long Twelfth Century*, ed. Thomas F. X. Noble and John Van Engen (Notre Dame, IN: University of Notre Dame Press, 2012), 18.

11. Peter did invoke the inspiration of the church fathers, who could not remain silent in the face of heretical teachings, but he did not call upon the authority of anyone from his own day. See Peter the Venerable, *Contra sectam Saracenorum*, prologue 1–9, ed. Glei, 30–44.

familiarity with this text and the polemical tradition that it represented, the *Apology of al-Kindi* does not seem to have inspired the abbot of Cluny to adopt the pastoral approach toward his Muslim audience that characterizes his treatise *Against the Sect of the Saracens*. Rather, it is clear that Peter employed the *Apology* primarily as an authority on the Muslim religion, which he mined with great enthusiasm to find raw material to forward his arguments against Islam. In short, the *Apology* was more important as a source of information than as a model for a polemical methodology. As we will see, Peter's approach in his treatise against Islam had much more in common with Syrus's account of Maiolus's debate with his Muslim captors than it did with any of the Eastern or Western traditions of Christian polemic known at twelfth-century Cluny.

The influence of this hagiographical vignette on Peter the Venerable's direct address to a Muslim audience rests on the claim that the abbot of Cluny was familiar with Syrus's account of Maiolus's dispute with his captors. This claim is not difficult to make. Peter's many writings speak to his familiarity with a wide range of saints' lives. The abbot took a special interest in the tales told about his abbatial predecessors and even ordered the composition of new accounts of the virtuous lives of Odo and Maiolus. Moreover, by the twelfth century, Maiolus was a towering figure in the Cluniac imagination, one whose sanctity the monks celebrated with great solemnity on his feast day. Peter himself attested to the abundance of stories that recounted the miracles he performed on behalf of the faithful. The prominence of the cult of Maiolus at Cluny and Peter's familiarity with the literary traditions that supported it strengthen the argument that he owed his method of direct address to a Muslim audience to the depiction of Maiolus challenging the authority of Muhammed that he had read in Syrus's *Life of Maiolus*.

✒ Reasoning with Unbelievers in the Decades around 1100

Peter the Venerable was not alone in his application of reason in polemical discourse with unbelievers in the early twelfth century. Several of the most renowned Christian thinkers of his generation had already applied the same intellectual approach in their confrontations with the most tenacious opponents of Christianity, the Jews.[12] Polemics against Judaism had a long his-

---

12. For a useful overview of reason and the authority of scripture as "les deux axes fondamentaux de la méthode de polémique contre les juifs," see Gilbert Dahan, *Les intellectuels chrétiens et les juifs au moyen âge* (Paris: Éditions du Cerf, 1990), 423–71; quotation at 470.

tory in the early Middle Ages.[13] For centuries Christian authors had criticized the Jews for their obstinate loyalty to the literal sense of the Old Testament, which blinded them to the spiritual truth of the Hebrew prophets whose messianic proclamations found their fulfillment in the coming of Jesus Christ. Despite these errors Christians believed that the Jews played an important role in salvation history as witnesses to the crucifixion of Christ and the guarantors of the antiquity of the claims made by their prophets about the significance of his death. Augustine of Hippo (d. 430) was the leading proponent of this tradition, which became known as the "Doctrine of Jewish Witness."[14] While the destruction of the Second Temple in 70 CE by the Romans and the subsequent exile of the Hebrews from the Holy Land were divine punishments for the role of the Jews in Christ's death, Augustine argued forcefully that they were nonetheless "marked by God"—that is, granted special protection by their maker so that they could play their role in the fulfillment of his divine plan, just as God had protected the murderous Cain to advance his own grander purpose.[15] Although they were stubborn in their disbelief and wretched in their exile, the Jews were still purposeful in Christian salvation history and therefore should not be destroyed, a view foretold and affirmed in the ancient words of the Psalmist: "Slay them not lest at any time they forget your law; scatter them in your might" (Ps. 58:12).[16]

The influence of Augustine's writings in the early Middle Ages resulted in the widespread adoption of his teaching about the place of the Jews in salvation history throughout western Europe, but their standing as "those marked by God" did not protect them from polemical attacks.[17] Generation

---

13. The classic work on the topic remains Bernhard Blumenkranz, *Juifs et chrétiens dans le monde occidental, 430–1096* (Paris: Peeters, 1960). See also Bat-Sheva Albert, "*Adversus Iudaeos* in the Carolingian Empire," in *Contra Iudaeos: Ancient and Medieval Polemics between Christians and Jews*, ed. Ora Limor and Guy G. Stroumsa (Tübingen, Germany: J. C. B. Mohr, 1996), 119–42.

14. See Jeremy Cohen, "Slay Them Not: Augustine and the Jews in Modern Scholarship," *Medieval Encounters* 4 (1998): 78–92; Jeremy Cohen, *Living Letters of the Law: Ideas of the Jew in Medieval Christianity* (Berkeley: University of California Press, 1999), 19–71; and Paula Frederiksen, *Augustine and the Jews: A Christian Defense of Jews and Judaism*, 2nd ed. (New Haven, CT: Yale University Press, 2010).

15. Augustine, *Contra Faustum*, 13.10, ed. Joseph Zycha, CSEL 25:389.

16. Augustine, *De civitate Dei*, 18.46, ed. Bernard Dombart and Alphonse Kalb, CCSL 48:644: "Deus meus demonstrauit mihi in inimicis meis, ne occideris eos, ne quando obliuiscantur legem tuam; disperge eos in uirtute tua." Augustine's reading of Psalm 59:12 differs from the Vulgate translations of the Septuagint and the Hebrew. Jerome summarizes his own encounters with alternative readings of this psalm in *Epistola* 106.33, ed. Isidore Hilberg, in *Sancti Eusebii Hieronymi Epistolae*, CSEL 55:263–64.

17. On the reception of Augustine's work in the early Middle Ages, see Conrad Leyser, "Augustine in the Latin West, 430–ca. 900," in *A Companion to Augustine*, ed. Mark Vessey (Oxford: Wiley-Blackwell, 2012), 450–64.

after generation, Christian authors marshaled the same lists of biblical authorities in the service of the same argument: the Old Testament, when read spiritually rather than literally, affirmed the true nature of the Trinity and foretold the coming of Christ. It was only in the last decades of the eleventh century that the conceptual armature of Christian polemics against unbelievers underwent an intellectual shift with the introduction of reason (ratio) to a tradition of dispute that had relied for centuries solely on the authority of scripture.

Peter Damian (c. 1007–72) provides the earliest known example of the application of reason to polemical debates with non-Christians in the Latin tradition.[18] The cardinal-bishop of Ostia was no stranger to controversy. In 1049 he addressed his *Book of Gomorrah* (*Liber Gomorrhianus*), a withering critique of homosexual practices among the secular clergy, to Pope Leo IX and argued strongly for the deposition of priests who had polluted their office in this way.[19] He was, however, by his own account a very reluctant polemicist.[20] Nevertheless, around 1040, Damian composed a treatise against the Jews at the request of an Egyptian bishop named Honestus who had written to enlist his aid in defending the Christian faith from the arguments of a local Jewish community.[21] The content of this treatise differs little from the enduring clichés of the early medieval *adversus Iudaeos* tradition: Damian built the case for the reality of the Trinity and the fulfillment of Old Testament prophecy in Christ through the accumulation of scriptural passages that supported his truth claims. But, in

---

18. On the life and works of Peter Damian, see William McCready, *Odiosa Sanctitas: St. Peter Damian, Simony, and Reform* (Toronto: PIMS, 2011). The exact date of his death is contested; see John Howe, "Did St. Peter Damian Die in 1073? A New Perspective on His Final Days," *Analecta Bollandiana* 128 (2010): 67–86.

19. Peter Damian, *Liber Gomorrhianus*, in PL 145, cols. 159–90. Insightful works amid a vast secondary literature on this treatise include Conrad Leyser, "Cities of the Plain: The Rhetoric of Sodomy in Peter Damian's *Book of Gomorrah*," *Romanic Review* 86 (1995): 191–211; and Glenn W. Olsen, *Of Sodomites, Effeminates, Hermaphrodites and Androgynes: Sodomy in the Age of Peter Damian* (Toronto: PIMS, 2011).

20. The fundamental study by David Berger has not been superceded; see Berger, "St. Peter Damian: His Attitude toward the Jews and the Old Testament," *Yavneh Review* 4 (1965): 80–112, reprinted in David Berger, *Persecution, Polemic and Dialogue: Essays in Jewish-Christian Relations* (Boston: Academic Studies Press, 2010), 261–88.

21. Peter Damian, *Epistola 1*, in *Die Briefe des Petrus Damiani*, ed. Kurt Reindel, MGH Die Briefe der deutschen Kaiserzeit (Munich, 1983), 1:63–102. For useful discussions of this text, see Bernhard Blumenkranz, *Les auteurs chrétiens latins du moyen âge sur les juifs et le judaïsme* (Paris: Peeters, 1963), 265–72; and Berger, "St. Peter Damian."

addition to this, he also made an appeal to reason that was unprecedented in any genre of medieval interfaith polemic.[22]

For their role in the murder of Jesus Christ, Peter Damian argued that God had punished the Jews with their ongoing exile, one that would surely last until the end of time.[23] Since he could marshal no biblical texts to support this claim directly, Peter implored the Jews to consider the litany of terrible crimes that they had committed in the past, as recorded in the Old Testament, and the punishments meted out by God on those occasions: the murmuring of the Israelites after their emancipation from Egypt earned them a forty-year exile in the harsh wilderness (Num. 14:26–35), while their adoption of the idolatrous rites of the god Ba'al at the instigation of Moabite women angered God to such a degree that he brought down a plague that killed thousands of them (Num. 25:1–9). The very worst example of God's indignation with the Jews came from the testimony of the prophet Zachariah, who foretold the return of God's favor to Jerusalem and the cities of Judah after suffering his displeasure for a full seventy years (Zach. 1:1–17). In light of these examples, Damian then urged the Jews to use reason to deduce what atrocity they had committed that had earned them their millennium-long wretchedness and concluded for them that it was their role in the death of Christ, a crime that transcended all other crimes, "the deepest abyss of your wickedness."[24]

A few decades after Peter Damian's foray into religious polemics, Archbishop Anselm of Canterbury (c. 1033–1109) marshaled the forces of reason in defense of the Christian faith in *Why God Became Man* (*Cur Deus Homo*), which he completed in the 1090s.[25] The purpose of this treatise was to

---

22. Peter Damian, *Epistola* 1, ed. Reindel, 99: "[L]ibet adhuc postpositis scilicet prophetarum exemplis sola tecum ratiocinatione contendere, et unam tecum in calce huius opusculi quaestiunculam breviter agitare." See also the prologue where Peter promises to "decertantium tibi Iudaeorum ora rationabilibus argumentis obstruere" (Ibid., 65).

23. For what follows, see Peter Damian, *Epistola* 1, ed. Reindel, 99–101.

24. Peter Damian, *Epistola* 1, ed. Reindel, 101: "Quae est ergo haec vestra tam insanabilis culpa? Unde vobis tam inremediabilis poena? Unde, inquam, nisi quia Christum Dei Filium occidistis, et post peractum facinus ad fontem vitae recurrere noluistis? Hoc enim profundissimum vestrae iniquitatis baratrum omnium flagitiorum transcendit modum, omnium superat immanitatem criminum."

25. Anselm of Canterbury, *Cur Deus Homo*, in *Sancti Anselmi Cantuariensis archiepiscopi opera omnia*, ed. Franciscus Salesius Schmitt (Rome: n.p., 1946), 2:37–133. On the career and works of Anselm, Richard W. Southern, *Saint Anselm: A Portrait in a Landscape* (Cambridge: Cambridge University Press, 1990), remains unsurpassed. For the influence of Anselm and his circle on the rise of Christian disputation in twelfth-century scholastic thought, see Alex J. Novikoff, "Anselm, Dialogue, and the Rise of Scholastic Disputation," *Speculum* 86 (2011): 387–418.

argue that the salvation of humankind depended entirely on the Incarnation of Christ. Why was it necessary for God to become a man, some people had asked, when he could have chosen another intermediary to do his bidding or simply exercised his omnipotent will to save the human race? To answer these inquiries, Anselm attempted to prove by arguing from reason alone that even if Christ was removed from consideration, as though no trace of him had ever existed, it is impossible for any person to be saved without him.[26] The treatise laid out the problem as follows: Through their inability to obey the will of God, human beings forfeited the condition of eternal blessedness for which they were created and they are powerless to return themselves to their blessed state without help. The solution to this problem was the Incarnation. Only an offering of obedience greater than the sum of all of the past offenses of humankind could restore the harmony lost by their willful disobedience. Human beings are not capable of such an offering. It is possible for God, however, but since the debt belonged to mortals, it was the obligation of a human being to make satisfaction for it. Therefore, Anselm argued, the act of obedience that would restore humankind to its blessedness could only be accomplished by one who is both human and God. For this reason, it was necessary for God to become a man in the person of Jesus Christ in order to redeem the human race.

Scholars have argued at great length about the identity of those con-temporaries of Anselm who doubted the necessity of the Incarnation. The vagueness of his terminology has played no small part in the difficulty of reconstructing the audience of *Why God Became Man*. Throughout the trea-tise, Anselm called his detractors "unbelievers" (*infideles*). At the end of the work, however, the archbishop's student Boso, who plays the role of his in-terlocutor throughout the treatise, refers directly to Jews and pagans when he congratulates the archbishop on the successful completion of his argu-ment: "For so well do you prove that God did, out of necessity, become a man, that even if the few things which you have taken from our books—such as what you have stated concerning the three persons of God and concerning Adam—were to be removed, you would satisfy not only the Jews but also the pagans with rational argument alone."[27] On the basis of this passage, some

---

26. Anselm, *Cur Deus Homo*, preface, ed. Schmitt, 2:42.

27. Anselm, *Cur Deus Homo*, 2.22, ed. Schmitt, 2:133: "Cum enim sic probes deum fieri homi-nem ex necessitate, ut etiam si removeantur pauca quae de nostris libris posuisti, ut quod de tribus dei personis et de ADAM tetigisti, non solum Iudaeis sed etiam paganis sola ratione satisfacias." Translation in Cohen, *Living Letters of the Law*, 175.

historians have interpreted *Why God Became Man* as a response to Jewish criticism of the Christian doctrine of the Incarnation.[28] Anselm's close association at this time with his friend and former pupil Gilbert Crispin, monk of Bec and abbot of Westminster, lends weight to this argument, for Gilbert was an active participant in religious polemic in the 1090s, writing two anti-Jewish treatises at the same time that Anselm was preparing *Why God Became Man*.[29]

Other scholars have gone even further, however, to suggest that the pagans (*pagani*) mentioned in Anselm's treatise alluded to Muslims and that the archbishop was attempting to refute Islamic polemics against the Christian faith.[30] But, in fact, neither of these religious constituencies—Jews or Muslims—was the most plausible audience of *Why God Became Man*. Anselm's "unbelievers" were most likely fellow Christians whose reckless application of reason to the teachings of the Church had raised doubts in their minds about the necessity of the Incarnation.[31] In the opening chapters of the treatise, Anselm characterized his opponents as "those who do not wish to

---

28. See, for example, Southern, *Saint Anselm*, 198–202; and Cohen, *Living Letters of the Law*, 167–79. Cf. Amos Funkenstein, *Perceptions of Jewish History* (Berkeley: University of California Press, 1993), 178, who notes with some caution that Anselm's *Cur Deus Homo* "though arguably not written for immediate polemical purposes, influenced the polemical literature directly and indirectly."

29. Anna Sapir Abulafia, "An Attempt by Gilbert Crispin, Abbot of Westminster, at Rational Argument in the Jewish-Christian Debate," *Studia Monastica* 26 (1984): 55–74; reprinted in Anna Sapir Abulafia, *Christians and Jews in Dispute: Disputational Literature and the Rise of Anti-Judaism in the West (c. 1000–1150)* (Aldershot, England: Variorum, 1998), no. 8. Gilbert's *Disputatio Iudei et Christiani* (which was dedicated to Anselm) and its continuation have been edited by Abulafia and G. R. Evans in *The Works of Gilbert of Crispin, Abbot of Westminster* (London: Oxford University Press, 1986), 8–61.

30. See, for example, René Roques, "Les *Pagani* dans le *Cur Deus Homo* de Saint Anselm," *Miscellanea Mediaevalia* 2 (1963): 192–206, and reiterated in the introduction to his edition of *Cur Deus Homo*; see Anselm of Canterbury, *Pourquoi Dieu s'est fait homme*, ed. René Roques, SC 91:65–74. See also Julia Gauss, "Anselmus von Canterbury zur Begegnung und Auseinandersetzung der Religionen," *Saeculum* 17 (1966): 277–363; and Julia Gauss, "Die Auseinandersetzung mit Judentum und Islam bei Anselm," in *Die Wirkungsgeschichte Anselms von Canterbury*, ed. Helmut Kohlenberger (Frankfurt am Main: Minerva, 1975), 2:101–9.

31. Anna Sapir Abulafia, "St. Anselm and Those outside the Church," in *Faith and Unity: Christian Political Experience*, ed. David Loades and Katherine Walsh, Studies in Church History 6 (Oxford: Ecclesiastical History Society, 1990), 11–37, reprinted in Abulafia, *Christians and Jews in Dispute*, no. 4. Abulafia, "St. Anselm and Those outside the Church," 31, does not deny the possibility, however, that "Jewish rejection of Christianity may well have stimulated the composition of *Cur Deus Homo*" but maintains that "the *infideles* are not specifically Jews and pagans, and that the *Cur Deus Homo* was not, in the first instance, addressed to them." For a response to Abulafia's position vis-à-vis Anselm and the Jews, see Cohen, *Living Letters of the Law*, 176–79, which points out some inconsistencies in Abulafia's argument and argues that Anselm had in mind "a contrived, hermeneutically crafted Jew" when writing *Cur Deus Homo* (178).

approach the faith without recourse to reason," a qualification that would apply to neither Jews nor Muslims.[32] Moreover, the treatise takes for granted that its readers hold in common the belief that human beings bear the burden of original sin, a supposition that would find no support among Jews or Muslims.[33] It is therefore much more likely that Anselm composed his treatise on the necessity of the Incarnation in response to doubts raised by fellow Christians and not as a work of polemic directed against Jews or Muslims.

Why God Became Man is best understood as a work of theology addressed to Christians who were teetering on the brink of heresy. The culprit in this case was probably a wandering teacher named Roscelin of Compiègne, who was active in northern France in the late 1080s and early 1090s.[34] This dangerous thinker first came to Anselm's attention in 1089. According to Roscelin, the application of reason to the doctrine of the Trinity raised doubts about the traditional teaching of the equality and coexistence of the three persons who comprised it. By his reckless logic, the Father, the Son, and the Holy Spirit were either three separate gods or one indivisible god who was incarnate in Christ. To make matters worse, Roscelin falsely claimed that Anselm had endorsed his teachings on the Trinity. In the early 1090s, the abbot of Bec denied this association and refuted the heretic's teachings in a short treatise known as *A Letter Concerning the Incarnation of the Word* (*Epistola de Incarnatione Verbi*), which argued that only one person of the Trinity could ever become incarnate and moreover that person was necessarily the Son.[35] The tenacity of the doubts raised by the teachings of Roscelin and the threat to the faith posed by the application of reason to Christian doctrine by charismatic teachers were the issues foremost in Anselm's mind when he composed *Why God Became Man* later that same decade.

The reasoning apparatus employed by Damian and Anselm to refute the doubts raised by the stubborn literalism of the Jews and the dark calculus of Christian heretics was also brought to bear against the errors of the Muslims. In the first decade of the 1100s, an educated Jew from Spain named Moses Sefardi converted to Christianity, changed his name to Peter Alfonsi, and composed a treatise to justify his decision to abandon Judaism (ca.

---

32. Anselm, *Cur Deus Homo*, 1.1, ed. Schmitt, 2:47: "Quod petunt, non ut per rationem ad fidem accedant."

33. Abulafia, "Saint Anselm and Those outside the Church," 31.

34. For what follows, see Southern, *Saint Anselm*, 175–81.

35. Anselm of Canterbury, *Epistola de incarnatione verbi*, in *Sancti Anselmi Cantuariensis archiepiscopi opera omnia*, ed. Schmitt, 2:3–35. Southern, *Saint Anselm*, 179, describes this treatise as "laboriously hammered out over a period of three or four years."

1110).[36] He couched his *Dialogue Against the Jews* (*Dialogus contra Judaeos*) as a conversation between his former Jewish self (Moses) and his new Christian persona (Peter).[37] This treatise was a work of Christian apology, written in answer to Jewish critics who had accused Alfonsi of abandoning the law of their God, misconstruing the message of God's prophets, and seeking worldly honor through his conversion because he understood that Christians were more powerful than Jews.[38] Like other Christian intellectuals of the early twelfth century, Alfonsi believed that he could demonstrate the truth value of Christianity through the application of reason and the authority of sacred scripture: "I have set down all the objections of any adversary of the Christian law and, having set them down, have destroyed them with reason and authority according to my understanding."[39] At the end of the *Dialogue* Alfonsi's Jewish alter ego conceded his defeat in the following terms: "God gave a great deal of his wisdom to you and illuminated you with a great reasoning power that I am unable to vanquish. Instead you have confounded my objections with reason."[40]

While it was becoming increasingly common for Christian thinkers to evoke reason in their debates with Jews and heretics in the decades around 1100, Alfonsi's religious and cultural background—particularly his proficiency in Hebrew and Arabic and his familiarity with both the Talmud and the Qur'an—set his *Dialogue* apart from other anti-Jewish polemics of his time in several important ways. Alfonsi broke with the conventions of the *adversus Judaeos* tradition by claiming that the Jews had committed deicide—that is, they had willfully murdered God incarnated in the person of Jesus Christ. Throughout the early Middle Ages, from Augustine to Anselm, Christian polemicists had always given the Jews the benefit of the doubt that they were

36. On the life and works of Peter Alfonsi, see John V. Tolan, *Petrus Alfonsi and His Medieval Readers* (Gainesville: University Press of Florida, 1993); and John V. Tolan, "Petrus Alfonsi," in CMR 3:356–62. In a chapter already running rampant with Peters, I will for the sake of clarity refer to Peter Alfonsi as Alfonsi in the text.

37. Peter Alfonsi, *Dialogus contra Iudaeos*, ed. Klaus-Peter Mieth and trans. Esperanza Ducay as *Pedro Alfonso de Huesca, Diálogo contra los Judíos* (Huesca: Instituto de Estudios Altoaragoneses, 1996); trans. Irven M. Resnick as *Petrus Alfonsi, Dialogue Against the Jews* (Washington, DC: Catholic University of America Press, 2006).

38. Alfonsi, *Dialogus contra Iudaeos*, prologue, ed. Mieth, 6–7.

39. Alfonsi, *Dialogus contra Iudaeos*, prologue, ed. Mieth, 7: "Ad ultimum etiam omnes cuiuslibet Christiane legis adversarii obiectiones posui positasque pro meo sapere cum ratione et auctoritate destruxi." Translation in Resnick, *Petrus Alfonsi*, 41.

40. Alfonsi, *Dialogus contra Iudaeos*, 12, ed. Mieth, 193: "Multum certe suae tibi deus dedit sapientiae et te magna illustravit ratione, quem vincere nequeo, immo tu obiectiones meas confutasti ratione." Translation in Resnick, *Petrus Alfonsi*, 273.

ignorant of the divinity of Christ when they plotted his death.[41] Anselm weighed this issue with the gravity it deserved: "For no member of the human race would ever wish to kill God, at least no one would knowingly wish it, and therefore those who killed him unknowingly did not fall headlong into that infinite sin with which no other sins can be compared."[42] Alfonsi departed from this view in his accusation that a handful of Jewish rabbis had in fact recognized Jesus as the Messiah, but killed him out of envy "because they were afraid of losing their rank and reputation on account of Him."[43] The destruction of the Temple in 70 CE and the subsequent diaspora of the Jews throughout the Mediterranean world were their punishments for this unspeakable crime: "For the envy and malice of the Jews was the cause of the death of Christ and the death of Christ was the cause of their captivity."[44] With the Temple in ruins, the Jews could no longer satisfy the precepts of the law of Moses. As a result, they were exiles not only from the Promised Land but also from God.

In addition to laying the charge of deicide against the Jews, Alfonsi was also the first Christian polemicist to attack the authority of the tradition of rabbinical commentaries on the Bible known as the Talmud—in particular those stories in the Haggadah that depicted God as a corporeal being.[45] The Old Testament is replete with stories that refer to God in corporeal terms, beginning with the statement in Genesis 1:27 that he created human beings in his own image. Many Christian and Jewish thinkers interpreted such passages allegorically in the belief that any attribution of physical dimensions or characteristics to God was an insult to his divine majesty because it implied

---

41. For examples of this tradition, but with no reference to Alfonsi himself, see Jeremy Cohen, "The Jews as the Killers of Christ in the Latin Tradition, from Augustine to the Friars," *Traditio* 39 (1983): 1–27.

42. Anselm, *Cur Deus Homo*, 2.15, ed. Schmitt, 2:115: "Deum enim occidere nullus homo umquam scienter saltem velle posset, et ideo qui illum occiderunt ignoranter, non in illud infinitum peccatum, cui nulla alia comparari peccata possunt, proruerunt."

43. Alfonsi, *Dialogus contra Iudaeos*, 10, ed. Mieth, 163: "Sane sicut prediximus ex invidia hoc fecerunt, quia videlicet per eum dignitatem suam ac famam amittere timuerunt." Translation in Resnick, *Petrus Alfonsi*, 263.

44. Alfonsi, *Dialogus contra Iudaeos*, 2, ed. Mieth, 59: "Invidia quippe Iudeorum et malitia causa mortis Christi fuit mors autem Christi causa captivitatis." Translation in Resnick, *Petrus Alfonsi*, 107.

45. Peter the Venerable expressed comparable concerns a generation later in his treatise against the Jews; see chapter 3 of the present volume. There are many similiarities between the presentation of Talmudic material in the respective works of Alfonsi and the abbot of Cluny, but not enough to make a convincing case that Peter copied Alfonsi's *Dialogus* directly. For a summary of the evidence, see Yvonne Friedman's introduction to her edition of Peter's *Adversus Iudeorum inveteratam duritiem*, CCCM 58:xv, where she concludes, "The hypothesis that Peter the Venerable's source was Alphonsi's book leaves many legends unaccounted for."

a limitation to his omnipresence. The same interpretative strategy was probably true of most Jewish readings of the depiction of God in the Talmud,
but Alfonsi presented these stories at face value and took great offense at their
presumptions.[46] He brought to bear not only reason but also his knowledge of
natural science to refute the image of God presented in the Talmud. For
example, Alfonsi took issue with the Talmudic assertion that God dwelled
in the westernmost sky.[47] Deploying his expert knowledge of astronomy,
he disproved this dubious claim with a long discourse on the relativity of the
term *west* that took into account both the roundness of the earth and the
movement of the sun and stars around it. Alfonsi's criticisms of the Talmud
served a larger purpose in his polemical work. For him, these rabbinical
commentaries had usurped the role of the Hebrew scriptures in the Jewish
religion. The Jews of his time were no longer true adherents to the law of
Moses; instead, they were enslaved to the teachings of an absurd tradition
of biblical interpretation that had no claim to divine authority. This attack
on the Talmud inaugurated a new era of anti-Jewish polemic in the medieval West.

Alfonsi was also the first Christian intellectual of his generation to refute
the Muslim religion in Latin. In the fifth book of his *Dialogues*, Moses asked
Peter why he had chosen the faith of the Christians over the faith of the
Muslims.[48] As his Jewish alter ego explained, "you were always, as I said, associated with them and you were raised among them; you read [their]
books, and you understand the language."[49] Moreover, Moses continued,
the law of the Saracens was built upon "an unshakable foundation of reason" (*fundamentum rationis fundatam*). He then proceeded to characterize the
devotional practices and beliefs of the Muslims in favorable terms, drawn
with accuracy from his knowledge of the Qur'an: their attention to prayer
and the bodily ablutions that preceded it; their declamation that there is one
God and Muhammed is his prophet; their fasting during the month of
Ramadan; the pilgrimage to Mecca; their dietary restrictions; their practice
of polygamy and other aspects of their legal culture; and the promise of an

---

46. Early twelfth-century Jewish communities were divided in their opinions regarding the an-
thropomorphism of God. See chapter 3 of the present volume.

47. For what follows, see Alfonsi, *Dialogus contra Iudaeos*, 1, ed. Mieth, 15–26. On Alfonsi's knowledge of natural science, and particularly astronomy, see Tolan, *Petrus Alfonsi and His Medieval Readers*, 42–72.

48. Alfonsi, *Dialogus contra Iudaeos*, 5, ed. Mieth, 91–103.

49. Ibid., ed. Mieth, 91: "Semper enim, ut dixi, in eis conversatus et nutritus es, libros legisti,
linguam intelligis." Translation in Resnick, *Petrus Alfonsi*, 146.

afterlife in a sensual paradise for those who believe in God and in his prophet Muhammed.

Peter's response to Moses was not a formal condemnation of Islamic theology. He did not address their monotheism or their criticism of the Trinity but chose instead to slander the character and career of Muhammed and to condemn the pagan pedigree of Muslim devotional practices. Peter began with an indictment of the prophetic claims of Muhammed, who he argued was in league with Jews and Christian heretics in his deception of the Arab people. Popular stories about the prophet's miracles were not only trivial but also untrue because they were not attested in the Qur'an. After arguing that Muhammed was a fraud, Peter then attacked the Muslim rituals enumerated by Moses by drawing from the deep well of Hispano-Jewish writings about Muslims and in particular from the ninth-century *Apology of al-Kindi*, the Christian polemic against Islam couched as an exchange of letters between two members of the 'Abbasid court, which Alfonsi had read in the original Arabic.[50]

By couching his polemic as a dialogue rather than a monologue, Alfonsi was able to present Muslim beliefs on two separate registers.[51] In the voice of Moses the Jew, he offered a literal and somewhat sympathetic account of Islamic doctrine informed by his firsthand reading of the Qur'an. In the voice of Peter the Christian, he countered this view with a critique of the character of Muhammed and the tainted legacy of Muslim rituals. Alfonsi had a polemical purpose for presenting these two views of Islam in this way. As a Jew, the character of Moses was unable to present anything other than the most literal interpretation of the Muslim texts that he had read. His inability to read for spiritual or allegorical significance conformed to the stereotype of Jews as stubbornly literal readers that was prevalent in early medieval polemical literature. The Christian readers of Alfonsi's *Dialogue* would have identified strongly with the character of Peter, who systematically defaced the image of Islam presented by his Jewish counterpart with arguments grounded both in reason and in the presumption that Christianity was the superior faith. By making the case against Islam in a dialogue couched in two distinct voices—one literal and informative, the

---

50. On Alfonsi's sources for his criticism of Islamic practices see, in particular, Bernard Septimus, "Petrus Alfonsi on the Cult at Mecca," *Speculum* 56 (1981): 517–33.

51. For what follows, I am indebted to the perceptive reading of Alfonsi's *Dialogus* in Leor Halevi, "*Lex Mahometi*: Carnal and Spiritual Representations of Islamic Law and Ritual in a Twelfth-Century Dialogue by a Jewish Convert to Christianity," in *The Islamic Scholarly Tradition: Studies in History, Law, and Thought in Honor of Professor Michael Allan Cook*, ed. Asad Q. Ahmed, Behnam Sadeghi, and Michael Bonner (Leiden: Brill, 2011), 315–42.

other critical and condescending—Alfonsi provided Western Christian readers with a statement of Muslim doctrine in Latin that was unprecedented in its clarity and accuracy, despite its polemical framework.

Recourse to reason by these Christian polemicists found the fullest range of its expression among the schoolmasters of the twelfth century. The career of Peter Abelard (1079–1142), one of the most brilliant and controversial thinkers of his time, has successfully eroded modern presumptions about the strict separation between the cloister and the world in this period. Charismatic teacher and failed abbot, condemned heretic and redeemed monk, Abelard moved fitfully but seamlessly between monastic and scholastic environments over the course of his tumultuous life.[52] When he was the abbot of the Monastery of Saint Gildas de Rhuys in Brittany (1127–32), Abelard composed his *Conferences* (*Collationes*), a fictional account of two conversations about moral philosophy: one between an ancient philosopher and a Jew, the other between the same philosopher and a Christian.[53] The work as a whole was an intellectual inquiry into "the greatest good and the greatest evil, and what makes a person truly happy or wretched."[54] Aside from their presentation in the form of a dialogue, Abelard's *Conferences* departed significantly from the expectations of anti-Jewish polemics in the early Middle Ages. As many scholars have noted, Abelard defied the conventions of his time with an unusually sympathetic portrait of the worldly plight of his Jewish character, who also broke the stereotype of the carnal Jewish reader by insisting in his dialogue with the philosopher that the Old Testament be read allegorically.

The most novel character in the *Conferences*, however, is the philosopher. Informed by Abelard's reading of Cicero and Seneca, this character is an ingenious imagining of an ancient philosopher in a twelfth-century milieu. A follower of "natural law" with no recourse to an authoritative sacred text, he relied on reason alone to guide his questions about moral philosophy. What is striking for our purposes is Abelard's decision to provide the philosopher with a twelfth-century identity by describing him as a circumcised descen-

---

52. For perspectives on Abelard's life and relationships, see Michael Clanchy, *Abelard: A Medieval Life* (Oxford: Wiley-Blackwell, 1997); and Constant Mews, *Abelard and Heloise* (Oxford: Oxford University Press, 2005).

53. Peter Abelard, *Collationes*, ed. and trans. John Marenbon and Giovanni Orlandi (Oxford: Clarendon Press, 2001).

54. Peter Abelard, *Collationes*, 2, ed. Marenbon and Orlandi, 2–3: "Hinc de summo bono et de summo malo et de his que uere beatum hominem uel miserum faciunt quoad potui instructus, statui apud me diuersas etiam fidei sectas, quibus nunc mundus diuisus est, studiose scrutari et omnibus inspectis et inuicem collatis illud sequi quod consentaneum magis sit rationi."

dant of Ishmael—that is, as a person who was born and raised in a land governed by the laws of Islam. Scholars have taken a variety of stances on the significance of this statement.[55] Some believe that Abelard deliberately modeled his character on a contemporary Muslim thinker, the philosopher Ibn Bajjah, who lived in Spain and allegedly preferred the application of reason independent of the authority of a sacred text. Others have argued the opposite—namely, that historians have misconstrued the wording of Abelard's text, which in their opinion does not imply that the philosopher was circumcised and therefore does not identify him as a Muslim. But even if Abelard had some general notion of the Dar al-Islam as a biographical setting for this fictional character, the philosopher's thoughts on moral matters were informed primarily by Abelard's reading of Roman Stoics and betrayed no evidence that he was familiar with or remotely interested in Muslim doctrines and the refutation of them.[56]

Peter the Venerable came of age in the shadow of these towering intellectuals, but their writings against unbelievers had very little impact on his enterprise to confront Islam. While the abbot of Cluny shared with them the lineaments of what could be called a polemical methodology—namely, that an argument for the religious truth of Christianity based on reason could silence the ravings of Jews and heretics—he inflected his treatise against Islam in ways that departed markedly from the combative works of his contemporaries. As we have seen, Peter was the first to write a refutation of Muhammed's prophetic authority and other Islamic beliefs that made its appeal to a Muslim audience. Unlike other Christian polemicists of his time, the abbot of Cluny did not prop up an imaginary interlocutor or conjure a make-believe dialogue in order to make his point; rather, he spoke directly to his religious opponents in the hopes of converting them to Christianity. No Christian author in northern Europe had ever openly entreated Muslim listeners in this way. Even Alfonsi's well-informed depiction of Islamic traditions, the only comparable text from this period, was part of a dialogue between a Jew and a Christian; it betrayed no concern for Muslims as potential converts to Christianity. In short, while Peter employed the rea-

---

55. For what follows, see the summary provided by Marenbon and Orlandi in the introduction to their edition of Abelard's *Collationes*, l–li.

56. See James Kritzeck, "De l'influence de Pierre Abélard sur Pierre le Vénérable dans ses œuvres sur l'Islam," in *Pierre Abélard—Pierre Vénérable: Les courants philosophiques, littéraires et artistiques en Occident au milieu du XIIe siècle: actes et mémoires du colloque international, Abbaye de Cluny, 2 au 9 juillet 1972* (Paris: L'Éditions du Centre National de la Recherche Scientifique, 1975), 205–12, esp. 212: "Pierre Abélard n'eut pas et ne put pas avoir aucune part dans la publication de la «Collectio Toletana» ou dans les écrits de Pierre le Vénérable sur l'Islam qui la suivirent."

soning apparatus that had become common among Christian polemicists at the turn of the twelfth century, he differed from his contemporaries in that his concern with Islam was outspokenly pastoral and couched as a direct discourse with a Muslim audience. As we will see, other traditions at the Abbey of Cluny provided the inspiration for Peter's novel approach to Muslims in his treatise *Against the Sect of the Saracens.*

A Reservoir of Eastern Censure

We cannot rule out the possibility that polemical views of Islam formulated by Arab Christians living under Muslim rule exerted an influence on the formulation of the Muslim policy of Peter the Venerable. While the abbot of Cluny spent less than a year in Spain and did not visit any other region with such close cultural ties to the Islamic world, he was nonetheless intimately familiar with the *Apology of al-Kindi*, the polemical treatise against Islam written in the ninth or tenth century, allegedly at the court of the Abbasid caliph al-Ma'mun (813–33), the son of Harun al-Rashid, who ruled in Baghdad.[57] When Peter of Toledo translated this epistolary exchange from Arabic into Latin for the Toledan Collection in 1142–43, he made available for the first time in western Europe one of the most widely read works of religious polemic against Islam composed by an Arab Christian. Despite Peter's knowledge of the *Apology of al-Kindi*, neither the structure of the text or the method of argument employed by its Christian author seems to have exerted a direct influence on the abbot's *Against the Sect of the Saracens.*

Unlike Peter the Venerable's direct, personal appeal to a Muslim audience, the anonymous author of the *Apology of al-Kindi* structured his argument as an epistolary exchange between two fictional characters, a Muslim named al-Hashimi and a Christian named al-Kindi, both of whom were allegedly learned courtiers in the service of Caliph al-Ma'mun. The treatise comprises two parts: a short letter from al-Hashimi inviting his Christian friend to convert to Islam (*Epistula sarraceni*) and a much longer response from al-Kindi (*Rescriptum christiani*). Al-Hashimi's letter explains the fundamental tenets and traditions of the Islamic faith, including belief in Muhammed as the prophet of God, the fast of Ramadan, and the pilgrimage to Mecca, and invites al-Kindi either to convert or to offer an explanation of the superior-

---

57. *Exposición y refutación del Islam: La versión latina de las epístolas de al'Hasimi y al-Kindi*, ed. and trans. Fernando González Muñoz (A Coruña, Spain: Universidade da Coruña, 2005); and Laura Bottini, "The Apology of al-Kindī," CMR 1:585–94.

ity of his religion. Al-Kindi complies with a response that systematically rejects the religious claims of his Muslim friend, particularly the notion that Muhammed was a prophet, and at the same time offers a defense of those aspects of Christianity that most confound Muslims, principally the doctrine of the Trinity. Al-Kindi's letter concludes with an invitation to al-Hashimi to embrace the correct faith.

While Peter the Venerable's *Against the Sect of the Saracens* shared a tantamount concern with the *Apology of al-Kindi* to prove that Muhammed was not a true prophet of God, the similarities between the two texts end there. The first section of the *Rescriptum christiani* is relentlessly theological and devotes considerable space to a defense of the Christian doctrine of the Trinity.[58] It begins with an argument based on a Christian reading of allusions to the threefold nature of God found in the Hebrew scriptures. Al-Kindi draws his evidence from the Old Testament both to establish the antiquity of belief in the Trinity and also to counter the claim of al-Hashimi that Abraham was the first monotheist and thus the first Muslim. There follows an examination of the oneness of God, which makes the argument that God is one with respect to his substance but threefold with respect to his number. God remains perfect in both respects, al-Kindi argues, because his substance is singular and pure, while his number (3) contains both an odd number (1) and an even number (2) and thus comprises every kind of number. After this defense of the Trinity, al-Kindi makes an argument about the attributes of the essence of God prompted by the allegation of al-Hashimi that God had a marital relationship or adopted a son in the literal sense. This section marshals more evidence from the Hebrew scriptures to make the case that God's primary attributes are his eternal word and spirit, which are synonymous with wisdom and life.

In contrast, Peter the Venerable had little interest in sparring with his Muslim audience on the nature of God. For him the value of al-Kindi's response lay in the fact that it was a convenient digest of information about the fallacies of the Muslim religion. When Peter evoked the *Apology of al-Kindi* in his treatise against Islam, his strategy often involved the censure or subversion of the authority of the words of Muhammed in the service of his arguments against Muslim beliefs. Instead of drawing his evidence directly from the Latin Qur'an, however, we often find the abbot of Cluny echoing the voice of Muhammed as he read it redacted in the response of al-Kindi. For example, when Peter ridicules the prophet's assertion that one should not dispute with those who have knowledge of the law and indeed it is bet-

---

58. For what follows, see *Rescriptum christiani*, 1–17, ed. Muñoz, 29–42.

ter to die than to contest their authority, the words of Muhammed follow the phrasing not of the Latin Qur'an but those of the paraphrase of al-Kindi.[59] Similarly, when dismissing the spurious claim of the Latin *Book of the Birth of Muhammad and his Upbringing* regarding an alleged prophecy foretelling the number of Muhammed's successors, the abbot of Cluny reproduced Muhammed's assertion that the Qur'an was the only source of truth from the *Apology of al-Kindi*.[60]

While the Latin translation of the *Apology of al-Kindi* provided the abbot of Cluny with a deep reservoir of religious polemic against Islam current in the tradition of Arab Christians living under Muslim rule, this work seems to have had little impact on the formulation of his treatise *Against the Sect of the Saracens*. To be sure, al-Kindi's response exposed Peter the Venerable to a refutation of Islamic beliefs that demonstrated a deep familiarity with Christian and Muslim scriptures, but neither the formal presentation of the argument as an exchange of letters nor the content of the treatise with its prevalent theological concerns seem to have inspired the abbot's own work against Islam. Moreover, where the concerns of the *Apology of al-Kindi* intersect with those of Peter, as is the case in their mutual refutation of the prophetic claims of Muhammed, the abbot of Cluny did not borrow directly from this source in crafting his argument. The novelty of Peter's pastoral appeal to a Muslim audience suggests that he drew his inspiration from a source outside of the broad discourse of religious polemic. A model for this approach was, in fact, only an arm's length away, in the library of his very own abbey.

✎ Nalgod's Industry

Despite the administrative burdens of his abbacy, Peter the Venerable was an engaged reader of pagan and Christian literature. As a child oblate at the Abbey of Sauxillanges, he was nurtured on a curriculum of Christian and secular learning mediated through the study of books. Later, as abbot of Cluny, the formidable contents of his community's library were an invaluable

---

59. Peter the Venerable, *Contra sectam Saracenorum*, 35, ed. Glei, 78: "Et iterum: 'Nolite disputare cum legem habentibus. Melior est enim caedes quam lis.'" See also the discussion by Glei on 273–74n278.

60. Peter the Venerable, *Contra sectam Saracenorum*, 121, ed. Glei, 188: "Et ne diutius vos protrahens plus nimio suspensos teneam, audite ipsum loquentem in Alkorano vestro, cui scripturae ab aliquo contradici nefas putatis: 'Quicquid,' ait, 'inveneritis pro me scriptum, conferte illud cum Alkorano, et si ei non concordaverit, scitote quia innocens sum ab illa scriptura et non est mea.' Conferatur ergo scriptura iam dicta cum isto Alkorano, et videatur utrum concors cum illa aut discors ab ipsa sit." See also the discussion by Glei on 292n500.

resource in the composition of his many letters and treatises. Only a few dozen of these books survived the destruction of monastic archives that took place during the French Revolution, but we can reconstruct the scope of the abbey's manuscript holdings both from a precious library catalog compiled at Cluny in the eleventh or twelfth century and from the writings of Peter himself.[61] Taken together these sources provide an index of the ancient and medieval authors known to the abbot of Cluny, either from his recollection of texts that he had studied as a boy or through his familiarity with authors whose works he had taken the time to read during his abbacy.

Peter the Venerable knew from memory a rich repertoire of stories about Christian holy men ranging from the deeds of the saints of antiquity to the activities of his predecessors as abbot of Cluny. Alongside frequent allusions to important Christian texts familiar to most monks, like Sulpicius Severus's *Life of Martin*, the *Rule of Benedict*, and the *Dialogues* of Gregory the Great, resonances of Cluniac saints' lives are conspicuous throughout the works of the abbot, most notably in the treatise *On Miracles* that he composed in the 1140s. By the time of Peter's abbacy, several monks of Cluny had already collected dozens of stories about the miracles performed by Abbot Hugh the Great (1049–1109), some of which he appropriated and retold in his own collection.[62] Moreover, Peter was also familiar with even older Cluniac traditions stretching back to the early tenth century, like John of Salerno's *Life of Odo*, composed around 943, which commemorated the second abbot of Cluny as a saint, as well as Odo's own account of the virtuous life of the warrior-saint Gerald of Aurillac, written around 930.[63]

By the twelfth century, however, the legacy of these Cluniac fathers paled before the traditions surrounding Maiolus, who was foremost among the earliest abbots of Cluny in terms of the sheer number of works devoted to celebrating his sanctity. By the year 1050 there was already an impressive corpus of hagiographical texts that commemorated the manifest virtue of

61. On the Cluniac library catalog, see Veronika von Büren, "Le grand catalogue de la Bibliothèque de Cluny," in *Le gouvernement d'Hugues de Semur à Cluny: Actes du Colloque scientifique international (Cluny, septembre 1988)* (Mâcon: Musée Ochier, 1990), 245–63.

62. Dominique Iogna-Prat, "Panorama de l'hagiographie abbatiale clunisienne," in *Manuscrits hagiographiques et travail des hagiographes*, ed. Martin Heinzelmann (Sigmaringen, Germany: Jan Thorbecke, 1991), 77–118, esp. 97–102; reprinted in Dominique Iogna-Prat, *Études clunisiennes* (Paris: Picard, 2002), 35–73, esp 55–58. For Peter's use of one of these stories, see *De miraculis*, 1.15, ed. Denise Bouthillier, CCCM 83:50–52.

63. See, for example, Peter the Venerable, *De miraculis*, 1.20 (John of Salerno's *Vita Odonis*), ed. Bouthillier, 61; and 2.24 (Odo's *Vita Geraldi*), ed. Bouthillier, 142.

God's power within him, both during his lifetime and after his death.[64] In addition, Odilo of Cluny composed several hymns to confect the new feast day (11 May) that he instituted in honor of Maiolus, which was celebrated at Cluny and its dependencies across Europe.[65] Moreover, at Odilo's request, the brethren of Souvigny collected over fifty accounts of miracles witnessed at his tomb, for the abbot had died among them while en route from Cluny to Paris and graced their church with his holy remains before their translation back to Burgundy in the late eleventh century.[66]

Maiolus was also renowned during the abbacy of Peter the Venerable as the witness to a miracle involving an army of the dead that came to the aid of a pious duke who had given over the income of an entire city to fund the release of souls suffering in purgatory. Known in the manuscript tradition as the story of Maiolus concerning the two dukes (*relatio Maioli de duobus ducibus*), this tale about the efficacy of prayer for the faithful departed circulated widely as an exemplum in Benedictine and Cisterican circles in the twelfth and thirteenth centuries.[67] A verse redaction of the story written at a Cluniac monastery around the year 1150 celebrated at length the legacy of Maiolus as an exemplary monastic leader:

> With an energetic spirit, [Maiolus] governed at Cluny, with watchful care he provided for so great a fold, safeguarding those happy sheep who were voluntarily shorn. Through their tonsure he cast away transitory goods [and] worldly pomp, like wool beneath the shears. His strict custom for cloisters lives on, a custom well tailored, a sacred discipline that guards the black cowls in their dignity, an untainted devotion that cleanses many ills, a pure devotion purer than the water

---

64. See chapter 2 of the present volume.

65. For the text of the hymns, see BC, cols. 291–92. See also the newly discovered poem concerning the death of Maiolus edited by Franz Dolveck in "Un poème passé inaperçu: Contribution au dossier hagiographique de saint Maieul, quatrième abbé de Cluny," *Archivum Latinitatis Medii Aevi* 70 (2013): 257–63. On the incorporation of Maiolus into the Cluniac liturgy in the early eleventh century, see Dominique Iogna-Prat, "Le saint Maieul à Cluny d'après le *Liber Tramitis aevi Odilonis*," in *Saint Mayeul et son temps: Actes du congrès international de Valensole, 2–14 mai 1994* (Dignes-les-Bains, France: Société Scientifique et Littéraire des Alpes de Haute-Provence, 1997), 219–32.

66. BHL 5186, in BC, cols. 1787–1814. Rodulphus Glaber provides early evidence of the cult of Maiolus at Souvigny in his *Five Books of Histories*, 2.14, ed. and trans. John France, in *Rodulphus Glaber: The Five Books of Histories and the Life of St. William* (Oxford: Clarendon Press, 1989), 76.

67. A study of this story cycle in the Benedictine tradition is in preparation by Scott G. Bruce and Christopher A. Jones. Cistercian sources for the tale include *Collectaneum Clarevallense*, 2.10, ed. Olivier Legendre, in *Collectaneum exemplorum et visionum Clarevallense e codice Trecensi 946*, CCCM 208:231–35 (no. 39); and *Collectio exemplorum cisterciensis*, 33, ed. Jacques Berlioz and Marie Anne Polo de Beaulieu, in *Collectio exemplorum Cisterciensis in codice Parisiensi 15912 asseruata*, CCCM 243:128–29 with commentary on 439–40 (no. 404 [XXXIII, 2]).

of a spring, a chaste devotion that sets human beings above the stars. The solicitude of Maiolus gave to cloisters laws of gold.[68]

The currency of tales about Maiolus was so strong during Peter's abbacy that he could credibly claim that more legends were told about the virtues of his predecessor throughout all of Europe (*in tota Europa*) than any other saint in Christendom besides the Virgin Mary.[69]

Peter the Venerable took an active interest in shaping and controlling the legacy of his saintly predecessors at Cluny, including stories about Maiolus. One clear indication of this is the hagiographical industry that Peter sponsored during his abbacy. Under his direction, a monk named Nalgod composed new accounts of the lives of Cluny's two most illustrious tenth-century leaders, Odo and Maiolus.[70] We can glean one of the rationales for this rewriting of abbatial hagiography from the prologues that Nalgod wrote to justify the enterprise. His concern as an author was first and foremost aesthetic. In the prologue of his revised *Life of Odo*, Nalgod complained at length about the literary ineptness of its original author, John of Salerno, who had been part of Odo's entourage during a trip through Italy in the 930s.[71] Redundancy and confusion burdened the tenth-century text. To make matters worse, the order of events presented in the work defied reason. John

---

68. Charleville-Mézières, Médiathèque Voyelles 190, fol. 144r, lines 19–30: "Pectore uiuaci tenuit regimen Cluniaci; / cura peruigili tanto prouidit ouili, / seruans gaudentes attonsas sponte bidentes. / Quorum tonsura bona proiecti peritura, / pompam mundanam ueluti sub forcipe lanam. / Spirat mos artus claustrorum, mos bene sartus, / ordo sacer pullas seruans in honore cucullas, / religio pura purgans contagia plura, / religio munda fontana mundior unda, / religio casta statuens homines super astra. / Maioli cura claustris dedit aurea iura." I am grateful to Christopher A. Jones for translating these verses.

69. Peter the Venerable, *De miraculis*, 2.32, ed. Bouthillier, 162: "Hac miraculorum gratia in tantum iam per centum sexaginta et duos annos, hoc est a tempore mortis sue claruit, ut post sanctum Dei genitricem, nullum sanctorum in tota Europa nostra in huiusmodi operibus parem habeat."

70. Nalgod, *Vita Odonis* (BHL 6299), ed. Jean Mabillon, in *Acta sanctorum ordinis sancti Benedicti in saeculorum classes distributa* (Paris: Colet, 1685), 5:186–199, reprinted in PL 133, cols. 85–104; and Nalgod, *Vita Maioli* (BHL 5181), edited under the title *Vita ex prolixoribus coaevorum actis a Nalgodo monacho post sesqui secum contracta*, in AASS Maii 2:657–67. Nothing is known about Nalgod himself apart from what he tells us in the prologues of the *vitae* he composed at Peter's request. For a brief account of his career, see Rémy Ceillier, *Histoire générale des auteurs sacrés et ecclésiastiques* (Paris: Louis Vivès, 1757), 21:412–13. The dates of his compositions are likewise unknown, though the case has been made that his *Vita Maioli* predated his *Vita Odonis*; see Maria Luisa Fini, "Studio sulla *Vita Odonis reformata* di Nalgodo: Il *fragmentum mutilum* del codice latino NA 1496 della Bibliotheque Nationale di Parigi," *Atti della Accademia delle Scienze dell'Istituto di Bologna* 63 (1974–75): 38–42.

71. On the career of John of Salerno and the composition of the original *Vita Odonis*, see chapter 2 of the present volume.

had leapt back and forth among episodes in the abbot's life with no regard for their temporal relationship.[72] It was Nalgod's task to impose order and clarity on this unruly text by pruning anecdotal material and other digressions that he deemed useless for contemporary readers. John's original work was a rambling affair, comprising eighty-three long chapters divided into three books of unequal length. When Nalgod was through with his editing, his revision presented the details of the abbot's holy life in fifty-three concise chapters arranged in chronological order.

The rewriting of early Cluniac hagiography under Peter the Venerable served another purpose beyond Nalgod's outspoken cosmetic concerns. Medieval hagiographers often seized the opportunity when rewriting saints' lives to address topical issues, and Nalgod was no exception.[73] Dominique Iogna-Prat has shown how Nalgod's reworking of John of Salerno's *Life of Odo* presented twelfth-century readers with anachronistic accounts of Cluny's foundation and Odo's succession as abbot.[74] Nalgod also emphasized the sovereignty of the abbey and its strong ties to Rome to harmonize the early history of Cluny with its contemporary standing with the papacy in the aftermath of Gregorian reform. For Peter, the rewriting of abbatial hagiography allowed him to harness the hallowed histories of his saintly predecessors to present an idealized portrait of the Abbey of Cluny that had been sanitized in style as well as in content. Thanks to Nalgod's industry, the brethren of Cluny could hear and read the stories of one of their tenth-century heroes couched in clear and well-ordered Latin and liberated from historical details that may have raised disconcerting questions about the nature and legitimacy of Cluny's foundation, the succession of its earliest abbots, and its relationship to Rome.

Unlike the task of revising the tenth-century *Life of Odo*, which required Nalgod to edit one long work by a single author, the multiple surviving *vitae* of Maiolus presented a much more daunting challenge. As we have seen, by the twelfth century the hagiographical dossier of this tenth-century Cluniac saint comprised numerous texts in a variety of genres. Faced with such an abundance of information from so many different sources, Nalgod had to make choices in preparation for producing a clear and concise narrative of

---

72. Nalgod, *Vita Odonis*, 1, in PL 133, col. 85b.

73. For more on this topic, see the introduction to the present volume.

74. Dominique Iogna-Prat, "La geste des origines dans l'historiographie clunisienne des XIe et XIIe siècles," *Revue bénédictine* 102 (1992): 135–91, esp. 183–87; reprinted in Iogna-Prat, *Études clunisiennes*, 161–200.

the abbot's virtuous life.[75] His retelling of the abduction episode borrowed many of its narrative features from the early eleventh-century *vitae* of Maiolus: the capture of the abbot and his entourage high on the Alpine passes, the miraculous healing of the wound that Maiolus received when he protected a monk from a sword stroke, the power of prayer to unlock the heavy chains that bound the captives, the raising of the ransom at Cluny, and the extirpation of the Muslim community at the hands of a Christian host.[76] But Nalgod also embroidered his account with new details that were unprecedented in the story's century-old history. For example, we learn for the first time that Maiolus and his entourage took flight when the Muslims attacked them and managed to reach the town of Pons-Ursariae (present-day Orsières, in Switzerland) before they were captured and hauled away to the brigands' mountain lair.[77] And while earlier accounts of the story had emphasized the miraculous healing of the wound that the abbot received from a sword thrust, Nalgod claimed that Maiolus thereafter carried a scar on his hand as a witness to his compassion.[78] And finally, Nalgod related a miracle that began with the unexpected discovery of a book. Maiolus apparently traveled with several manuscripts in his possession. While in captivity, he marveled to find hidden in the folds of his cloak a short treatise on the Assumption of the Virgin because he presumed that it had been lost, like all of his other books.[79] Seized with a great joy, he calculated the number of days until the Feast of the Assumption (15 August) and prayed to Mary that he would be set free by then in order to celebrate it in the company of fellow Christians.[80] Sure enough, when he woke up the next morning, his chains had fallen away and

---

75. Nalgod, *Vita Maioli*, prologue, in AASS Maii 2:656: "Vitam beatissime patris Maioli, confusa diffusione dispersam potius quam digestam, ut simplici brevitate colligerem et expedirem fratum studiosa caritas imperavit."

76. Nalgod, *Vita Maioli*, 22–25, in AASS Maii 2:662–63.

77. Nalgod, *Vita Maioli*, 22, in AASS Maii 2:662.

78. Ibid.

79. Nalgod, *Vita Maioli*, 23, in AASS Maii 2:662: "Cumque ablatis sibi aliis libris suis, libellum beati Hieronymi de Assumptione perpetuae Virginis, quem in sinu suo familiari reverentia circumferre solebat, sub amictu suo repositum invenisset." This book was in fact not the work of Jerome, but rather in all likelihood the apocryphal treatise known as *Cogitis me*, composed in Jerome's name by the ninth-century Carolingian theologian Paschasius Radbertus. The Latin text of this work has been edited by Albert Ripberger as "Paschasii Radberti Epistula Hieronymi ad Paulam et Eustochium de Assumptione Sanctae Mariae Virginis" in CCCM 55C:97–162. There is helpful commentary on this treatise in E. Ann Matter, *The Voice of My Beloved: The Song of Songs in Western Medieval Christianity* (Philadelphia: University of Pennsylvania Press, 1990), 152–53.

80. Ibid. In the next chapter, Nalgod related that the abbot's prayer was answered, for a delegation of monks from Cluny soon arrived with the ransom and allowed him to return home before the Feast of the Assumption. If this episode has any historical veracity, then it implies that Maiolus was

all subsequent attempts by his captors to bind him again failed when he made the sign of the cross.

Amid these new details, Nalgod emphasized an aspect of the abduction episode that only appeared in Syrus's *Life of Maiolus*: the conversion of the abbot's captors to Christianity. According to Nalgod, after the release of Maiolus and the defeat of the Muslims of La Garde-Freinet by a vengeful Christian army, "the few remaining Saracens who had survived from that vanquished horde confessed that they had been justly punished because they had unjustly abused the man of God and flew to the grace of baptism."[81] Unlike Syrus's account, however, which credited the conversion of the Muslims to the influence of the "life-giving words" spoken to them by Maiolus during his captivity, Nalgod's version of the story attributed their change of heart to a miracle. When Maiolus was chained up alone in the middle of the night he would sing to himself, and his captors swore they could hear other voices singing along with him. Nalgod took this to mean that angels were keeping the saint company during his captivity.[82] His retelling of the abduction of Maiolus made the claim that portentous events have the power to draw even the most barbarous unbelievers into the fold of Christianity. It was the miraculous unbinding of the abbot's chains when he made the sign of the cross that softened their feelings for him, but when they heard his solitary singing accompanied by angelic voices, their conversion was complete.[83]

Nalgod's use of a miracle to sway the hearts of the abbot's Muslim captors was consistent with a major theme that preoccupied Peter the Venerable in the mid-1140s. In his treatises *Against the Long-Standing Stubbornness of the Jews* and *On Miracles*, the abbot argued that the efficacy of miracles performed by the saints set Christianity apart from Judaism and Islam and drew unbelievers to the faith.[84] In the absence of any other temporal markers, Nalgod's decision to depict the conversion of the Muslims of La Garde-Freinet as the result of a miracle provides a strong indication that he was rewriting the *Life of Maiolus* during the 1140s when the power of miracles as a tool for conversion was foremost on his abbot's mind. A few years later, however, in the dark days following the end of the Second

---

in captivity for less than three weeks, since he was taken on 23–24 July and freed in time to return to Cluny by 15 August.

81. Nalgod, *Vita Maioli*, 25, in AASS Maii 2:663: "Pauci vero residui, qui ex illa perversa multitudine superesse potuerunt, confitentes se juste puniri, quia injuste vexaverant virum Dei, ad baptismi gratiam convolarunt."

82. Nalgod, *Vita Maioli*, 25, in AASS Maii 2:663.

83. Nalgod, *Vita Maioli*, 23, in AASS Maii 2:663; and 25, in AASS Maii 2:664.

84. See chapter 3 of the present volume.

Crusade in 1149, miracles like this one were in short supply. From the vantage point of the 1150s, Nalgod's wishful account of the miraculous conversion of the Muslims of La Garde-Freinet would have been cold comfort in the face of the grim reality of Christian defeat in the Holy Land.

When weapons proved worthless against the might of the Muslims and the prospect of a new expedition against them faded after the death of Bernard of Clairvaux in 1153, Peter the Venerable contemplated a new means of rapprochement with his Muslim adversaries. It was only at this time, at the very end of his life, that he decided to confront the threat of Islam "not . . . with arms, but with words, not with force, but with reason."[85] Alone among his contemporaries, he directed his voice to a Muslim audience with an appeal in defense of the Christian faith. The abbot's approach to the perceived problem of Islam was strikingly similar in its methodology to the example of Maiolus both as a relentless preacher of the faith and as a direct and successful interlocutor with Muslims on issues of religious truth as presented in the early eleventh-century *vita* composed by Syrus.

That Maiolus loomed large in Peter the Venerable's imagination is beyond question. For more than a century before Peter became abbot of Cluny in 1122, Maiolus had long been one of the brightest stars in the constellation of saints who received special veneration at the abbey. Under the guidance of Abbot Odilo, the brethren of Cluny had institutionalized their remembrance of him in several ways. From perhaps as early as 1002, there was a church dedicated to Maiolus on the grounds of the abbey, a monumental reminder of his abiding presence in the community.[86] Relics of the saint played a similar commemorative role. Although Maiolus had been buried at Souvigny upon his death in 994, an eleventh-century relic list from Cluny boasted the possession of a portion of his hair kept in a glass container.[87] The church dedicated to Maiolus became an important venue for the solemnities surrounding the abbot's feast day instituted on 11 May by Odilo, just as the precious remains of his mortal body promised to manifest his intercessory power for the benefit of his devout brethren.[88] Moreover, a rich tradition of stories embroidered the memory of him. Legends about the miracles performed by Maiolus promoted his reputation as a holy man well into

---

85. *Contra sectam Saracenorum*, 1.24, ed. Glei, 62: "Aggredior inquam vos, non, ut nostri saepe faciunt, armis sed verbis, non vi sed ratione, non odio sed amore."

86. Didier Méhu, *Paix et communautés autour de l'abbaye de Cluny (Xe–XVe siècle)* (Lyon: Presses Universitaires de France, 2001), 223.

87. *Liber tramitis aevi Odilonis abbatis* 180, ed. Peter Dinter, CCM 10:261: "portio capillorum sancti Maioli in uase uitreo."

88. Iogna-Prat, "Le saint Maieul à Cluny d'après le *Liber Tramitis aevi Odilonis*."

the twelfth century at Cluny and beyond. Peter knew these stories well, claiming that "none of the other saints in all of our Europe was his equal in works of this kind."[89]

Maiolus was clearly a towering figure in the mind of Peter the Venerable when the failure of the Second Crusade in 1149 prompted the abbot of Cluny to consider a new approach to the problem of Islam. In the aftermath of this humiliating defeat, Peter wrote his treatise *Against the Sect of the Saracens* as a open appeal to a Muslim audience. In doing so he was unique among twelfth-century polemicists, none of whom addressed their criticisms of Islam directly to Muslims. He was not, however, unique in this regard among abbots of Cluny, for over a century earlier Maiolus himself had likewise defended the Christian faith against Muslim reproach. That Peter was familiar with this story from Syrus's early eleventh-century *Life of Maiolus* is clear from the work of Nalgod, whom the abbot commissioned to write a new account of his predecessor's life for a twelfth-century audience. Nalgod's industry presupposes that Peter had been reading different accounts of Maiolus's life during his abbacy, including the one told by Syrus. It is thus very plausible that the battle of words between Maiolus and his Muslim captors in the summer of 972 informed and inspired Peter when he adopted a similar stance toward his religious adversaries in the middle of the twelfth century.

In all likelihood, Syrus's early eleventh-century account of Maiolus's dispute with the Muslims of La Garde-Freinet had a powerful influence on Peter the Venerable's method of direct address to his religious adversaries in the 1150s, but it may have also inflected the content of his treatise *Against the Sect of the Saracens*. Syrus's rendering of Maiolus's defense of the Christian faith against the disparaging remarks of his captors is laconic, but it clearly relates that the foundation of the abbot's refutation of Islam was the credibility of Muhammed as a religious authority with intercessory power: "[Maiolus] attempted to demonstrate with proven and most credible arguments that the one whom they worshipped as God did not have the power to free himself from punishment, let alone to help them in any way."[90] Over a century later, Peter devoted the second half of his treatise against Islam to the presentation of arguments that rejected the authenticity of Muhammed as a prophet, largely on the basis of the fact that the Qur'an

---

89. Peter the Venerable, *De miraculis*, 2.32, ed. Bouthillier, 162: "[N]ullum sanctorum in tota Europa nostra in huiusmodi operibus parem habeat."

90. Syrus, *Vita sancti Maioli*, 3.2, ed. Dominique Iogna-Prat, in *Agni Immaculati: Recherches sur les sources hagiographiques relatives à saint Maieul de Cluny (954–994)* (Paris: Éditions du Cerf, 1988), 249–50: "[E]um quem deum colebant, nec se a supplicio liberare, nec illos in aliquo posse adiuuare certis et euidentissimis adgressus est rationibus demonstrare."

provided no evidence that this so-called prophet of God ever had the divinely inspired ability "to reveal to mortals things unknown either of the past or the present or the future taught not by human reasoning."[91] Calling into doubt the integrity of Muhammed as a holy man was a common approach in Christian polemics against Islam, but if Peter did in fact borrow his method of direct address to Muslims from Syrus's portrait of Maiolus, then the details of this same narrative may have informed the content of his argument as well.

The influence of hagiographical narratives on the intellectual formation of monastic thinkers like Peter the Venerable cannot be underestimated. While their purpose was primarily devotional, important saints' lives saturated the imagination of medieval monks like few other genres due to their near constant repetition in the fabric of the liturgy and as favored texts read publically and privately in the cloister. While historians of religious polemic have been at pains to explain the novelty of Peter's direct address to a Muslim audience in his final treatise *Against the Sect of the Saracens*, a successful model for this approach had been well known to Cluniac monks for over a century in the hagiographical tradition inspired by the virtues of their late tenth-century abbot Maiolus. Like his distant predecessor, Peter brandished the word of God as a weapon against his Muslim foes in the prospect that reason would succeed where violent conflict had failed. Just as Maiolus's vanquished captors accepted baptism due to the "life-giving words" of their captive, in the last months of his life Peter harbored the hope that his appeal to reason would inspire the same response among the Muslims addressed directly in his treatise.

Peter the Venerable was alone among his contemporaries in his effort to refute the prophetic claims of Muhammed in a treatise written to call Muslims to the saving grace of baptism through a reasoned disputation with them about the truth claims of Christianity. While many Christian intellectuals of the late eleventh and early twelfth centuries had applied their energy to the refutation of heresy and Judaism, none of them was inspired to employ a reasoning apparatus to defend Christian interests against the threat of Islam. The reason for this is clear: until the translation into Latin of the Toledan Collection, western Europeans had very little knowledge about Muslim beliefs and traditions on which to found a defense of Christianity.

---

91. *Contra sectam Saracenorum*, 97, ed. Glei, 160: "Propheta est, qui res ignotas aut praeteriti temporis aut praesentis vel futuri non humana cognitione edoctus, sed spiritu dei inspiratus mortalibus manifestat."

As the patron of this translation project, the abbot of Cluny had firsthand exposure to the "contagion" of Islam, but he was not moved to write a formal refutation until the failure of the Second Crusade unmasked the futility of armed conflict against these enemies of Christ. It was only then that he adopted a pastoral approach to the Muslims, to win with words a struggle that had been lost with arms. He found his inspiration for this novel approach to his religious adversaries not in the polemical currents of his own time but in the hagiographical tradition of his own abbey. The kidnapping of Maiolus of Cluny by the Muslims of La Garde-Freinet in the summer of 972 had loomed large in the imagination of his brethren for generations. From an early eleventh-century version of this story, Peter knew that his saintly predecessor had preached successfully to his kidnappers during his confinement in the Alps. Over a century after its composition, this tale of reasoned debate about matters of faith between Maiolus and his Muslim captors offered the aged abbot of Cluny a new approach to the problem of Islam in the aftermath of the Second Crusade. It was his last measure of hope in a world turned upside down by humiliating defeat.

Conclusion

Saints' lives were ubiquitous in the libraries of medieval abbeys, but historians have tended to consider their influence narrowly in the context of their primary devotional and commemorative purposes. This book has argued that stories about the saints in fact had a much wider influence on the formation of medieval approaches to Islam than we have previously recognized. The tales told by the monks of Cluny about the tribulations of Abbot Maiolus and his captivity in the summer of 972 are a case in point. The Muslims of La Garde-Freinet were never recognized as a polity by any Islamic government, but this small community of entrepreneurs on the northern edge of the Dar al-Islam played an important role in the political calculus of Provence, northern Italy, and the Alpine passes for several decades of the tenth century until the summer of 972, when their kidnapping of Maiolus of Cluny led to their destruction. The stories told about the hardships of the abbot's captivity were popular among monastic readers in the orbit of Cluny in the eleventh century, but the authors of these stories were not consistent in their representation of the abbot's Muslim captors. It is clear that they shaped their depiction of them based on the devotional aims of their narratives and their respective knowledge of Islam.

Despite their inconsistencies, many of these tales remained in circulation well into the twelfth century, when western military expeditions to win back the Holy Land from the Muslims gave the narrative of Maiolus's captivity a new relevance. One of these stories provided Abbot Peter the Venerable with an example of interfaith dialogue between Christians and Muslims that was unprecedented in early medieval hagiography. In the account of Maiolus's captivity composed by Syrus of Cluny around 1010, Peter found the tale of his saintly predecessor successfully preaching the Christian faith to his Muslim captors by means of "proven and most credible arguments." In the aftermath of the Second Crusade, when it was painfully clear that the force of arms would not prevail against the might of Islam, the abbot of Cluny composed a reasoned refutation of the prophetic claims of Muhammed in a treatise addressed to a Muslim audience. In doing so he was participating in a millennium-old tradition of Christian censure of dissenting religious views, for in his mind the religion of Islam was yet another in a long succession of heresies. But his inspiration for this particular approach to the problem of Islam—an impassioned appeal directly to Muslims—derived not from the polemical writings of his contemporaries or from the eastern Christian traditions revealed to the abbot in the newly translated *Apology of al-Kindi*, but instead from a saint's life that lauded a tenth-century abbot of Cluny who successfully called his Muslim adversaries to baptism with reasoned arguments in favor of the Christian faith. In short, it was a work of Cluniac hagiography that provided Peter with an approach to Islam that was unprecedented in the Christian polemical tradition.

The legacy of Peter the Venerable's undertaking is difficult to evaluate. In the later Middle Ages, mendicants were the most active missionaries in Islamic principalities, where they preached to Christians and Muslims alike.[1] Peter's most important contribution to their efforts was undoubtedly his translation of the Qur'an, the keystone of the Toledan Collection. The Latin Qur'an survives in many late medieval manuscript copies, almost all of which were framed by polemical annotations and ancillary texts that were hostile to Islam.[2] Some of these books clearly served the needs of Christian missionaries, like the tiny thirteenth-century Latin Qur'an preserved in the Bibliothèque nationale in Paris (MS Latin 3668). Designed as much for reading as for reference, "pocket Qur'ans" like this one had indexes organized around polemical and apologetic themes, which made these

---

1. On the industry of mendicant preachers in this period, see the articles collected in *Franciscans and Preaching: Every Miracle from the Beginning of the World Came About through Words*, ed. Timothy J. Johnson (Leiden: Brill Academic, 2012).

2. See Thomas Burman, *Reading the Qur'an in Latin Christendom, 1140–1560* (Philadelphia: University of Pennsylvania Press, 2007), esp. 88, where Burman characterizes Robert of Ketton's translation of the Qur'an as "something of a best seller" that has survived in twenty-four medieval manuscripts.

books formidable instruments of religious debate.[3] Owing to the efforts of the abbot of Cluny, the owners of these manuscripts could boast an extensive knowledge of the tenets of Islam without the need to learn Arabic.

While the Latin Qur'an was a powerful tool in the Christian arsenal that Peter the Venerable assembled to confront the advance of Islam, there is little evidence to suggest that his other works were as influential in the later Middle Ages. Very few copies of his treatise *Against the Sect of the Saracens* survive, no doubt because later Christian readers did not identify with its direct address to a Muslim audience. Despite the abbot's hopes, his appeal was never translated into Arabic and thus failed to reach the very constituency he aimed to address.[4] Moreover, while it is clear that late medieval thinkers shared Peter's notion that preaching with recourse to reason could win over Muslim audiences and fortify the faith of wavering Christians abroad, they generally undertook their work without direct reference to the groundbreaking initiatives expressed in the abbot's treatise. For example, when Francis of Assisi preached before al-Kamil, the Sultan of Egypt, in 1219, he did so with no knowledge that he was acting out a scenario of interfaith dialogue conjured by the abbot of Cluny in the prologue of his treatise against Islam some six decades earlier.[5] Likewise, when Thomas Aquinas expressed his optimism in his *Summa Against the Pagans* (*Summa contra gentiles*; ca. 1270) that Christians could persuade Muslims to adopt the correct faith because Muslims were, like all human beings, endowed with reason, he betrayed no hint that he was familiar with Peter's treatise or the contents of the Toledan Collection.[6] It is likely that the realities of thirteenth-century missionary ambitions rendered the armchair approach of the abbot of Cluny somewhat antiquated and out of touch. While Peter the Venerable commissioned the translation of Muslim texts into Latin, a century later Franciscans like Roger Bacon (d. 1292) and Raymond Llull (d. ca. 1315) encouraged the most ambitious missionaries to learn Arabic for themselves.

---

3. Burman, *Reading the Qur'an in Latin Christendom*, 91–98, figs. 4–5.

4. The only Western medieval Latin work to be translated into Arabic before 1600 was the early fifth-century *Historiae adversus paganos libri septem* by Paul Orosius, which appeared in an Arabic translation in tenth-century Spain and survives in a unique fourteenth-century manuscript. See Christian C. Sahner, "From Augustine to Islam: Translation and History in the Arabic Orosius," *Speculum* 88 (2013): 905–31, esp. 907n8.

5. John V. Tolan, *Saint Francis and the Sultan: The Curious History of a Christian-Muslim Encounter* (Oxford: Oxford University Press, 2009).

6. John V. Tolan, "Thomas Aquinas," in CMR 4:521–29, with ample references to recent literature.

The reasoned approach to Muslims first endorsed by the abbot of Cluny in the twelfth century found a renewed relevance in the later Middle Ages. Just as Peter the Venerable sought recourse to reason in the aftermath of the Second Crusade, so too did fifteenth-century humanists place their faith in the persuasive power of words after the fall of Constantinople in 1453 to the Ottoman Turks.[7] Christian intellectuals responded to this humiliating defeat by composing elaborate fantasies of interfaith reconciliation and by renewing efforts to open dialogue with Muslim leaders on the topic of conversion to Christianity. In his treatise *On the Peace of Faith* (*De pace fidei*), Nicolas of Cusa (d. 1464) imagined a council in heaven attended by the representatives of all religions, including Islam. The result of this conclave in the audience of God was the declaration that there is in fact only one faith expressed in a plurality of different rituals (*una religio in varietate rituum*). Cusa coupled this vision of a worldwide community of faith with a renewed scrutiny of the text of the Latin Qur'an with the aim of finding a common ground of belief from which to pursue new missionary overtures among the Muslims. He published this work in 1461 as *The Sifting of the Qur'an* (*Cribratio Alkorani*).[8] That very same year, Pope Pius II addressed a letter to Mehmed II (*Epistula ad Mahumetem*), inviting the Sultan to convert to Christianity after a reasoned deliberation on the true nature of God.[9] Both works have in common their presumption that all human beings are rational and respond more favorably to sound arguments than to harsh censure.

This marriage of military defeat and reasoned rapprochement in the wake of the fall of Constantinople is remarkably similar to the context in which Peter the Venerable wrote *Against the Sect of the Saracens*, so it is not surprising to see a renewed interest in his treatise in the fifteenth century after several centuries of relative neglect. The Bibliothèque nationale in Paris preserves one of the few surviving manuscripts of the Toledan Collection

---

7. For what follows, see Nancy Bisaha, *Creating East and West: Renaissance Humanists and the Ottoman Turks* (Philadelphia: University of Pennsylvania Press, 2004).

8. *Nicholas of Cusa's De pace fidei and Cribratio Alkorani: Translation and Analysis*, ed. and trans. Jasper Hopkins (Notre Dame, IN: A. J. Banning Press, 1990).

9. Aeneas Silvius Piccolomini [Pope Pius II], *Epistola ad Mahometam II (Epistle to Mohammad II)*, ed. and trans. Albert R. Baca (New York: Peter Lang, 1990). See also Albert R. Baca, "On the Sources of Pius II's *Epistula ad Mahometam II*," in *Paradigms in Medieval Thought, Applications in Medieval Disciplines: A Symposium*, ed. Nancy Van Deusen and Alvin E. Ford (Lewiston, NY: Edwin Mellon Press, 1990), 27–36; Nancy Bisaha, "Pope Pius II's Letter to Sultan Mehmed II: A Reexamination," *Crusades* 1 (2002): 183–200; and, more generally, Thomas M. Izbicki, "The Possibility of Dialogue with Islam in the Fifteenth Century," in *Nicholas of Cusa in Search of God and Wisdom*, ed. Gerald Christianson and Thomas M. Izbicki (Leiden: Brill Academic, 1991), 175–83.

(MS Latin 3669), which was copied precisely in this period.[10] What is so striking about this manuscript, however, is not the appeal of the abbot's reasoned approach to Islam to a fifteenth-century audience but instead the discordant tone struck by a poem that a prelate named Martin of Lausanne added to the first folio of the book sometime after its creation and probably toward the end of the century. The message of this poem is completely at odds with the contents of the manuscript that it glosses, for it replaces reasoned dialogue with a harsh rebuke of the Qur'an:

> Depart, O book, into the darkness of the abyss thick with smoke and remain open no longer before our eyes! Conceived in the cavern of Hell, you are not worthy of the sunlight. That Beelzebub—or another, more deceitful than he, if possible—was made known in you, his son, and you in him, as a father. Your falsehood creeps stealthily beneath the guise of truth, but it is discerned by even a slight exercise of judgment. You tear down sacred law, openly making up blasphemies. You follow Abraham alone, whereas Christ contains all. You promise an end where woman is the highest form of pleasure; if there exists nothing better, she would have been paradise. O snare of death! O foulest pit of evils! You amass every abomination of infectious error. Depart, never to return; depart to be branded by burning coal; or let Muhammad, along with his nation, devour you![11]

In contrast to the naive and ultimately misplaced optimism of Nicholas of Cusa and Pope Pius II, the poet Martin of Lausanne poured forth a torrent of abuse that betrays, in the view of at least one learned contemporary, the collapse of reason as a means of finding common ground with the Ottoman Turks.

The unhindered progress of Muslim armies across the Bosporus and the inexorable tide of conquest that advanced their forces slowly up the Danube Valley in the early sixteenth century prolonged the relevance of Peter the Venerable's Muslim enterprise even further. In the aftermath of the siege of Vienna in 1529, which marked the farthest encroachment of the Ottoman Turks into western Europe, a Swiss Protestant scholar named Theodore Bibliander (1504–64) published the contents of the Toledan Collection in an encyclopedic compendium of polemical texts against Islam.[12] The first

---

10. *Catalogue général des manuscrits latins de la Bibliothèque nationale* (Paris, 1975), 6:489–91.

11. For a transcription of this poem, see the appendix of the present volume.

12. See Hartmut Bobzin, *Der Koran im Zeitalter der Reformation: Studien zur frühgeschichte der Arabistik und Islamkunde in Europa* (Beirut: Ergon, 1995), 158–275; Burman, *Reading the Qur'an in Latin*

edition of *The Lives and Teaching and the Very Qur'an of Muhammad, Prince of the Saracens, and His Successors* (*Machumetis saracenorum principis eiusque successorum vitae, doctrina ac ipse alcoran*) appeared in 1543; a second edition followed in 1550. In the shadow of the military threat posed by the Ottoman Turks, Bibliander's anthology had a pastoral purpose. The defense of Christendom and the conversion of Muslims to the true faith demanded extensive knowledge of the religion of the Turks among Latin Europeans, which the initiative of the abbot of Cluny had provided in the twelfth century. Given the dangerous content of the Latin Qur'an, however, Bibliander felt obliged to surround the text with "an overwhelming army of authors who both refute and disprove and slaughter and kill" the teachings of Muhammed.[13]

The vehemence of Theodore Bibliander's gruesome image of the Christian censure of Islamic belief as slaughter and murder calls to mind Peter of Poitier's praise of his abbot several centuries earlier as a champion of the faith who "butchered with the sword of the divine word" all of those who opposed belief in Christ.[14] Despite the centuries that separated these utterances, they invite comparison as the bluster of angry men frustrated by the military success of the followers of a false prophet against whom, by all logic, Christians should have prevailed in war. Fear inflected the shrillness of their words, but shame fueled it as well—shame that the sins of Christians were ultimately responsible for the withdrawal of God's grace, which left Europe vulnerable to the inexorable advance of Islam. Like the abbot of Cluny, Theodore Bibliander only placed his faith in reasoned discourse when it was clear that the force of arms had failed. With the futility of their violent ambitions unmasked, these prelates played their final gambit in the hope that words would sway the hearts of their adversaries. In the end, their belated attempts at rapprochement went unheeded or unheard.

Christendom, 110–21; and Gregory J. Miller, "Theodor Bibliander's *Machumetis saracenorum principis eiusque successorum vitae, doctrina ac ipse alcoran* (1543) as the Sixteenth-Century 'Encyclopedia' of Islam," *Islam and Christian-Muslim Relations* 24 (2013): 241–54.

13. Theodore Bibliander, *Apologia pro editione Alcorani*, cited from the 1550 edition, in Burman, *Reading the Qur'an in Latin Christendom*, 111–12.

14. See chapter 3 of the present volume.

Martin of Lausanne's Invective Poem against the Qur'an

This unique poem, titled "In alchoran Macometi," appears on one of the opening pages (fol. 3v) of a fifteenth-century manuscript of Peter the Venerable's works against Islam, which also contains an anonymous list of Quranic errors grouped by topic (Paris, Bibliothèque nationale, MS Latin 3669).[1] Written slightly later than the rest of the manuscript, the poem comprises sixteen lines of elegaic couplets (alternating lines of dactylic hexameter and pentameter) brimming with contempt for the Qur'an. Martin's poem is first and foremost a work of religious invective directed against the main source of textual authority for the Muslim religion, but it is also, in fact, a clever parody of an epilogue or *envoi* that Roman and medieval poets often placed at the end of their work. The most famous example is the epilogue to Geoffrey Chaucer's *Troilus and Criseyde*:

> Go, litel book, go, litel myn tragedye,
> Ther god thi makere yit, [e]r that he dye,
> So sende might to make in som comedye!
> But, litel book, no makying thow nenvie,
> But subgit be to alle poesie;

---

1. *Catalogue général des manuscrits latins de la Bibliothèque nationale* (Paris: Bibliothèque nationale, 1975), 6:489–91.

> And kis the steppes, where as thow seest space
> Virgile, Ovide, Omer, Lucan, and Stace.[2]

But while Chaucer bids a fond farewell to his "litel book" and encourages it to kiss the steps of the great poets of pagan antiquity, Martin consigns the book of Muhammed, the Qur'an, to the darkness of an abyss thick with smoke in the hope that no one will ever read it again.

In alchoran Macometi

Martinus praepositus Lausanensis

> 1 I, liber, in tenebras dense fumantis abissi
> nec pateas nostros amplius ante oculos
> non sole es dignus baratri conceptus in antro
> nam qui te genuit Belzebuth ipse fuit
> 5 Belzebuth ille fuit uel si mendatior ipso est
> te genito notus tu patre notus eo
> fraus tua sub quedam veri simulachra latenter
> serpit sed paruo cognita iudicio
> legi detrectus sacre obrius impia fingens
> 10 solum Abraham sequeris omnia Christus habet
> finem promittis ubi femina summa voluptas
> si nichil est melius hec paradisus erat
> o mortis lanqueus spurcissima fossa malorum
> pestifera erroris congeris omne nephas
> 15 irrediturus abi ardenti carbone notandus
> aut cum gente sua te Mathometus edat.

---

2. *Troilus and Criseyde*, 5.1786–92, ed. R. K. Root (Princeton, NJ: Princeton University Press, 1945), 402. See J. S. P. Tatlock, "The Epilog of Chaucer's *Troilus*," *Modern Philology* 18 (1920–21): 625–59, esp. 627–30, where he traces the *envoi* tradition back to the poems of Ovid.

⟡ BIBLIOGRAPHY

Primary Sources

Abelard, Peter. *Collationes*. Edited and translated by John Marenbon and Giovanni Orlandi. Oxford: Clarendon Press, 2001.

——. *Theologia "Scholarium."* In PL 178, cols. 979–1114.

Agobard of Lyons. *De iudaicis superstitionibus et erroribus (ad Ludouicum)*. In *Agobardi Lugdunensis Opera Omnia*, edited by Lieven Van Acker, CCCM 52: 197–221. Turnhout, Belgium: Brepols, 1981.

Annales Bertiniani. Edited by Georg Waitz. MGH SRG 5. Hanover: Impensis Bibliopolii Hahniani, 1883.

Annales Fuldenses. Edited by Friedrich Kurze. MGH SRG 7. Hanover: Impensis Bibliopolii Hahniani, 1891.

Annales Magdeburgensis. Edited by Georg Pertz. MGH SS 16. Hanover: Impensis Bibliopolii Aulici Hahniani, 1859.

Annales Regni Francorum. Edited by Georg Pertz. MGH SRG 6. Hanover: Impensis Bibliopolii Hahniani, 1895.

Annales Xantenses. Edited by Bernhard von Simon. MGH SRG 12. Hanover: Impensis Bibliopolii Hahniani, 1909.

Anselm of Canterbury. *Cur Deus Homo*. In *Sancti Anselmi Cantuariensis archiepiscopi opera omnia*, edited by Franciscus Salesius Schmitt, 2:37–133. Rome, n.p., 1946.

——. *Epistola de incarnatione verbi*. In *Sancti Anselmi Cantuariensis archiepiscopi opera omnia*, edited by Franciscus Salesius Schmitt, 2:3–35. Rome, n.p., 1946.

The Apology of al-Kindi. In *Exposición y refutación del Islam: La versión latina de las epístolas de al'Hasimi y al-Kindi*, edited and translated by Fernando González Muñoz. A Coruña: Universidade da Coruña, Servizo de Publicacións, 2005.

Augustine. *De civitate Dei*. Edited by Bernard Dombart and Alphonse Kalb. 2 vols. CCSL 47–48. Turnhout, Belgium: Brepols, 1955.

——. *Contra Faustum*, edited by Joseph Zycha. CSEL 25: 251–797. Vienna, 1891.

Bede. *Historia abbatum*. In *Abbots of Wearmouth and Jarrow*, edited and translated by Christopher Grocock and I. N. Wood, 22–75. Oxford: Clarendon Press, 2013.

——. *Historia Ecclesiastica*. In *Bede's Ecclesiastical History of the English People*, edited by Bertram Colgrave and R. A. B. Mynors. Oxford: Clarendon Press, 1969.

——. *In samuelem prophetam allegorica expositio*, in PL 91, cols. 499–714.

Bernard. *Itinerarium*. In *Das "Itinerarum Bernardi Monachi": Edition—Übersetzung—Kommentar*, edited by Josef Ackermann, 115–27. MGH Studien und Texte 50. Hanover: Hahnsche Buchhandlung, 2011.

Bernard of Clairvaux. *Epistolae*. Edited by Jean Leclercq. *Sancti Bernardi Opera*, vol. 8. Rome: Editiones Cistercienses, 1977.

Bibliander, Theodore. *Machumetis saracenorum principis eiusque successorum vitae, doctrina ac ipse alcoran*, 3 vols. Basel: Johann Oporinus, 1543.

Boniface. *Epistolae*. Edited by Michael Tangl. MGH Epistolae Selectae 1. Berlin: Apud Weidmannos, 1955.

La Chanson de Roland. Edited by Luis Cortés. Paris: Nizet, 1994.

Charlemagne. *Capitulare missorum generale* (802). Edited by Alfred Boretius. MGH Capitularia regum Francorum 1. Hanover: Impensis Bibliopolii Hahniani, 1883.

Chaucer, Geoffrey. *Troilus and Criseyde*. Edited by R. K. Root. Princeton, NJ: Princeton University Press, 1945.

Chronicon novaliciense. Edited by Georg Pertz. MGH SS 7. Hanover: Impensis Bibliopolii Aulici Hahniani, 1846.

Codex Diplomaticus: Sammlung der Urkunden zur Geschichte Cur-Rätiens und der Republik Graubünden. 2 vols. Edited by Theodor von Mohr. Cur, Switzerland: L. Hitz, 1848–52.

Collectaneum exemplorum et visionum Clarevallense e codice Trecensi 946. Edited by Olivier Legendre. CCCM 208. Turnhout, Belgium: Brepols, 2005.

Collectio exemplorum Cisterciensis in codice Parisiensi 15912 asseruata. Edited by Jacques Berlioz and Marie Anne Polo de Beaulieu. CCCM 243. Turnhout, Belgium: Brepols, 2012.

"Diplôme de Charles le Simple pour l'abbaye de Psalmodi." In *Histoire générale de Languedoc avec des notes et les pièces justificatives*, vol. 5, edited by Claude de Vic and Joseph Vaissete, cols. 127–30 (no. 37). Toulouse: J.P. Paya, 1840.

Einhard. *Translatio et miracula sanctorum Marcellini et Petri*. Edited by Georg Waitz. MGH SS 15.1. Hanover: Impensis Bibliopolii Hahniani, 1888.

———. *Vita Karoli*. Edited by Oswald Holder-Egger. MGH SRG 25. Hanover: Impensis Bibliopolii Hahniani, 1911.

Ekkehard. *Casus Santi Galli*. In *St. Galler Klostergeschichten*, edited by Hans F. Haefle. Darmstadt, Germany: Wissenschaftliche Buchgesellschaft, 1980.

Flodoard. *Les Annales de Flodoard*. Edited by Philippe Lauer. Paris: Alphonse Picard et Fils, 1905.

Gallia Christiana in provincias ecclesiasticas distributa. Edited by the Monks of the Congregation of Saint-Maur. 16 vols. Paris: Coignard, 1715–1865.

Galterius. *Vita Anastasii*. In PL 149, cols. 427–32. Translated by Scott G. Bruce in *The Renaissance of the Twelfth Century: A Reader*, edited by Alex J. Novikoff. Toronto: University of Toronto Press, 2015 (forthcoming).

Gilbert Crispin. *Disputatio Iudei et Christiani*. In *The Works of Gibert of Crispin, Abbot of Westminster*, edited by Anna Sapir Abulafia and G. R. Evans, 8–61. London: Oxford University Press, 1986.

Gilo. *Vita Hugonis*. Edited by H. E. J. Cowdrey in "Two Studies in Cluniac History 1049–1126." *Studi Gregoriani* 11 (1978): 45–109.

Gislebertus of Saint-Trond. *Gesta Abbatum Trudonensium VIII–XIII*. Edited by Paul Tombeur, CCCM 257A. Turnhout, Belgium: Brepols, 2013.

Glaber, Rodulfus. *Historiarum libri quinque*. In *Rodulphus Glaber: The Five Books of Histories and the Life of St. William*, edited and translated by John France, 1–253. Oxford: Clarendon Press, 1989.

Gregory VII. *Registrum*. Edited by Erich Caspar as *Das Register Gregors VII*. MGH Epistolae selectae 2. Berlin: Apud Weidmannos, 1920.

Gregory the Great. *Homilia*. Edited by Charles Morel as *Grégoire le Grand, Homélies sur Ézéchiel*. 2 vols. SC 327, 360. Paris: Éditions du Cerf, 1986, 1990.

Hildebert of Lavardin. *Epistolae*. In PL 171, cols. 141–312.

[Ibrahim ibn Ya'qub al'Isra'ili al'Turtushi.] *Ein arabischer Berichterstatter aus dem 10. Jahrhundert über Fulda, Schleswig, Soest, Paderborn und andere Städte des Abendlandes: Artikel aus Qazwînîs Âthâr al-bilâd*. 3rd ed. Translated by Georg Jacob. Berlin: Mayer & Müller, 1896.

Instituta regalia et ministeria camerae regum Longobardorum et honorantiae civitatis Papiae, edited by Adolf Hofmeister. In MGH SS 30.2:1444–60. Leipzig: Impensis Karoli W. Hiersemann, 1934.

Jerome. *Epistolae*. Edited by Isidore Hilberg as *Sancti Eusebii Hieronymi Epistolae*. 2 vols. CSEL 54–55. Vienna: Verlag der Österreichischen Akademie der Wissenschaften, 1996.

——. [*Vita Malchi*] *De monacho captivo*. In *Jérôme: Trois vies des moines (Paul, Malchus, Hilarion)*, edited by Edgardo Morales and Pierre Leclerc, 184–211. SC 508. Paris: Éditions du Cerf, 2007.

John the Deacon. *Gesta Episcoporum Neapolitanorum*. Edited by Georg Waitz. MGH SSRL. Hanover: Impensis Bibliopolii Hahniani, 1878.

John of Saint Arnulf. *Vita Iohannis Gorziensis*. Edited and translated by Michel Parisse as *La Vie de Jean, Abbé de Gorze*. Paris: Picard, 1999.

John of Salerno. *Vita Odonis*. In PL 133, cols. 43–86.

Jotsaldus. *Vita Odilonis*. Edited by Johannes Staub as *Iotsald von Saint-Claude, Vita des Abtes Odilo von Cluny*. MGH SRG 68. Hanover: Hahnsche Buchhandlung, 1999.

Lampert of Hersfeld. *Annales*. Edited by Oswald Holder-Egger. MGH SRG 38. Hanover: Impensis Bibliopolii Hahniani, 1894.

Liber pontificalis. Edited by Louis Marie Olivier Duchesne. 2 vols. Paris: Ernest Thorin, 1886–92.

Liber Tramitis Aevi Odilowis Abbatis. Edited by Peter Dinter. CCM 10. Siegburg: Franz Schmitt, 1980.

Liudprand. *Antapodosis*, edited by Paolo Chiesa, in *Liudprandi Cremonensis Opera Omnia*, CCCM 156:1–150. Turnhout, Belgium: Brepols, 1998. Translated by Paolo Squatriti in *The Complete Works of Liudprand of Cremona*, 41–202. Washington, DC: Catholic University of America Press, 2007.

Louis II. *De rebus vero saecularibus*, edited by Georg Pertz, in MGH Capitularia regum Francorum 2. Hanover: Impensis Bibliopolii Hahniani, 1897.

Martin I, Pope. *Epistolae*, in PL 87, cols. 119–204.

Nalgod. *Vita Maioli*. In *Vita ex prolixoribus coaevorum actis a Nalgodo monacho post sesqui secum contracta*, AASS Maii 2, 657–67.

——. *Vita Odonis*. In *Acta sanctorum ordinis sancti Benedicti in saeculorum classes distributa*, edited by Jean Mabillon, 5:186–199. Paris: Colet, 1685. Reprinted in PL 133, cols. 85–104.

Nicholas of Cusa. *Nicholas of Cusa's De pace fidei and Cribratio Alkorani: Translation and Analysis*. Edited and translated by Jasper Hopkins. Notre Dame, IN: A. J. Banning Press, 1990.

Odilo. *Vita sancti Maioli*. AASS Maii 2, 683–88. Reprinted in PL 142, cols. 959–62. Translated by Paul Dutton in *Medieval Saints: A Reader*, edited by Mary-Ann Stouck, 250–64. Peterborough, Ontario: Broadview Press, 1999.

Odo of Cluny. *Sermo 3 (De sancto Benedicto abbate)*. In PL 133, cols. 721–29.

——. *Vita sancti Geraldi Auriliacensis*. Edited by Anne-Marie Bultot-Verleysen as *Odon de Cluny, Vita sancti Geraldi Auriliacensis: Édition critique, traduction français, introduction et commentaires*. Brussels: Société des Bollandistes, 2009.

Orderic Vitalis. *Historia ecclesiastica*. Edited and translated by Marjorie Chibnall as *The Ecclesiastical History of Orderic Vitalis*. 6 vols. Oxford: Clarendon Press, 1969–80.

"Paschasii Radberti Epistula Hieronymi ad Paulam et Eustochium de Assumptione Sanctae Mariae Virginis." In *Pascasius Radbertus, De partu Virginis, De assumptione sanctae Mariae Virginis*, edited by Albert Ripberger, CCCM 55C: 97–162. Turnhout, Belgium: Brepols, 1985.

Peter Alfonsi. *Dialogus contra Iudaeos*. Edited by Klaus-Peter Mieth and translated by Esperanza Ducay, as *Pedro Alfonso de Huesca, Diálogo contra los Judíos*. Huesca, Spain: Instituto de Estudios Altoaragoneses, 1996. Translated by Irven M. Resnick as *Petrus Alfonsi, Dialogue against the Jews*. Washington, DC: Catholic University of America Press, 2006.

Peter Damian. *Epistolae*. Edited by Kurt Reindel. In *Die Briefe des Petrus Damiani*, MGH Die Briefe der deutschen Kaiserzeit 4. Munich: Monumenta Germaniae Historica, 1983.

——. *Liber Gomorrhianus*. In PL 145, cols. 159–90.

Peter the Venerable, *Adversus Iudeorum inveteratam duritiem*. Edited by Yvonne Friedman. CCCM 58. Turnhout, Belgium: Brepols, 1985. Translated by Irven M. Resnick as *Peter the Venerable, Against the Inveterate Obduracy of the Jews*. Washington, DC: Catholic University of America Press, 2013.

——. *Contra Petrobrusianos hereticos*. Edited by James Fearns. CCCM 10. Turnhout, Belgium: Brepols, 1968.

——. *Contra sectam Saracenorum*. In *Petrus Venerabilis, Schriften zum Islam*, edited by Reinhold Glei, 30–239. Altenberge, Germany: CIS Verlag, 1985.

——. *De miraculis libri duos*. Edited by Denise Bouthillier. CCM 83. Turnhout, Belgium: Brepols, 1988.

——. *Epistola de translatione sua*. In *Petrus Venerabilis, Schriften zum Islam*, edited by Reinhold Glei, 22–29. Altenberge, Germany: CIS Verlag, 1985.

——. *Epistolae*. Edited by Giles Constable as *The Letters of Peter the Venerable*. 2 vols. Cambridge, MA: Harvard University Press, 1967.

——. *Statuta Petri Venerabili abbatis Cluniacensis*. Edited by Giles Constable. CCM 6. Siegburg, Germany: Franz Schmitt, 1975.

——. *Summa totius haeresis Sarracenorum*. In *Petrus Venerabilis, Schriften zum Islam*, edited by Reinhold Glei, 2–22. Altenberge, Germany: CIS Verlag, 1985.

Piccolomini, Aeneas Silvius [Pope Pius II]. *Epistola ad Mahomatem II (Epistle to Mohammad II)*. Edited and translated by Albert R. Baca. New York: Peter Lang, 1990.

Pippin. *Capitulare* (754–55). Edited by Alfred Boretius. MGH Capitularia regum Francorum 1. Hanover: Impensis Bibliopolii Hahniani, 1883.

Polyptyque de l'abbé Irminon ou dénombrement des manses, des serfs et des revenus de l'abbaye de Saint-Germain-des-Prés sous le règne de Charlemagne. Edited by Benjamin Guérard. 2 vols. Paris: A l'Imprimerie Royale, 1844.

Praeceptum Ottonis imperatoris de sancto Maiolo de Papia (dated 999). In BC, col. 409. Paris, n.p., 1614; reprinted, Mâcon: Protat, 1915. Also in PL 142, col. 1039.

Quodvultdeus. *Contra Iudaeos, paganos et Arrianos.* In *Opera Quodvultdeo Carthaginiensi Episcopo Tributa*, edited by René Braun, 227–58. CCSL 60. Turnhout, Belgium: Brepols, 1976.

Radelgisi et Siginulfi Divisio Ducatus Beneventani. Edited by Georg Pertz. In MGH Leges 4:221–25. Hanover: Impensis Bibliopolii Aulici Hahniani, 1868.

Recueil des chartes de l'abbaye de Cluny. Edited by Auguste Bernard and Alexandre Bruel. 6 vols. Paris: Imprimerie Nationale, 1876–1903.

Regino of Prüm. *Chronicon.* Edited by Friedrich Kurze. MGH SRG 50. Hanover, 1890. Translated by Simon MacLean in *History and Politics in Late Carolingian and Ottonian Europe: The Chronicle of Regino of Prüm and Adalbert of Magdeburg.* Manchester: Manchester University Press, 2009.

Regula Benedicti. Edited by Adalbert de Vogüé as *La règle de saint Benoît.* 7 vols. SC 181–87. Paris: Éditions du Cerf, 1971–72.

Sulpicius Severus. *Vita Martini.* Edited by Jacques Fontaine as *Sulpice Sévère: Vie de saint Martin.* 3 vols. SC 133–35. Paris: Éditions du Cerf, 1967–69.

Symmachus, *Epistolae.* Edited by Jean-Pierre Callu as *Symmaque: Lettres.* 4 vols. Paris: Les Belles Lettres, 1972–2002.

Syrus. *Vita sancti Maioli.* In *Agni Immaculati: Recherches sur les sources hagiographiques relatives à saint Maieul de Cluny (954–994)*, edited by Dominique Iogna-Prat, 163–285. Paris: Éditions du Cerf, 1988.

"Testament de Rostang, archevêque d'Arles." In *Gallia christiana novissima: Histoire des archevêchés, évêchés et abbayes de France d'après les documents authentiques recueillis dans les registres du Vatican et les archives locales*, edited by J.-H. Albanés and Ulysse Chevalier, vol. 3, cols. 94–95 (no. 233). Valence, France: Valentinoise, 1901.

Thietmar of Merseberg. *Chronicon.* Edited by Robert Holtzmann. MGH SRG, n.s. 9. Berlin: Apud Weidmannos, 1935.

Three Treatises from Bec on the Nature of Monastic Life. Edited by Giles Constable. Toronto: University of Toronto Press, 2008.

Virgil. *Aeneid.* Edited by Gian Biagio Conte. Berlin: De Gruyter, 2009.

Vita breuior sancti Maioli. In BC, cols. 1763–82. Paris, n.p., 1614; reprinted, Mâcon: Protat, 1915.

Widukind. *Res Gestae Saxonicae.* Edited by Georg Waitz and K. A. Kehr. MGH SRG 60. Hanover: Impensis Bibliopolii Hahniani, 1935.

Secondary Sources

Abulafia, Anna Sapir. "An Attempt by Gilbert Crispin, Abbot of Westminster, at Rational Argument in the Jewish–Christian Debate." *Studia Monastica* 26 (1984): 55–74.

——. *Christians and Jews in Dispute: Disputational Literature and the Rise of Anti-Judaism in the West (c. 1000–1150)*. Aldershot, England: Variorum, 1998.

——. "St. Anselm and Those outside the Church." In *Faith and Unity: Christian Political Experience*, edited by D. Loades and K. Walsh, 11–37. Studies in Church History 6. Oxford: Ecclesiastical History Society, 1990.

Albert, Bat-Sheva. "*Adversus Iudaeos* in the Carolingian Empire." In *Contra Iudaeos: Ancient and Medieval Polemics between Christians and Jews*, edited by Ora Limor and Guy G. Stroumsa, 119–42. Tübingen, Germany: J. C. B. Mohr, 1996.

Amargier, Paul. "La capture de saint Maieul de Cluny et l'expulsion des Sarrasins de Provence." *Revue bénédictine* 73 (1963): 316–23.

Arnoux, Mathieu, "Un Vénitien au Mont-Saint-Michel: Anastase, moine, ermite et confesseur († vers 1085)." *Médiévales* 28 (1995): 55–78.

Atti del 4° congresso internazionale di studi sull'alto medioevo, Pavia-Scaldasole-Monza-Bobbio, 10–14 settembre 1967. Spoleto, Italy: Centro Italiano di Studi sull'Alto Medioevo, 1969.

Atwood, Margaret. *Strange Things: The Malevolent North in Canadian Literature*. Oxford: Clarendon Press, 1995.

Baca, Albert R. "On the Sources of Pius II's *Epistula ad Mahometam II*." In *Paradigms in Medieval Thought, Applications in Medieval Disciplines: A Symposium*, edited by Nancy Van Deusen and Alvin E. Ford, 27–36. Lewiston, NY: Edwin Mellon Press, 1990.

Ballan, Mohammad. "Fraxinetum: An Islamic Frontier State in Tenth-Century Provence." *Comitatus* 41 (2010): 23–76.

Barret, Sébastien. "Cluny et les Ottoniens." In *Ottone III e Romualdo di Ravenna: Impero, monasteri e santi asceti, atti del XXIV convegno del Centro Studi Avellaniti, Fonte Avellana, 2002*, 179–213. Verona: Gabrielli Editori, 2003.

Beckett, Katharine Scarfe. *Anglo-Saxon Perceptions of the Islamic World*. Cambridge: Cambridge University Press, 2003.

Benson, Robert L., and Giles Constable, with Carol D. Lanham, eds. *Renaissance and Renewal in the Twelfth Century*. Cambridge, MA: Harvard University Press, 1982.

Berger, David. "St. Peter Damian: His Attitude toward the Jews and the Old Testament." *Yavneh Review* 4 (1965): 80–112. Reprinted in David Berger, *Persecution, Polemic and Dialogue: Essays in Jewish-Christian Relations*, 261–88. Boston: Academic Studies Press, 2010.

Berry, Virginia. "Peter the Venerable and the Crusades." In *Petrus Venerabilis 1156–1956: Studies and Texts Commemorating the Eighth Centenary of His Death*, edited by Giles Constable and James Kritzeck, 141–62. Rome: Herder, 1956.

Besson, Joseph-Antoine. *Mémoires pour l'histoire ecclésiastique des diocèses de Genève, Tarantaise, Aoste, et Maurienne, et du décanat de Savoye*. Nancy, France: Sebastien Henault, 1759.

Bisaha, Nancy. *Creating East and West: Renaissance Humanists and the Ottoman Turks*. Philadelphia: University of Pennsylvania Press, 2004.

———. "Pope Pius II's Letter to Sultan Mehmed II: A Reexamination." *Crusades* 1 (2002): 183–200.

Bishko, Charles Julian. "Liturgical Intercession at Cluny for the King-Emperors of Leon." *Studi Monastica* 3 (1961): 53–76.

———. "Peter the Venerable's Journey to Spain." In *Petrus Venerabilis 1156–1956: Studies and Texts Commemorating the Eighth Centenary of His Death*, edited by Giles Constable and James Kritzeck, 163–75. Rome: Herder, 1956.

———. "The Spanish Journey of Abbot Ponce of Cluny." *Richerche di Storia Religiosa* 1 (1957): 311–19.

———. *Spanish and Portugese Monasticism, 600–1300*. London: Variorum, 1984.

Blumenkranz, Bernhard. *Les auteurs chrétiens latins du moyen âge sur les juifs et le judaïsme*. Paris: Peeters, 1963.

———. *Juifs et chrétiens dans le monde occidental, 430–1096*. Paris: Peeters, 1960.

Bobzin, Hartmut. *Der Koran im Zeitalter der Reformation: Studien zur frühgeschichte der Arabistik und Islamkunde in Europa*. Beirut: Ergon, 1995.

Bourdon, Léon. "Les voyages de Saint Mayeul en Italie: Itinéraires et chronologie." *Mélanges d'archéologie et d'histoire* 43 (1926): 63–89.

Boynton, Susan, and Isabelle Cochelin, eds. *From Dead of Night to End of Day: The Medieval Customs of Cluny / Du coeur de la nuit à la fin du jour: Les coutumes clunisiennes au moyen âge*. Leiden: Brepols, 2005.

Brentchaloff, Daniel, and Philippe Sénac. "Note sur l'épave sarrasine de la rade d'Agay (Saint-Raphaël, Var)." *Archeologie islamique* 2 (1991): 71–79.

Bruce, Scott G. "Lurking with Spiritual Intent: A Note on the Origin and Functions of the Monastic Roundsman (*Circator*)." *Revue bénédictine* 109 (1999): 75–89.

———. *Silence and Sign Language in Medieval Monasticism: The Cluniac Tradition (c. 900–c. 1200)*. Cambridge: Cambridge University Press, 2007.

Bullough, Donald A. "Urban Change in Early Medieval Italy: The Example of Pavia." *Papers of the British School at Rome* 34 (1966): 82–130.

Büren, Veronika von. "Le grand catalogue de la Bibliothèque de Cluny." In *Le gouvernement d'Hugues de Semur à Cluny: Actes du Colloque scientifique international (Cluny, septembre 1988)*, 245–63. Mâcon: Musée Ochier, 1990.

Burman, Thomas E. *Reading the Qur'an in Latin Christendom, 1140–1560*. Philadelphia: University of Pennsylvania Press, 2007.

Burns, Robert I. "The Coherence of the Arabic-Latin Translation Program in Toledo in the Twelfth Century." *Science in Context* 14 (2001): 249–88.

Carozzi, Claude. "La vie de saint Bobon: un modèle clunisien de sainteté laïque." In *Guerriers et moines: Conversion et sainteté aristocratiques dans l'occident médiéval (IXe–XIIe siècle)*, edited by Michel Lauwers, 467–91. Antibes, France: APDCA, 2002.

Carraz, Damien. *L'ordre du temple dans la basse vallée du Rhône (1124–1312): Ordres militaires, croisades et sociétés méridionales*. Lyon: Presses Universitaires de Lyon, 2005.

Casagrande, Maria Antonietta. "Fondazione e suiluppo del monasterio cluniacense di San Maiolo di Pavia nei primi secoli." In *Atti del 4° congresso internazionale di studi sull'alto medioevo, Pavia-Scaldasole-Monza-Bobbio, 10–14 settembre*

1967, 335–51. Spoleto, Italy: Centro Italiano di Studi sull'Alto Medioevo, 1969.

Catalogue des manuscrits de la bibliothèque de l'Arsenal. 9 vols. Paris: Plon, 1885–99.

Catalogue général des manuscrits latins de la Bibliothèque nationale. 7 vols. Paris: Bibliothèque nationale, 1939–88.

Ceillier, Rémy. *Histoire générale des auteurs sacrés et ecclésiastiques.* 23 vols. Paris: Louis Vivès, 1729–63.

Chachuat, Germaine. "L'érémitisme à Cluny sous l'abbatiat de Pierre le Vénérable." *Annales de l'académie de Mâcon* 58 (1982): 89–96.

Chazan, Robert. *European Jewry and the First Crusade.* Berkeley: University of California Press, 1987.

Ciggaar, Krijnie. *Western Travellers to Constantinople: The West and Byzantium, 962–1204: Cultural and Political Relations.* Leiden: Brill, 1996.

Clanchy, Michael. *Abelard: A Medieval Life.* Oxford: Wiley-Blackwell, 1997.

Cohen, Jeremy. "The Jews as the Killers of Christ in the Latin Tradition, from Augustine to the Friars." *Traditio* 39 (1983): 1–27.

——. *Living Letters of the Law: Ideas of the Jew in Medieval Christianity.* Berkeley: University of California Press, 1999.

——. *Sanctifying the Name of God: Jewish Martyrs and Jewish Memories of the First Crusade.* Philadelphia: University of Pennsylvania Press, 2004.

——. "Slay Them Not: Augustine and the Jews in Modern Scholarship." *Medieval Encounters* 4 (1998): 78–92.

Colombo, Alessandro. "I diplomi ottoniani e adelaidini e la fondazione del monastero di S. Salvatore di Pavia." *Biblioteca della Societa storica subalpina* 130 (1932): 1–39.

Constable, Giles. *Cluniac Studies.* London: Variorum, 1980.

——. *Cluny from the Tenth to the Twelfth Centuries: Further Studies.* Aldershot, England: Ashgate, 2000.

——. "Cluny in the Monastic World of the Tenth Century." In *Il secolo di ferro: Mito e realtà del secolo X (Spoleto, 19–25 aprile 1990),* Settimane di studio del Centro italiano di studi sull'alto medioevo 38, 391–437. Spoleto, Italy: Centro Italiano di Studi sull'Alto Medioevo, 1991.

——. *Crusaders and Crusading in the Twelfth Century.* Burlington, VT: Ashgate, 2009.

——. "The Crusading Project of 1150." In *Montjoie: Studies in Crusading History in Honour of Hans Eberhard Mayer,* edited by Benjamin Z. Kedar, Jonathan Riley-Smith, and Rudolf Hiestand, 67–75. Aldershot, England: Variorum, 1997.

——. "The Monastic Policy of Peter the Venerable." In *Pierre Abélard—Pierre Vénérable: Les courants philosophiques, littéraires et artistiques en Occident au milieu du XIIe siècle: actes et mémoires du colloque international, Abbaye de Cluny, 2 au 9 juillet 1972,* 119–41. Paris: Éditions du Centre national de la recherche scientifique, 1975.

——. "The Second Crusade as Seen by Contemporaries." *Traditio* 9 (1952): 213–79.

Constable, Giles, and James Kritzeck, eds. *Petrus Venerabilis 1156–1956: Studies and Texts Commemorating the Eighth Centenary of His Death.* Rome: Herder, 1956.

Coolidge, W. A. B. *Josias Simler et les origines de l'alpinisme jusqu'en 1600*. Grenoble, France: Allier Frères, 1904.

Cowdrey, H. E. J. *Pope Gregory VII, 1073–1085*. Oxford: Clarendon Press, 1998.

Cucarella, Sarrió. "Corresponding across Religious Borders: Al-Bājī's Response to a Missionary Letter from France." *Medieval Encounters* 18 (2012): 1–35.

Cutler, Anthony. "Gifts and Gift Exchange as Aspects of the Byzantine, Arab, and Related Economies." *Dumbarton Oaks Papers* 55 (2001): 247–78.

——. "Who Was the 'Monk of France' and When Did He Write?" *Al-Andalus* 28 (1963): 249–69.

Dahan, Gilbert. *Les intellectuels chrétiens et les juifs au moyen âge*. Paris: Éditions du Cerf, 1990.

D'Alverny, Marie-Thérèse. *La connaissance de l'Islam dans l'Occident médiéval*. Aldershot, England: Variorum, 1994.

——. "La connaissance de l'Islam en Occident du IXe au milieu du XIIe siècle." In *L'Occidente e l'Islam nell'alto medioevo: Spoleto 2–8 aprile 1964*, 1:577–602. Spoleto, Italy: Centro Italiano di Studi sull'Alto Medioevo, 1965.

——. "Deux traductions latines du Coran au Moyen Âge." *Archives d'histoire doctrinale et littéraire du Moyen Âge* 22–23 (1947–48): 69–131.

——. "Translations and Translators." In *Renaissance and Renewal in the Twelfth Century*, edited by Robert L. Benson and Giles Constable with Carol D. Lanham, 421–62. Cambridge, MA: Harvard University Press, 1982.

Daniel, Norman. *Islam and the West: The Making of an Image*. Rev. ed., Oxford, 1993.

Defourneaux, Marcelin. *Les Français en Espagne aux XIe et XIIe siècles*. Paris: Presses Universitaires de France, 1949.

Delisle, Léopold. *Inventaire des manuscrits de la Bibliothèque nationale: Fonds de Cluni*. Paris: Librairie H. Champion, 1884.

Dolveck, Franz. "Un poème passé inaperçu: contribution au dossier hagiographique de saint Maieul, quatrième abbé de Cluny." *Archivum Latinitatis Medii Aevi* 70 (2013): 257–63.

Drocourt, Nicholas. "Christian-Muslim Diplomatic Relations: An Overview of the Main Sources and Themes of Encounter (600–1000)." In *Christian-Muslim Relations: A Bibliographical History*, edited by David Thomas and Alex Mallett, 2: 29–72. Leiden: Brill, 2010.

Duby, Georges. "Le budget de l'abbaye de Cluny entre 1080 et 1155: Économie domaniale et économie monétaire." *Annales: Économies, Sociétés, Civilisations* 7 (1952): 155–71. Reprinted in Georges Duby, *Hommes et structures du moyen âge: Recueil d'articles*, 61–82. Paris: Mouton, 1973.

Duc, Joseph Auguste. "À quelle date est mort Saint Bernard de Menthon?" *Miscellanea di storia Italiana* 31 (1894): 341–68.

Dunlop, D. M. "A Christian Mission to Muslim Spain in the Eleventh Century." *Al-Andalus* 17 (1952): 259–310.

Eickhoff, Ekkehard. *Seekrieg und Seepolitik zwischen Islam und Abendland: Das Mittelmeer unter byzantinischer und arabischer Hegemonie (650–1040)*. Berlin: De Gruyter, 1966.

El-Hajji, Abdurrahman Ali. *Andalusian Diplomatic Relations with Western Europe during the Umayyad Period (A.H. 138–366/A.D. 755–976): An Historical Survey*. Beirut: Dar al-Irshad, 1970.

————. "Ibrahim ibn Ya'qub at-Tartushi and His Diplomatic Activity." *Islamic Quarterly* 14 (1970): 22–40.

Euw, Anton von, and Peter Schreiner, eds. *Kaiserin Theophanu: Begegnung des Ostens und Westens um die Wende des ersten Jahrtausends.* 2 vols. Cologne: Schnütgen-Museum, 1991.

Fearns, James. "Peter von Bruis und die religiöse Bewegung des 12. Jahrhunderts." *Archiv für Kulturgeschichte* 48 (1966): 311–35.

Férotin, Marius. "Complément de la lettre de Saint Hugues." *Bibliothèque de l'École des Chartes* 63 (1902): 682–86.

————. "Une lettre inédite de Saint Hugues, abbé de Cluny, à Bernard d'Agen, archevêque de Tolède (1087)." *Bibliothèque de l'École des Chartes* 61 (1900): 339–45.

Février, Paul-Albert. *La Provence des origines à l'an mil: Histoire et archéologie.* Rennes: Ouest-France Université, 1989.

Fichtenau, Heinrich. "Reisen und Reisende." In *Beiträge zur Mediävistik: Ausgewählte Aufsätze,* 3:1–79. Stuttgart: Hiersemann, 1975–86.

Fini, Maria Luisa. "Studio sulla *Vita Odonis reformata* di Nalgodo: Il *fragmentum mutilum* del codice latino NA 1496 della Bibliotheque Nationale di Parigi." *Atti della Accademia delle Scienze dell'Istituto di Bologna* 63 (1974–75): 33–147.

Fouracre, Paul. *Frankish History: Studies in the Construction of Power.* Farnham, England: Variorum, 2013.

————. "Merovingian History and Merovingian Hagiography." *Past and Present* 127 (1990): 3–38.

France, John. "Glaber as a Reformer." *Studia Monastica* 34 (1992): 41–51.

————. "Rodulphus Glaber and the Cluniacs." *Journal of Ecclesiastical History* 39 (1988): 497–508.

Franz, Adolph. *Die kirchlichen Benediktionen im Mittelalter.* 2 vols. Graz, Austria: Akademische Druckund Verlagsanstalt, 1960.

Frederiksen, Paula. *Augustine and the Jews: A Christian Defense of Jews and Judaism.* 2nd ed. New Haven, CT: Yale University Press, 2010.

Friedman, Yvonne. "An Anatomy of Anti-Semitism: Peter the Venerable's Letter to Louis VII, King of France (1146)." *Bar-Ilan Studies in History* 1 (1978): 87–102.

Funkenstein, Amos. *Perceptions of Jewish History.* Berkeley: University of California Press, 1993.

Garand, Monique-Cécile. "Copistes de Cluny au temps de saint Maieul (948–994)." *Bibliothèque de l'École des Chartes* 136 (1978): 5–36.

Gauss, Julia. "Anselmus von Canterbury zur Begegnung und Auseinandersetzung der Religionen." *Saeculum* 17 (1966): 277–363.

————. "Die Auseinandersetzung mit Judentum und Islam bei Anselm." In *Die Wirkungsgeschichte Anselms von Canterbury,* edited by Helmut Kohlenberger, 2:101–9. Frankfurt am Main: Minerva, 1975.

Geary, Patrick J. *Furta Sacra: Thefts of Relics in the Central Middle Ages.* 2nd ed. Princeton, NJ: Princeton University Press, 1990.

————. *Living with the Dead in the Middle Ages.* Ithaca, NY: Cornell University Press, 1994.

——. *Phantoms of Remembrance: Memory and Oblivion at the End of the First Millenium*. Princeton, NJ: Princeton University Press, 1996.

——. "Saints, Scholars, and Society: The Elusive Goal." In *Living with the Dead in the Middle Ages*, edited by Patrick J. Geary, 9–29. Ithaca, NY: Cornell University Press, 1994.

Goullet, Monique, Martin Heinzelmann, and Christiane Veyrard-Cosme, eds. *L'hagiographie mérovingienne à travers ses réécritures*. Ostfildern, Germany: Thorbecke, 2010.

Graboïs, Aryeh. *Les sources hébraïques médiévales*, vol. 2: *Les commentaires exégétiques*. Typologie des sources du moyen âge occidental 66. Turnhout, Belgium: Brepols, 1993.

Gussone, Nikolaus. "Trauung und Krönung: Zur Hochzeit der byzantinischen Prinzessin Theophanu mit Kaiser Otto II." In *Kaiserin Theophanu: Begegnung des Ostens und Westens um die Wende des ersten Jahrtausends*, edited by Anton von Euw and Peter Schreiner, 2:161–74. Cologne: Schnütgen-Museum, 1991.

Halevi, Leor. "*Lex Mahomethi*: Carnal and Spiritual Representations of Islamic Law and Ritual in a Twelfth-Century Dialogue by a Jewish Convert to Christianity." In *The Islamic Scholarly Tradition: Studies in History, Law, and Thought in Honor of Professor Michael Allan Cook*, edited by Asad Q. Ahmed, Behnam Sadeghi, and Michael Bonner, 315–42. Leiden: Brill, 2011.

Hall, Hubert. *Studies in English Official Historical Documents*. Cambridge: Cambridge University Press, 1908.

Hallinger, Kassius. "Überlieferung und Steigerung im Mönchtum des 8. bis 12. Jahrhunderts." In *Eulogia: Miscellanea liturgica in onore di P. Burckhard Neunheuser O.S.B.*, 125–87. Rome: Anselmiana, 1979.

Harvey, Susan Ashbrook. "Martyr Passions and Hagiography." In *The Oxford Handbook of Early Christian Studies*, edited by Susan Ashbrook Harvey and David G. Hunter, 603–27. Oxford: Oxford University Press, 2008.

Heath, Robert G. *Crux Imperatorum Philosophia: Imperial Horizons of the Cluniac Confraternitas, 964–1109*. Pittsburgh: Pickwick Press, 1976.

Hefele, Charles-Joseph. *Histoire des Conciles d'après les documents originaux*, trans. Henri Leclercq, 11 vols. Paris: Letouzey et Ané, 1907–.

Heinzelmann, Martin. *Translationsberichte und andere Quellen des Reliquienkultes*. Typologie des sources du moyen âge occidental 33. Turnhout, Belgium: Brepols, 1979.

Heyd, Wilhelm. *Histoire du commerce du Levant au moyen âge*. 2 vols. Leipzig, Germany: O. Harrassowitz, 1923.

Hofmann, Petra. "Infernal Imagery in Anglo-Saxon Charters." PhD diss., University of St. Andrews, 2008.

Hourlier, Jacques. *Saint Odilon, Abbé de Cluny*. Leuven, Belgium: Bibliothèque de l'Université, Bureaux de la Revue, 1964.

——. "Saint Odilon bâtisseur." *Revue Mabillon* 51 (1961): 303–24.

Howe, John. "Did St. Peter Damian Die in 1073? A New Perspective on His Final Days." *Analecta Bollandiana* 128 (2010): 67–86.

Hunt, Noreen. *Cluny under Saint Hugh, 1049–1109*. Notre Dame, IN: University of Notre Dame Press, 1967.

Iogna-Prat, Dominique. *Agni Immaculati: Recherches sur les sources hagiographiques relatives à saint Maieul de Cluny (954–994)*. Paris: Éditions du Cerf, 1988.

———. *Études clunisiennes*. Paris: Picard, 2002.

———. "La geste des origines dans l'historiographie clunisienne des XIe et XIIe siècles." *Revue bénédictine* 102 (1992): 135–91.

———. "Les morts dans la compatibilité céleste des moines clunisiens autour l'an mil." In *Religion et culture autour de l'an mil: Royaume capétien et Lotharingie*, edited by Dominique Iogna-Prat and Jean-Charles Picard, 55–69. Paris: Picard, 1990. Translated as "The Dead in the Celestial Bookkeeping of the Cluniac Monks around the Year 1000." In *Debating the Middle Ages: Issues and Readings*, edited by Lester Little and Barbara H. Rosenwein, 340–62. Oxford: Wiley, 1998.

———. *Ordonner et exclure: Cluny et la société chrétienne face à l'hérésie, au judaïsme et à l'islam, 1000–1150*. Paris: Aubier, 1998. Translated by Graham Robert Edwards as *Order and Exclusion: Cluny and Christendom Face Heresy, Judaism, and Islam (1000–1150)*. Ithaca, NY: Cornell University Press, 2002.

———. "Panorama de l'hagiographie abbatiale clunisienne." In *Manuscrits hagiographiques et travail des hagiographes*, edited by Martin Heinzelmann, 77–118. Sigmaringen, Germany: Jan Thorbecke, 1991.

———. "Le saint Maieul à Cluny d'après le *Liber Tramitis aevi Odilonis*." In *Saint Mayeul et son temps: Actes du congrès international de Valensole, 2–14 mai 1994*, 219–32. Dignes-les-Bains, France: Société Scientifique et Littéraire des Alpes de Haute-Provence, 1997.

Izbicki, Thomas M. "The Possibility of Dialogue with Islam in the Fifteenth Century." In *Nicholas of Cusa in Search of God and Wisdom*, edited by Gerald Christianson and Thomas M. Izbicki, 175–83. Leiden: Brill Academic, 1991.

Jensen, Lloyd B. "Royal Purple of Tyre." *Journal of Near Eastern Studies* 22 (1963): 104–18.

Jézégou, Marie-Pierre, Anne Joncheray, and Jean-Pierre Joncheray. "Les épaves sarrasines d'Agay et de Cannes." *Archéologia* 377 (1997): 32–39.

Johnson, Timothy J., ed. *Franciscans and Preaching: Every Miracle from the Beginning of the World Came About through Words*. Leiden: Brill Academic, 2012.

Joncheray, Jean-Pierre. "The Four Saracen Shipwrecks of Provence." In *Barbarian Seas: Late Rome to Islam*, edited by Sean Kingsley, 102–7. London: Periplus, 2004.

Joncheray, Jean-Pierre, and Philippe Sénac. "Une nouvelle épave sarrasine du haut moyen âge." *Archeologie islamique* 5 (1995): 25–34.

Kedar, Benjamin. *Crusade and Mission: European Approaches toward the Muslims*. Princeton, NJ: Princeton University Press, 1984.

Kennedy, Hugh. "The Muslims in Europe." In *The New Cambridge Medieval History*, vol. 2: *c. 700–c. 900*, edited by Rosamond McKitterick, 249–71. Cambridge: Cambridge University Press, 1995.

Kohnle, Armin. *Abt Hugo von Cluny, 1049–1109*. Sigmaringen, Germany: Thorbecke, 1993.

Kreutz, Barbara M. *Before the Normans: Southern Italy in the Ninth and Tenth Centuries*. Philadelphia: University of Pennsylvania Press, 1991.

Kritzeck, James. "De l'influence de Pierre Abélard sur Pierre le Vénérable dans ses œuvres sur l'Islam." In *Pierre Abélard—Pierre Vénérable: Les courants philosophiques, littéraires et artistiques en Occident au milieu du XIIe siècle: actes et mémoires du colloque international, Abbaye de Cluny, 2 au 9 juillet 1972,* 205–12. Paris: Editions du Centre national de la recherche scientifique, 1975.

———. *Peter the Venerable and Islam.* Princeton, NJ: Princeton University Press, 1964.

———. "Peter the Venerable and the Toledan Collection." In *Petrus Venerabilis 1156–1956: Studies and Texts Commemorating the Eighth Centenary of His Death,* edited by Giles Constable and James Kritzeck, 176–201. Rome: Herder, 1956.

Krönert, Klaus. "Le rôle de l'hagiographie dans la mise en place d'une identité locale aux Xe–XIe siècles: L'example de Trèves." In *Constructions de l'espace au Moyen Âge: Practique et représentations,* 379–89. Paris: Publications de la Sorbonne, 2007.

Langmuir, Gavin. *Toward a Definition of Antisemitism.* Berkeley: University of California Press, 1990.

Leclercq, Jean. *Pierre le Vénérable.* Paris: Éditions de Fontenelle, 1946.

———. "Pierre le Vénérable et l'érémitisme clunisien." In *Petrus Venerabilis 1156–1956: Studies and Texts Commemorating the Eighth Centenary of His Death,* edited by Giles Constable and James Kritzeck, 99–120. Rome: Herder, 1956.

———. "S. Maiolo fondatore e riformatore di monasteri a Pavia." In *Atti del 4° congresso internazionale di studi sull'alto medioevo, Pavia-Scaldasole-Monza-Bobbio, 10–14 settembre 1967,* 155–73. Spoleto, Italy: Centro Italiano di Studi sull'Alto Medioevo, 1969.

Lewis, Archibald R. *Naval Power and Trade in the Mediterranean, A.D. 500–1100.* Princeton, NJ: Princeton University Press, 1951.

Lewis, Bernard. *The Muslim Discovery of Europe.* New York: W. W. Norton, 1982.

Leyser, Conrad. "Augustine in the Latin West, 430–ca. 900." In *A Companion to Augustine,* edited by Mark Vessey, 450–64. Oxford: Wiley-Blackwell, 2012.

———. "Cities of the Plain: The Rhetoric of Sodomy in Peter Damian's *Book of Gomorrah.*" *Romanic Review* 86 (1995): 191–211.

Leyser, Karl. *Communications and Power in Medieval Europe: The Carolingian and Ottonian Centuries.* Edited by Timothy Reuter. London: Hambledon Press, 1994.

———. "Ends and Means in Liudprand of Cremona." In *Byzantium and the West, c. 850–c. 1200: Proceedings of the XVIII Spring Symposium of Byzantine Studies, Oxford, 30 March–1 April 1984,* edited by J. D. Howard-Johnston, 119–43. Amsterdam: Hakkert, 1988.

———. "Theophanu Divina Gratia Imperatrix Augusta: Western and Eastern Emperorship in the Later Tenth Century." In *Communications and Power in Medieval Europe: The Carolingian and Ottonian Centuries,* edited by Timothy Reuter, 143–64. London: Hambledon Press, 1994.

Longo, Umberto. "Riti e agiografia: L'istituzione della *commemoratio omnium fidelium defunctorum* nelle *Vitae* di Odilone di Cluny." *Bullettino dell'Istituto storico italiano per il Medio Evo e Archivio muratoriano* 103 (2002): 163–200.

Lopez, Robert. "An Aristocracy of Money in the Early Middle Ages." *Speculum* 28 (1953): 1–43.

Lorberbaum, Yair. "Anthropomorphisms in Early Rabbinic Literature: Maimonides and Modern Scholarship." In *Traditions of Maimonideanism*, edited by Carlos Fraenkel, 313–17. Leiden: Brill, 2009.

MacLean, Simon. *Kingship and Politics in the Late Ninth Century: Charles the Fat and the End of the Carolingian Empire.* Cambridge: Cambridge University Press, 2003.

Manaresi, Cesare. "La fondazione del monastero di S. Maiolo in Pavia." In *Spiritualità Cluniacense*, 274–85. Todi, Italy: Accademia Tudertina, 1960.

Manselli, Raoul. "Il monaco Enrico e la sua eresia." *Bulletino dell'Istituto storico italiano per il Medio Evo e Archivo muratoriano* 65 (1953): 1–62.

——. *Studi sulle eresie del secolo XII.* Rome: Nella sede dell'Istituto, 1953.

Martène, Edmond, and Ursin Durand. *Veterum scriptorum et monumentorum ecclesiasticorum et dogmaticorum amplissima collectio.* 9 vols. Paris: Apud Franciscum Montalant, 1724–33.

Matheus, Michael. "Borgo San Martino: An Early Medieval Pilgrimage Station on the Via Francigena Near Sutri." *Papers of the British School at Rome* 68 (2000): 185–99.

Matter, E. Ann. *The Voice of My Beloved: The Song of Songs in Western Medieval Christianity.* Philadelphia: University of Pennsylvania Press, 1990.

McCormick, Michael. *Origins of the European Economy: Communications and Commerce, AD 300–900.* Cambridge: Cambridge University Press, 2001.

——. "New Light on the Dark Ages: How the Slave Trade Fuelled the Carolingian Economy." *Past and Present* 177 (2002): 17–54.

McCready, William. *Odiosa Sanctitas: St. Peter Damian, Simony, and Reform.* Toronto: PIMS, 2011.

Meckler, Michael. "Wolves and Saracens in Odilo's *Life of Mayeul.*" In *Latin Culture in the Eleventh Century: Proceedings of the Third International Conference on Medieval Latin Studies, Cambridge, September 9–12 1998*, edited by Michael W. Herren, C. J. McDonough, and Ross Arthur, 2:116–28. Turnhout, Belgium: Brepols, 2002.

Méhu, Didier. *Paix et communautés autour de l'abbaye de Cluny (Xe–XVe siècle).* Lyon: Presses Universitaires de France, 2001.

Metcalfe, Alex. *The Muslims of Medieval Italy.* Edinburgh: Edinburgh University Press, 2009.

Mews, Constant. *Abelard and Heloise.* Oxford: Oxford University Press, 2005.

——. *Abelard and His Legacy.* Aldershot, England: Ashgate, 2001.

——. "On Dating the Works of Peter Abelard." *Archives d'histoire doctrinale et littéraire du moyen âge* 52 (1985): 73–134.

Miller, Gregory J. "Theodor Bibliander's *Machumetis saracenorum principis eiusque successorum vitae, doctrina ac ipse alcoran* (1543) as the Sixteenth-Century 'Encyclopedia' of Islam." *Islam and Christian-Muslim Relations* 24 (2013): 241–54.

Moore, R. I. *The War on Heresy.* Cambridge, MA: Belknap Press of Harvard University Press, 2012.

Moore, Wilfrid J. *The Saxon Pilgrims to Rome and the Schola Saxonum.* Fribourg, Switzerland: Society of St. Paul, 1937.

Muñoz, Fernando González. "La versión latina de la *Apología al-Kindi* y su tradición textual." In *Musulmanes y cristianos en Hispania durante las conquistas de los siglos XII y XIII,* edited by Miquel Barceló and José Martínez Gázquez, 25–40. Barcelona: Universidad Autónoma de Barcelona, 2005.

Nirenberg, David. "The Rhineland Massacres of Jews in the First Crusade: Memories Medieval and Modern." In *Medieval Concepts of the Past: Ritual, Memory, Historiography,* edited by Gerd Altoff, Johannes Fried, and Patrick Geary, 279–310. Cambridge: Cambridge University Press, 2002.

Novikoff, Alex J. "Anselm, Dialogue, and the Rise of Scholastic Disputation." *Speculum* 86 (2011): 387–418.

Olsen, Glenn W. *Of Sodomites, Effeminates, Hermaphrodites and Androgynes: Sodomy in the Age of Peter Damian.* Toronto: PIMS, 2011.

Ortenberg, Veronica. "Archbishop Sigeric's Journey to Rome in 990." *Anglo-Saxon England* 19 (1990): 197–246.

Parker, A. J. *Ancient Shipwrecks of the Mediterranean and the Roman Provinces.* Oxford: Tepus Reparatum, 1992.

Phillips, Jonathan. *The Second Crusade: Extending the Frontiers of Christendom.* New Haven, CT: Yale University Press, 2007.

Pick, Lucy. "Rethinking Cluny in Spain." *Journal of Medieval Iberian Studies* 5 (2013): 1–17.

Pierre Abélard—Pierre Vénérable: Les courants philosophiques, littéraires et artistiques en Occident au milieu du XIIe siècle: actes et mémoires du colloque international, Abbaye de Cluny, 2 au 9 juillet 1972. Paris: Éditions du Centre national de la recherche scientifique, 1975.

Pluskowski, Aleksander. *Wolves and the Wilderness in the Middle Ages.* Woodbridge, England: Boydell, 2006.

Poly, Jean-Pierre. *La Provence et la société féodale (879–1166): Contribution à l'étude des structures dites féodales dans le Midi.* Paris: Bordas, 1976.

Reilly, Bernard F. *The Contest of Christian and Muslim Spain, 1031–1157.* Cambridge, MA: Blackwell, 1992.

Reinaud, Joseph Toussaint. *Invasions des sarrazins en France et de France en Savoie, en Piémont et dans la Suisse, pendant les 8e, 9e et 10e siècles de notre ère.* Paris: À la libraire orientale de Vᵉ Dondey-Dupré, 1836. Translated by Haroon Khan Sherwani as *Muslim Colonies in France, Northern Italy and Switzerland.* Lahore, Pakistan: Ashraf, 1955.

Richter, Helmut. *Die Persönlichkeitsdarstellung in cluniazensischen Abtsviten.* Erlangen, Germany: H. Richter, 1972.

Rizzardi, Giuseppe. *Domande christiane sull'Islam nel medioevo: Edizioni e studi sul Corpus cluniacense a proposito dei saraceni.* San Cataldo, Italy: Lussografica, 2001.

Rodriguez, Jarbel. "Financing a Captive's Ransom in Late Medieval Aragon." *Medieval Encounters* 9 (2003): 164–81.

Roma fra oriente e occidente. 2 vols. Settimane di Studio del Centro Italiano di Studi sull'Alto Medioevo 49. Spoleto, Italy: Presso la Sede del Centro, 2002.

Roma nell'alto medioevo. 2 vols. Settimane di Studio del Centro Italiano di Studi sull'Alto Medioevo 48. Spoleto, Italy: Presso la Sede del Centro, 2001.

Roques, René. "Les *Pagani* dans le *Cur Deus Homo* de Saint Anselm." *Miscellanea Mediaevalia* 2 (1963): 192–206.

Rosé, Isabelle. *Construire une société seigneuriale: Itinéraire et ecclésiologie de l'abbé Odon de Cluny (fin du IXe–milieu du Xe siècle).* Turnhout, Belgium: Brepols, 2008.

Rosenwein, Barbara H. "The Family Politics of Berengar, King of Italy (888–924)." *Speculum* 71 (1996): 247–89.

———. *Rhinoceros Bound: Cluny in the Tenth Century.* Philadelphia: University of Pennsylvania Press, 1982.

Rotter, Ekkehart. *Abendland und Sarazenen: Das okzidentale Araberbild und seine Entstehung im Frühmittelalter.* Berlin: De Gruyter, 1983.

Russell, Jeffrey Burton. *The Devil: Perceptions of Evil from Antiquity to Primitive Christianity.* Ithaca, NY: Cornell University Press, 1977.

Sahner, Christian C. "From Augustine to Islam: Translation and History in the Arabic Orosius." *Speculum* 88 (2013): 905–31.

Saurette, Marc. "Rhetorics of Reform: Peter the Venerable and the Twelfth-Century Rewriting of the Cluniac Monastic Project." PhD diss., University of Toronto, 2005.

Schulte, Aloys. *Geschichte des mittelalterlichen Handels und Verkehrs zwischen Westdeutschland und Italien mit Ausschluss von Venedig.* 2 vols. Leipzig, Germany: Verlag von Duncker & Humblot, 1900.

Schulze, Hans K. *Heiratsurkunde der Kaiserin Theophanu: Die griechische Kaiserin und das römisch-deutsche Reich 972–991.* Hanover: Hahn, 2007.

Sénac, Philippe. "Contribution a l'étude des incursions musulmanes dans l'occident chrétien: La localisation du Gabel al-Qilal." *Revue de l'Occident Musulman et de la Méditerranée* 31 (1981): 7–12.

———. *Musulmans et sarrasins dans le sud de la Gaule du VIIIe au XIe siècle.* Paris: Sycomore, 1980.

———. *Provence et piraterie sarrasine.* Paris: Maisonneuve et Larose, 1982.

Septimus, Bernard. "Petrus Alfonsi on the Cult at Mecca." *Speculum* 56 (1981): 517–33.

Shatzmiller, Joseph. *Cultural Exchange: Jews, Christians and Art in the Medieval Marketplace.* Princeton, NJ: Princeton University Press, 2013.

Shaw, Brent. "Bandits in the Roman Empire." *Past and Present* 105 (1984): 3–52.

Smith, Julia M. H., ed. *Early Medieval Rome and the Christian West: Essays in Honour of Donald A. Bullough.* Leiden: Brill, 2000.

———. "Old Saints, New Cults: Roman Relics in Carolingian Francia." In *Early Medieval Rome and the Christian West: Essays in Honour of Donald A. Bullough,* edited by Julia M. H. Smith, 317–39. Leiden: Brill, 2000.

Smith, Katherine Allen. *War and the Making of Medieval Monastic Culture.* Woodbridge, England: Boydell Press, 2011.

Smith, L. M. *The Early History of the Monastery of Cluny.* Oxford: Oxford University Press, 1920.

Soares-Christen, Eliana Magnani. *Monastères et aristocratie en Provence milieu Xe–début XIIe siècle.* Münster, Germany: LIT Verlag, 1999.

Southern, Richard. *The Making of the Middle Ages*. New Haven, CT: Yale University Press, 1953.

——. *Saint Anselm: A Portrait in a Landscape*. Cambridge: Cambridge University Press, 1990.

——. *Western Views of Islam in the Middle Ages*. Cambridge, MA: Harvard University Press, 1962.

Steinsaltz, Adin. *The Essential Talmud*. Translated by Chaya Galai. London: Weidenfeld and Nicolson, 1976.

Stratford, Neil. "The Documentary Evidence for the Building of Cluny III." In *Studies in Burgundian Romanesque Sculpture*, 1:41–59. London: Pindar, 1998.

——. "Un grand clunisien, Henri de Blois." In *Cluny: Onze siècles de rayonnement*, edited by Neil Stratford, 238–45. Paris: Éditions du Patrimoine Centre des Monuments Nationaux, 2010.

Talbot, Alice-Mary. "Searching for Women on Mt. Athos: Insights from the Archives of the Holy Mountain." *Speculum* 87 (2012): 995–1014.

Tatlock, J. S. P. "The Epilog of Chaucer's *Troilus*." *Modern Philology* 18 (1920–21): 625–59.

Taylor, Larissa J., ed. *Encyclopedia of Medieval Pilgrimage*. Leiden: Brill, 2010.

Tolan, John V. "Peter the Venerable on the Diabolical Heresy of the Saracens." In *The Devil, Heresy and Witchcraft in the Middle Ages: Essays in Honor of Jeffrey B. Russell*, edited by Alberto Ferreiro, 345–67. Leiden: Brill, 1998.

——. *Petrus Alfonsi and His Medieval Readers*. Gainesville, FL: University Press of Florida, 1993.

——. *Saint Francis and the Sultan: The Curious History of a Christian-Muslim Encounter*. Oxford: Oxford University Press, 2009.

——. *Saracens: Islam in the Medieval European Imagination*. New York: Columbia University Press, 2002.

——. *Sons of Ishmael: Muslims through European Eyes in the Middle Ages*. Gainesville, FL: University Press of Florida, 2008.

Torrell, Jean-Pierre. "Les juifs dans l'oeuvre de Pierre le Vénérable." *Cahiers de civilisation médiévale* 30 (1987): 331–46.

——. "La notion de prophétie et la méthode apologétique dans le *Contra Sarracenos* de Pierre le Vénérable." *Studia monastica* 17 (1975): 257–82.

Torrell, Jean-Pierre, and Denise Bouthillier. "*Miraculum*: Une catégorie fondamentale chez Pierre le Vénérable." *Revue thomiste* 80 (1980): 357–86, 549–66.

——. *Pierre le Vénérable et sa vision du monde: Sa vie, son oeuvre, l'homme et le démon*. Leuven, Belgium: Spicilegium Sacrum Lovaniense, 1986.

Turki, Abdelmagid. "La lettre du 'Moine de France' à al-Muqtadir billah, roi de Saragosse, et la réponse d'al-Bayi, le faqih andalou." *Al-Andalus* 31 (1966): 73–153.

Tyler, John E. *The Alpine Passes: The Middle Ages (962–1250)*. Oxford: Basil Blackwell, 1930.

Van den Eynde, Damien. "Les principaux voyages de Pierre le Vénérable." *Benedictina* 15 (1968): 58–110.

Van der Toorn, Karel, Bob Becking, and Pieter W. van der Horst, eds. *Dictionary of Deities and Demons in the Bible*. Leiden: Brill, 1995.

Van Engen, John. "The Twelfth Century: Reading, Reason, and Revolt in a World of Custom." In *European Transformations: The Long Twelfth Century*, edited by Thomas F. X. Noble and John Van Engen, 17–44. Notre Dame, IN: University of Notre Dame Press, 2012.

Vauchez, André. *La sainteté en Occident aux derniers siècles du moyen âge d'après les procès de canonisation et les documents hagiographiques*. 2nd ed. Paris: École française de Rome, 1988. Translated by Jean Birrell as *Sainthood in the Later Middle Ages*. Cambridge: Cambridge University Press, 1997.

Voss, Lena. *Heinrich von Blois: Bischof von Winchester (1129–1171)*. Berlin: Ebering, 1932.

Wasserstein, David. *The Rise and Fall of the Party-Kings: Politics and Society in Islamic Spain 1002–1086*. Princeton, NJ: Princeton University Press, 1985.

Werblowsky, R. J. Zwi, and Geoffrey Wigoder, eds. *Oxford Dictionary of the Jewish Religion*. New York: Oxford University Press, 1997.

Wollasch, Joachim. *Cluny, Licht der Welt: Aufstieg und Niedergang der klösterlichen Gemeinschaft*. Düsseldorf, Germany: Patmos, 1996.

———. "Das Schisma des Abtes Pontius von Cluny." *Francia* 23 (1996): 31–52.

———, ed. *Synopse der cluniacensischen Necrologien*. 2 vols. Munich: Fink, 1982.

Zerner, Monique. "La capture de Maïeul et la guerre de libération de Provence: Le départ des sarrasins à travers les cartulaires provençaux." In *Saint Mayeul et son temps: Actes du congrès international de Valensole, 2–14 mai 1994*, 199–210. Dignes-les-Bains, France: Société Scientifique et Littéraire des Alpes de Haute-Provence, 1997.

♠ INDEX

Printed in the USA
CPSIA information can be obtained
at www.ICGtesting.com
LVHW051602141223
766375LV00004B/463